Winthrop 1/95

Man and Land in Chinese History

Man and Land
in Chinese History

An Economic Analysis

Kang Chao

Stanford University Press
Stanford, California   1986

Stanford University Press
Stanford, California
© 1986 by the Board of Trustees of the
Leland Stanford Junior University
Printed in the United States of America

CIP data appear at the end of the book

To Tonia and Connie

Preface

In the past few years, I have written a number of articles and unpublished conference papers revolving around a central theme: how did the Chinese people respond technologically and institutionally to population pressure during the course of history? In this book I would like to present my arguments and evidence in a more systematic—but still sufficiently succinct—manner. The issues themselves are by no means new. They have been dealt with in the studies of Professors Ping-ti Ho, Dwight H. Perkins, Mark Elvin, Cho-yun Hsu, and many others. Although I have been greatly inspired by their writings, my own views and interpretations do not always agree with theirs.

I have also been inspired by Professor Albert Feuerwerker's remark that the feudalism-capitalism dichotomy is a semantic nightmare, not only for the student of European history but also—indeed, more so—for the modern historian of China. Feuerwerker stated nearly 30 years ago, "While the search for traces of incipient capitalism is not an uninteresting quest, it distracts us from the equally interesting, probably more difficult, and certainly more important undertaking of producing a useful anatomy and physiology of this traditional economy." It is precisely the latter that I attempt in this volume.

The economic behavior of the people of a country, unlike their political system, tends not to alter sharply in the short term, as for example with a change of dynasty. In order to detect very gradual changes and contrasting patterns, hardly discernible in ordinary dynastic studies, I have extended my observations over a long period of history. This has been possible, of course, only at the sacrifice of some detail.

I fully recognize, and repeatedly remind the reader, that quantitative data from historical sources are much inferior to modern data and should not be judged by the same standards. Much larger margins of error must be allowed for. Their utility lies less in their exactitude than in their indication of definite trends.

Preface

I am grateful to the Committee on Scholarly Communication with the People's Republic of China and the Graduate School of the University of Wisconsin at Madison for research grants, and to Professors Cho-yun Hsu, Yen-chien Wang, Thomas Rawski, and Evelyn Rawski, as well as to Mr. Michael Laske, for their comments on an earlier draft of this book. I would also like to thank the Chinese Institute of Economics and the History Department of Nanjing University for their permission to use the Ming-Ch'ing materials on land institutions in their possession.

K.C.

Contents

Tables

Man and Land in Chinese History

I

Economic Adjustments Induced by Population Pressure

MANY EXISTING STUDIES of China's premodern economy and its development leave something to be desired. Specifically, the restrictive methodologies employed in these studies need to be reexamined. First, the overemphasis on dynastic studies seems unfortunate. Historians who specialize in the Ming-Ch'ing period, for example, have noted the flourishing commerce of the period, but few have attempted to make intertemporal comparisons to determine if Ming-Ch'ing commerce was more prosperous than, say, Han or Sung commerce. That economic evolution sometimes takes such a long time that it cannot be detected by means of ordinary dynastic studies is often forgotten.

Second, some scholars hold the deep-rooted conviction, implicit or explicit, that the history of any country always shows linear progress. Such scholars find it unnecessary to ask if the degree of commercialization in the Ming-Ch'ing was higher than in the Sung.

Third, the general applicability of the Marxist interpretation of economic history has been overstressed by a group of Chinese scholars who are impressed by its scale and depth, highly systematical presentation, and internal consistency. Marx described the stages of economic development as a natural process of forward movement that no social or political force could deter indefinitely. Thus, his theoretical framework also denies the possibility of historical regression and postulates the worst conceivable situation as a prolonged stagnation at any one of the historical stages. According to Marx, modern capitalist society must be preceded by a feudal natural economy. For those who accept this framework, the nature of the premodern Chinese economy is a foregone conclusion; the main task remaining is to identify and date the stages of its development.

Thus, in spite of lack of firm evidence, the Marxist historian believes that a counterpart system to European feudal manorism existed some-

1

time in Chinese history. Historical records show only that a political feudal system existed before the Ch'in unification in 221 B.C., but it is far from clear from surviving documents how production activities were managed during that period. Although there was no private ownership of land, it is likewise by no means certain whether the people who received allotments of public land for cultivation were serfs or free peasants.

Recorded history further shows that no later than 300 B.C., during the Warring States period, Chinese society already displayed the following basic characteristics of a market economy:

1. People could move fairly freely across state borders. Cases in which people moved to the areas ruled by so-called benevolent governments are frequently cited.

2. Most land became privately owned and could be transferred between consenting parties. By the time of the Han dynasty, the concept of property rights was firmly and unambiguously established. Surviving land transaction agreements from Han times provide complete descriptive details, including explicit statements that whatever existed on the ground or beneath the surface of the land that was legally transacted belonged to the new owner.

3. Rulers and prominent scholars alike were in favor of the social division of labor. The broadest classification of occupations was known as the "four categories of people," whereas a more detailed division referred to the "one hundred crafts." As early as the Shang dynasty (ca. 16th-11th centuries B.C.; see Appendix A), numerous clans specialized in various fields of handicraft production and eventually adopted the names of their professions as their family or clan names. The leaders of such specialist clans were later appointed by the government as the heads of offices supervising all craftsmen in those fields.

4. Because of the high degree of social division of labor and the prevalence of small peasant and craftsman households, each of whom was unable to produce a large variety of daily necessities because of the limited labor inputs available, exchange of products in China was imperative and developed very early. Instead of encouraging a self-sufficient subsistence economy, Chinese governments in most dynasties exerted great efforts to promote marketing activities. Before the Ch'in unification, the government in each state constructed at least one market district in each city as

2

a part of standard urban planning. In the state of Ch'i, the residential wards in each city were said to have been arranged in such a way that government employees lived near the palace, farmers near the city gates, and merchants and craftsmen near the market district.[1] Even outside cities, we are told, there was a rural market every 50 *li* along trunk roads.

5. Virtually everything had a price tag in ancient China. According to documents recorded on recently excavated wooden or bamboo tablets, the criminal codes of the Ch'in dynasty stipulated that burglary sentences were to be determined in accordance with the values of goods stolen.[2] All drafted workers were paid in cash rather than in kind. Written tablets from the Han also reveal that under the property registration system of the time, each family reported its household belongings in monetary terms. All these signs point to the omnipresence of markets in which prices of various articles were readily known.

An abundance of surviving historical material corroborates these features, but passages from two well-known works will suffice as examples. One is the debate between Mencius and a disciple of Hsü Hsing, an agricultural fundamentalist in the Warring States period, the other an argument by the great historian Ssu-ma Ch'ien. The Mencius debate is interesting and illuminating enough to deserve quotation in full:[3]

> There was a man by the name of Hsü Hsing who preached the teachings of Shen-nung. He came to T'eng from Ch'u, went up to the gate and told Duke Wen, "I, a man from a distant region, have heard that you, my lord, are practicing benevolent government. I wish to be given a place to live and become one of your subjects."
>
> The Duke gave him a place.
>
> His followers, numbering several score, all dressed in coarse cloth and earned a living by making sandals and weaving mats.
>
> Ch'en Hsiang, a follower of Ch'en Liang, and his brother Hsin came to T'eng from Sung carrying their ploughs on their backs. "We have heard," said they, "that you, my lord, practice the government of the sages. We believe you must be a sage yourself. We wish to become the subjects of a sage."
>
> Ch'en Hsiang met Hsü Hsing and was greatly pleased with him, so he abandoned what he had learned before and became a follower of Hsü Hsing.
>
> Ch'en Hsiang saw Mencius and cited the words of Hsü Hsing to the following effect: "The prince of T'eng is truly a worthy ruler. However, he

3

has never been taught the Way. A worthy ruler shares the work of tilling the land with his people to earn his keep, and he rules while cooking his own meals. But now T'eng has granaries and treasuries, which shows that the prince is oppressing the people in order to nourish himself. How can he be a worthy prince?"

"Does Hsü Tzu only eat the grain grown by himself?" asked Mencius. "Yes."

"Does Hsü Tzu only wear the cloth woven by himself?"

"No. He dresses in coarse cloth."

"Does Hsü Tzu wear a cap?"

"Yes."

"What kind of cap does he wear?"

"Plain raw silk."

"Does he weave it himself?"

"No. He gets it in exchange for his grain."

"Why does Hsü Tzu not weave it himself?"

"That would interfere with his field work."

"Does Hsü Tzu cook with an iron pot and an earthenware steamer and does he plow with iron implements?"

"Yes."

"Does he make them himself?"

"No. He gets them in exchange for his grain."

"To do so is not to oppress the potter and the blacksmith. The potter and the blacksmith, for their part, also exchange their wares for grain. Can it not be said that in doing this, they are not oppressing the farmer? Why does Hsü Tzu not be a potter and a blacksmith and get everything he needs from his own house? Why does he run confusedly about trading with the hundred crafts? Why does Hsü Tzu not loathe all the trouble?"

"It is naturally impossible to mix the work of a hundred crafts with the tilling of the land."

"Would you regard ruling the Empire as an exception that can be mixed with the work of tilling the land?"

This passage has several important implications. First, Hsü Hsing and his followers had the freedom to select their domiciles in an area known to be ruled by a "benevolent government." Second, even a dedicated agricultural fundamentalist like Hsü Hsing could not get everything he needed from his own house. Most important, however, is Mencius's defense of the prevailing system of social division of labor and product exchange.

A more pointed argument was made by the historian Ssu-ma Ch'ien

4

in support of the market economy he was about to describe in the "Chapter of the Money-Makers" from his *Records of the Historian*:

> There must be farmers to produce food, men to extract the wealth of
> mountains and marshes, artisans to process these things and merchants
> to circulate them. There is no need to wait for government orders; each
> man will play his part, doing his best to get what he desires. So cheap
> goods will go where they fetch more, while expensive goods will make
> men search for cheap ones. When all work willingly at their trades, just as
> water flows ceaselessly downhill day and night, things will appear un-
> sought and people will produce them without being asked. For clearly this
> accords with the Way and is in keeping with nature.[4]

Ssu-ma Ch'ien's likening of economic activities in a market economy to
water flowing downhill is a Chinese version of Adam Smith's "invisible
hand." In fact, there is no mention of a self-sufficient feudal manorial
economy in the chapter.

It is curious that economic historians have ignored for so long the
many important passages in well-known classics that describe the ancient
economy. The data point overwhelmingly to the fact that ancient China
was an atomistic market economy; indeed, it continued to be so until the
1950's. By atomistic I mean made up primarily of countless small production units making independent decisions. Such units were frequently described as "households with five persons tilling 100 *mou* of land." These
freeholders or tenants of the large landlords that figured in every period
were themselves independent, decision-making units.

A market economy is not necessarily a product of modern times, nor is
it necessarily a product of a politically democratic society. The modern
capitalist economy is merely a high stage into which a market economy
may eventually evolve. China was a market economy for more than two
millennia before the 1950's, though with varying degrees of development
and changing levels of technology. Under such an economic system individual units would make independent decisions to use their resources
in order to maximize their gains. In Ssu-ma Ch'ien's words, each man
played his part, doing his best to get what he desired.

Of course, the people made decisions subject to existing constraints;
whenever constraints changed, they had to revise their decisions accordingly. A formidable constraint for most societies is the availability of
resources, and in the case of China this constraint has manifested itself
as limited land for cultivation. In other words, the Chinese people had

to adjust their economic choices to respond to an increasing man-land ratio as population pressure gradually mounted. Among other adjustments, they eventually chose the types of economic organizations (operation units) that could accommodate a larger population and the type of production technology that could absorb more labor per unit of output.

This book is an inquiry into the historical response of the Chinese people to mounting population pressure and its economic consequences. Specifically, I will seek to perform three tasks:

1. If China was, or very closely resembled, a market economy, it will be possible to construct an abstract model based on conventional economic theories and to postulate the reactions of individual participants towards such a constraint.

2. I will examine (and adjust, where necessary), historical statistics of population and arable acreage to ascertain whether and to what degree the man-land ratio in the country increased.

3. I will assemble historical data to test my theoretical deductions.

In this introductory chapter I will construct a theoretical model to demonstrate why and how people in a market economy change their preferences for economic institutions and production techniques when population and cultivated acreage have failed to grow in the same proportions. I will show that drastic changes take place after surplus population appears.

The crucial turning point, where surplus population is concerned, is the point at which the marginal product of labor in agricultural production equals the subsistence cost. The population of a country at a given point of time may be too large relative to its total cultivated acreage, causing the marginal product of labor in agriculture to fall short of the subsistence cost. What I mean here by surplus population is the difference between the actual population and the population that would yield a marginal product of labor exactly equal to the subsistence cost.

This demarcation point differs conceptually from Mark Elvin's point of high-level equilibrium[5] as illustrated in Figure 1.1, in which the horizontal axis measures the quantity of labor L, which is assumed to be a function of the population size; the vertical axis measures the total output Q produced by labor. Curve P is the production function based on one variable productive factor—labor—that does not shift if we adopt the simplifying assumptions of a constant size of farmland and stable farming technology. Curve S denotes the subsistence consumption, which is

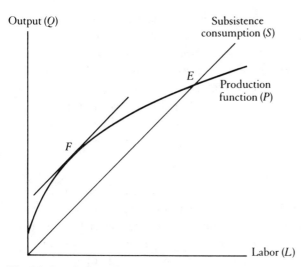

Fig. 1.1. Population and consumption.

also a linear function of the population size. Point E is Elvin's point of high-level equilibrium, except that the total quantity of farmland and the state of technology are assumed to be constant here. If the simplifying assumption is relaxed, the production function (P) gradually shifts upward as a result of the enlarged size of land and improved technology.

Point E is not a meaningful concept economically because it is defined by equality between total food supply and total subsistence requirement of food. This equality can be achieved only with the help of a redistributive mechanism so powerful as to be an impossibility in any society.

According to modern marginalistic analysis, which emphasizes decision making on the basis of marginal quantities, the crucial point is F, not E. At point F, the tangent line is parallel to S, signifying that the marginal product MP of labor is equal to subsistence. The economic relevance of point F is that production units with hired labor inputs will stop hiring when the marginal product of labor is equal to the subsistence wage level. If point F is taken as an equilibrium point, the population size associated with it should then be called the equilibrium population. Additional population beyond this point represents a surplus, meaning that those additional people cannot produce enough to feed themselves. Thus surplus population can exist only when there is a redistributive mechanism that transfers some of the product from those whose marginal product is above the subsistence level to those whose marginal product is below it. In other words, for one reason or another, the former have the "obligation" to support the latter despite their low marginal product; it is therefore in their interest to make use of the latter as labor until their marginal product drops to zero. That is—to speak simply—if you have to support someone, you may as well let him do some work; earning even below subsistence is still better than earning nothing. In a sense they become "fixed" inputs, rather than variable inputs, to those who have to support them.

In traditional China, especially in the agricultural sector, some redistributive mechanisms existed, and these enabled the population to expand beyond point F. But even if redistributive mechanisms rendered a degree of surplus population tolerable, they could never have been so strong as to push the country to point E (where everyone would have been eating at the subsistence level), let alone beyond that point.

The relevant point—in Europe as well as in China—is point F. The main difference between the histories of these two cultures is, however, that China's traditional economy was more resilient than Europe's in its institutions and was able to adjust itself in time to keep absorbing surplus labor. Increasing population pressure forced the Chinese people to make greater use of the built-in redistributive mechanisms of their society. In terms of Figure 1.1, traditional China could, and did, travel farther along curve P beyond point F than Europe did.

Before the Industrial Revolution, a strong tradition in European society prevented young men from considering marriage before securing steady employment or some other type of assured income. The total population was loosely regulated by economic conditions, at least in the long run, and thus could not surpass point F by a large margin. There was little possibility for a jobless person to depend indefinitely on others for subsistence. Stated another way, there was no effective mechanism that could transfer income from those who made enough to those who did not.

The Chinese traditional family system functioned quite differently, for two important reasons. One was the drive for family perpetuation, the obsession with having male heirs to carry on the family lineage. Marriage was a decision not dependent on one's economic condition, but on one's deepest obligation to one's whole family as well as to one's ancestors. The second was the strength of family feeling, the inescapable obligation of a family to support those members who had no income or jobs. The family as institution often became a multiworker business entity, provider of employment and basis for intrafamily income distribution. Consequently, instead of functioning as an automatic regulator, the Chinese family system tolerated overpopulation.

In a sense, the peasant riots so frequent in Chinese history were also a kind of redistributive mechanism, though of course compulsory and violent. Theoretically, even with the help of this redistribution by force, the population could not go beyond point E, because at that point the average food supply would equal the average subsistence consumption. There would be nothing left for redistribution.

The most powerful mechanism of redistribution in Chinese history, however, was not peasant rebellion but the family system. Though unable to check population growth, the family system could make necessary adjustments over time to accommodate surplus population by a process of domesticating production units. Managerial landlords and latifundia would stop hiring workers when the marginal product of labor dropped below the wage floor. But if a family unit acted as a production unit, there would be no wage floor; those with a marginal product below the subsistence consumption level could partake of the total family income with other members. In this regard, owner-peasants and tenants were alike, except that the latter owned no land.

Classical marginalists, at least after John Bates Clark, provide an unequivocal solution for the conventional factor market in which people sell the productive services of their resources to producers. The product exhaustion theorem says that if factors are priced according to their marginal products, the incomes of all resource owners will exactly exhaust the value of the total product in the long-run competitive equilibrium. This holds true regardless of which factor is variable and which is fixed, and regardless of which group of resource owners act as producers who buy productive services of other resources in the market and receive the residuals for themselves. In an agrarian economy with land and labor as the inputs, a landowner may cultivate his land and purchase labor from outside, paying a wage rate in accordance with labor's marginal product. In such a case the landowner is the residual claimant. Alternatively, he may lease out his land and receive a fixed rental rate per unit of area equal to the marginal product of the land. In this case the tenant is the producer and claims the residual. Income distribution between the two parties remains the same under each land arrangement. Wage and rent are, therefore, conceptually parallel.

Following precedent, we may assume that two homogeneous inputs, land and labor, are employed to produce a homogeneous product in an agrarian economy. For simplification, it is further assumed that agricultural production involves no uncertainty. The two inputs are owned by two separate groups of people, who may go to the competitive factor market to sell their own resources, to buy the input from others, or to form a partnership by contributing their complementary inputs. As a separate market unit, each landless person has the option of working as a wage laborer for a landowner, of leasing land at a fixed rent, or of sharing the crop with a landowner. By the same token, a landowner may choose from among the three alternative arrangements. It is assumed for the time being that no transaction costs are entailed in adopting any given tenure system. Thus, there are six quantity variables, two prices, and a pricelike parameter, defined as follows:

L_1 = the amount of labor devoted to wage-paid work
L_2 = the amount of labor devoted to the rented land
L_3 = the amount of labor devoted to sharecropping
H_1 = the amount of land cultivated by the owner
H_2 = the amount of land leased out to tenants at a fixed rental rate
H_3 = the amount of sharecropped land
w = the wage rate
r = the rental rate per acre
s = the share of output paid by the sharecropper to the landlord

With a uniform technology of production, the three production functions should be identical, all characterized by diminishing returns to any factor but constant returns to scale. The production functions are F_1 (L_1, H_1) for owner-cultivation, F_2 (L_2, H_2) for rented land, and F_3 (L_3, H_3) for sharecropping. The general equilibrium would require

$$\frac{\partial F_1}{\partial L_1} = \frac{\partial F_2}{\partial L_2} = \frac{\partial F_3}{\partial L_3} = w, \qquad \frac{\partial F_1}{\partial H_1} = \frac{\partial F_2}{\partial H_2} = \frac{\partial F_3}{\partial H_3} = r$$

For F_1 and F_2 the equilibrium is reached in the land market and labor market, respectively; for F_3 the equilibrium may be reached through negotiating the pricelike parameter s, or the proportion of land and labor contributions from the two partners, or both.

With these simplifying assumptions made—constant returns to scale, absence of uncertainty or risk, and absence of transaction cost—it would not matter to the resource owner which of the three tenurial arrangements or combination thereof he adopted. If the simplifying assumptions

10

were removed, however, he might have a specific preference. If agricultural production is characterized by substantial economies of scale, latifundia employing a large number of full-time laborers would be preferable to tenant farming, for the latter is generally confined to the family unit. Uncertainty in agricultural production is another determinant of tenure preference. Owner cultivation is preferable if landlords are less risk averse than tenants, whereas renting contracts are preferable if tenants are less risk averse than landlords. When the two parties have equal risk aversions, they may either engage in sharecropping or combine land renting and owner cultivation in appropriate proportions to disperse risk.

Transaction costs are a third factor influencing tenure preference. Such costs are broadly defined here to include (1) the cost of negotiating tenure contracts, (2) the cost of enforcing contracts, (3) the cost of making quick adjustments in the process of production, and (4) the cost of commuting between farms. It is generally agreed that negotiation cost does not vary greatly among different types of tenure contracts, but the difference in enforcement cost may be very substantial. Enforcement cost is usually associated with labor, for supervising labor requires greater effort than using land. Consequently, the issue of enforcement cost and the work incentive argument in evaluating various farm institutions are merely two sides of the same coin. Enforcement cost is highest on farms with hired hands because the lack of self-generated incentive on the part of workers entails close daily supervision; no such supervision is needed where the land is rented out because the producers use their own labor. In this respect, sharecropping is similar to the hiring of farm laborers: although the landowner need not supervise the daily operations of the sharecropper in every detail, he must ensure that the sharecropper contributes the labor stipulated in the contract. More important, under sharecropping contracts the landlord or his representative must be present in the field during harvest to verify the quantity actually harvested.

I have indicated earlier the manner in which population density is influenced by the production function and the redistributive mechanism. Over time, however, population density itself seems to be an explanatory variable that helps to account for certain secular changes in land institutions. With the increase in population density and the consequent fall in the marginal product of labor, agricultural production tends to adopt labor-intensive techniques to absorb more labor per unit of land. As long as the marginal product of labor is above the subsistence level, all three

11

farming systems described here would remain attractive even though the wage rate declines and the rental rate rises. General equilibrium is lost, however, as soon as the population has increased to the point where the marginal product of labor drops below the subsistence level. In that case, the subsistence cost forms a wage floor for farms employing full-time workers; they will stop hiring at the point where the marginal product of labor is equal to the subsistence wage. The original equilibrium condition now becomes

$$\frac{\partial F_1}{\partial L_1} = w_s$$

where w_s is the subsistence wage. The redundant or surplus labor will be absorbed by tenant farmers who have the obligation to support their family members. Thus

$$\frac{\partial F_2}{\partial L_2} = \frac{\partial F_3}{\partial L_3} < w_s$$

which suggests that the marginal product of labor in tenant farming is considerably below the subsistence level, a situation generally known as the Nurksian type of disguised unemployment or underemployment. Accordingly, the marginal products of land under the three land arrangements tend to shift in the opposite way so that

$$\frac{\partial F_1}{\partial H_1} < \frac{\partial F_2}{\partial H_2} = \frac{\partial F_3}{\partial H_3} = r$$

which indicates that the landlord would earn less from cultivating the land himself than from leasing it out. The predictable result of such a situation would be a gradual shift from owner cultivation of land to tenant farming.

The rising population density also affects the choice between fixed rate tenancy and sharecropping. As the man-land ratio rises, farmers tend to adopt more labor-intensive cropping systems and farming techniques. This in turn raises the transaction costs under share tenancy. For one thing, complex rotation systems, multiple crops, interplanting, and heterogeneous by-products considerably enhance the difficulty of defining "output shares" for the two parties. More important, the increased number of laborers per acre and the prolonged farming season entail greater supervisory efforts from landlords to enforce the stipulated quantity and quality of labor. Thus, the renting system based on self-generated work incentives appeared increasingly more attractive than the sharecropping system to Chinese landowners.

To depict traditional China realistically, however, the model provided here should allow for a number of occupational alternatives. Besides operating a farm, a person with capital may also operate a handicraft factory with full-time workers or a putting-out business supplying capital to rural subsidiary production. Similarly, a landless person may work full-time in a handicraft factory or engage in part-time nonagricultural subsidiary production in his rural home. A person with a small amount of capital and his own labor may be an owner-farmer engaged exclusively in agricultural production or may operate a family workshop.

To the three production functions mentioned earlier we must therefore add $F_4 (L_4, H_4)$ for rural subsidiary production and $F_5 (L_5, H_5)$ for handicraft factories, where H_4 and H_5 are the capital requirements in the two occupations measured in land units. (Land and capital are here assumed to be freely interchangeable.) If all resource owners try to maximize their incomes when there are no institutional restrictions, the first-order conditions are

$$\frac{\partial F_1}{\partial L_1} = \frac{\partial F_2}{\partial L_2} = \frac{\partial F_3}{\partial L_3} = \frac{\partial F_4}{\partial L_4} = \frac{\partial F_5}{\partial L_5} = w$$

and

$$\frac{\partial F_1}{\partial H_1} = \frac{\partial F_2}{\partial H_2} = \frac{\partial F_3}{\partial H_3} = \frac{\partial F_4}{\partial H_4} = \frac{\partial F_5}{\partial H_5} = r$$

In such an economy, various production institutions exist simultaneously and are mutually interchangeable until overall equilibrium is reached. Producers go to the factor markets to purchase the resources they do not possess. Owner-farming and family workshops are cases in which the owners possess both resources, capital and labor. Absentee landlords are those who wish to engage in more than one line of production.

The introduction of complicating elements and constraints, however, whether they are physical or institutional, may alter the general equilibrium solution. One important and well-known constraint is the natural growth season in agricultural production, which leaves sizeable amounts of unused labor in the off-season. Such idle labor cannot be reallo-

13

cated to F_5; it must be absorbed by F_4. It is not surprising that every country has experienced a long history of rural subsidiary production of one type or another during its preindustrialization era.

Another crucial complicating element is transaction cost, which is broadly defined to include all costs and inconveniences, monetary and psychic, that may be incurred after a good has been produced but before it is consumed by the user. No transaction cost is involved, therefore, if one uses what he himself has produced. Savings on transaction cost explain the prevalence of domestic production for home consumption in early human history. The so-called natural subsistence economy is merely an extreme case in which transaction cost is prohibitively high. Historically, transaction cost, especially its transportation and marketing components, declined over time so that the extent of production for self-consumption was gradually reduced. Where transaction cost is very low, even rural households can engage in the subsidiary production of goods intended for distant markets. In some cases the poor marketing ability of individual rural households can be compensated for by efficiently organized professional marketeers.

Economies of scale are another important factor, one that in many cases strongly favors handicraft factories over family production. Compared with family production, handicraft factories can practice division of labor, use more productive techniques and equipment, and more effectively train workers to a higher degree of skill. Unless the benefits of scale economies are offset by high transportation costs, family production is at a disadvantage. A division of labor often exists between handicraft factories and rural subsidiary production, with the latter specializing in goods that require relatively simple equipment and skills. Handicraft factories are usually more dynamic because they have the potential to breed new technology, thereby shifting the production function F_5 upward. It is in this sector that industrialization and mechanization eventually take place. In cases where handicraft factories and rural subsidiary production use more or less the same technology and neither has any special advantage, however, the two are in direct competition.

By the time population has grown to such a size that the marginal product of labor falls short of the subsistence level, the subsistence cost constitutes a wage floor for both latifundia and handicraft factories, both of which employ full-time workers. Both organizations must stop hiring at the point where the marginal product of labor is equal to the subsistence wage. The original equalities now become

$$\frac{\partial F_1}{\partial L_1} = \frac{\partial F_5}{\partial L_5} = w_s \quad \text{and} \quad \frac{\partial F_2}{\partial L_2} = \frac{\partial F_3}{\partial L_3} = \frac{\partial F_4}{\partial L_4} < w_s$$

where w_s is the subsistence wage. The redundant labor will be absorbed by individual households, which have the obligation to subsidize their family members. Consequently, the marginal products of labor in family farms, family workshops, tenant farming, and rural subsidiary production are below subsistence. This in turn leads to

$$\frac{\partial F_1}{\partial H_1} = \frac{\partial F_5}{\partial H_5} < \frac{\partial F_2}{\partial H_2} = \frac{\partial F_3}{\partial H_3} = \frac{\partial F_4}{\partial H_4}$$

In other words, persons possessing capital (or land) earn less from operating latifundia or running handicraft factories than from leasing out land to tenants or extending capital to rural households under the putting-out arrangement. Predictably, the result would be the disappearance of latifundia and some handicraft factories because they are less profitable than other uses of capital.

The putting-out system, it should be noted, does not involve hiring workers for a fixed wage. The contract between the household and the putter-out is not a wage-work contract but a sales agreement in which the putter-out specifies the selling price of the raw material supplied by him and the price of the finished product he collects from the household. The difference between the two prices is the earning rate of the household per unit of finished product. Unlike wage payments to full-time workers, this price differential is not limited by the subsistence cost; by minimizing the household's earning rate, the putter-out is thus able to get a rate of return on his capital comparable to that which he would gain from other profitable alternatives. In a sense, the family working for the putter-out is the residual claimant of the output value; it has to receive some income below the subsistence level as it has retained the redundant labor at home. The putter-out is equivalent to the landlord who maximizes his income by renting out his land at a rate of return equal to that which he would gain from alternative uses. He has no obligation to bear any loss caused by the use of redundant labor.

Unfortunately, however, the existence of a large amount of redundant labor has the tendency to thwart the development of the production in-

15

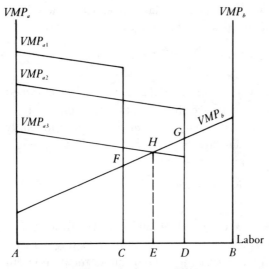

Fig. 1.2. Labor allocation of a rural family.

stitution most dynamic and effective in breeding new technology in the framework of preindustrialization. Redundant labor can also hamper the importation of advanced technology from abroad. Overpopulation therefore inevitably delays the process of industrialization.

Certain aspects of this argument are illustrated in Figure 1.2. Let us imagine a rural family that possesses a piece of land, not directly shown in the graph, and a total amount of labor from family members, as indicated by the distance on the horizontal axis between points A and B. The family attempts to allocate its total labor between agricultural production (A) and subsidiary production (B). The amount of labor allocated to agricultural production is measured by the horizontal distance to A, the amount of labor allocated to subsidiary production is measured by the horizontal distance to B, and the sum of the two is the total distance AB. The vertical axis on A indicates the value of the marginal product of labor engaged in agricultural production, whereas the vertical axis on B indicates the value of the marginal product of labor engaged in subsidiary production. The line VMP_b shows the diminishing returns in subsidiary production as more and more labor is applied. The line VMP_{a1}, which shows the diminishing marginal product in agricultural production, turns vertical and terminates at point C because of the limitation of the crop-

16

ping season. In other words, *CB* represents the amount of labor available during the off-season, which, when devoted to subsidiary production, yields a marginal product of *CF*.

As population density in the economy rises, the average farm size declines. This effect is reflected in the downward shift in the marginal product curve of agricultural production from VMP_{a1} to VMP_{a2}. To the extent that the family is induced to intensify farming, the cropping season may be lengthened, say, to point *D*, leaving *DB* to subsidiary production. Extension of the cropping season has its physical limit, however, beyond which any further increase in population, reduction in farm size, and lowering of the marginal product line to VMP_{a3} will lead to an expansion of subsidiary production. *HE* is the line on which the marginal products of the two types of family production activities become equal. As the population pressure continues to mount, this dividing line tends to shift further and further to the left, a phenomenon that may be called the domestication and ruralization of nonfarm goods production.

The development of the putting-out system and merchant activities in general makes a great contribution to the process of domestication and ruralization of nonfarm goods production in an overpopulated area or economy. The main barrier to the expansion of rural subsidiary production is usually not the lack of capital in rural households, because the capital required in most cases is negligible; it is rather the problem of marketing. Unless this problem is solved, rural families can hardly produce more nonagricultural goods than they themselves can consume. It is usually the putters-out and merchants who manage to establish the marketing networks for peasants so that rural households can produce nonagricultural goods for a large market. The contribution of the putting-out system is reflected in a upward shift in the line VMP_b because the prices of such goods tend to increase in an enlarged market.

We may go a step further in connecting rural subsidiary production with handicraft factories. If both of these production institutions use the same technology to manufacture a given product, they differ only in the following two respects: (1) labor is a fixed input for rural families and a variable input for handicraft factories, so that the latter can more easily adjust their output than the former, and (2) with zero opportunity cost for labor it is worthwhile for rural families to carry on subsidiary production at any price level for which the net revenue (price minus cost of materials) is above zero; handicraft factories, in contrast, can operate only

17

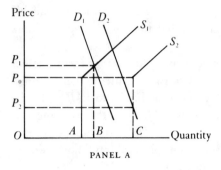

PANEL A

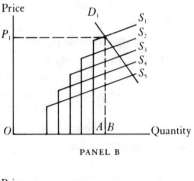

PANEL B

Fig. 1.3. Competition between factories and rural subsidiary production.

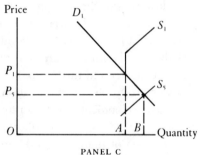

PANEL C

when the price of the commodity is high enough for them to pay at least a subsistence wage to full-time workers.

In panel A of Figure 1.3 the kinked curve S_1 shows the combined supply of both rural subsidiary production and handicraft factories for a given commodity. Given its nature, rural subsidiary production supplies a nearly fixed amount of OA and is price inelastic. To exaggerate this feature, a vertical supply schedule is drawn. The supply of handicraft factories begins at $P = P_0$ in cases where they receive a revenue barely sufficient to pay subsistence wages to workers. But their supply is price elastic: when the price rises, more output is forthcoming. If the current demand is D_1, the intersection of S_1 and D_1 yields an equilibrium quantity of OB and an equilibrium price P_1. The equilibrium quantity is made up of two parts: the output of OA from rural subsidiary production and the output of AB supplied by factories.

Population growth shifts the supply curve to S_2, which is also a vertical line kinked at the same P_0 (where the price allows payment of the subsistence wage rate). Rural families then provide a fixed output of OC with

18

their labor, which is available to them at zero cost. Although the demand schedule also shifts to the right as a result of the population increase, it does so only by a smaller horizontal distance because the per capita income fails to rise by the same proportion. Consequently, D_2 intersects S_2 at its vertical segment, indicating that the demand is barely sufficient to absorb the output OC at a price of P_2, which falls short of a price allowing a subsistence wage. Thus, factory production disappears, leaving only rural subsidiary production to meet the total demand. The latter survives merely because it is not constrained by any wage floor.

This effect is unfortunate, however, because handicraft factories are the type of organization that can potentially breed modern technology. Panel B of Figure 1.3 depicts a viable sector of handicraft factories that can successfully compete with rural subsidiary production. This is so because the economy is not yet overpopulated. The intersection of S_1 and D_1 yields an equilibrium price of P_1 that is above the wage floor (the kinked point). The factory sector profitably produces an output of AB. Through further division of labor and inventions of more specialized and efficient instruments, factories are capable of generating a series of technological improvements. Each step of technological progress reduces production cost (as manifested by the successive downward shifts in the supply curve to S_2, S_3, and S_4) until an industrial revolution is realized (at, say, the position of S_5). Moreover, as technology advances, labor productivity in factories tends to rise so that factory workers earn higher wages; these rising wages in urban areas will then entice more and more of the rural population to the cities, a process known as urbanization (or, as some scholars prefer, proletarianization), and the labor available to rural subsidiary production at zero cost will accordingly be reduced. This process is indicated in the graph in the form of successive shifts in the vertical segment of the supply curve to the left of point A.

The question that remains is simply this: How is a country suffering from overpopulation and the resulting domestication and ruralization of nonagricultural production finally able to import modern technology and advanced forms of industrial organization? Panel C of Figure 1.3 provides the answer. Here the initial situation of the economy is represented by D_1 and S_1; the equilibrium price is P_1, a state in which the handicraft factory sector was displaced completely by rural subsidiary production because of substantial population pressure. Consequently, the economy lost the opportunity of generating its own industrial revolution, as in panel B. But after an industrial revolution has taken place in countries in which the absence of population pressure has enabled the factory sector to develop uninterrupted, local producers may find it profitable to import modern forms of organization and mechanized production technology. The new technology reduces the cost of production to such a low level that the factories can successfully compete with the local supply from rural households. This situation is demonstrated by the new supply curve S_5 in panel C. The new factories can make profits even when the price is as low as P_5.

Even in this case, though, modernization and industrialization will initially meet with stubborn and formidable resistance from rural subsidiary producers, whose situation is so flexible that they can survive as long as their labor income from subsidiary production has not dropped to zero. As time passes, however, rural labor is likely to move to the modern sector because of the higher wages offered there. At that stage the modern sector may find it has actually benefited greatly from the enormous supply of cheap labor from the countryside that has enabled it to compete in the international market. In other words, even though overpopulation is an "absolute disadvantage" in a closed, traditional economy, it turns into a "comparative advantage" once the economy has embarked on modernization and opened up to international trade.

The changes described here by the theory of general equilibrium cannot be verified by short-term data or even by dynastic studies. Fortunately, however, because China has been a market economy for more than two thousand years and because its man-land ratio has so rapidly and seriously increased in recent centuries, Chinese history provides a wonderful opportunity to observe such changes.

Let us now turn from institutional to technological adjustments. Ester Boserup has convinced many economists that population growth leads to changes in agricultural technology.[6] In particular, this theory has been used to explain some significant agricultural developments in Chinese history. Dwight Perkins argues, for example, that rising population density after the eleventh century made possible widespread double cropping in southern and southeastern China by removing the bottleneck between the two crops caused by a shortage of labor.[7] In a more recent study, Cho-yun Hsu contends that high population density led the country to develop many intensive farming techniques as early as in the Han dynasty

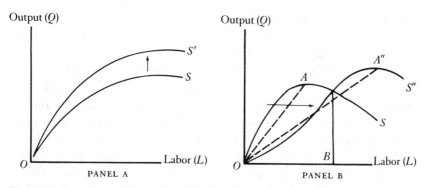

Fig. 1.4. Effects of new labor-saving technology (PANEL A) and new labor-using technology (PANEL B).

(206 B.C.-A.D. 220).[8] In general, I share their views and in the remaining pages of this chapter will construct a model by which the economic consequences of such technological adjustments may be conjectured.

In general and abstract terms, a distinction may be made between two types of innovations in farming technology—labor saving and labor using. Use of the latter is often referred to as intensification of farming. The two types are depicted in Figure 1.4 as two different ways of shifting the production function. In panels A and B, the horizontal axis measures the quantity of labor L and the vertical axis measures the total output Q produced by labor. In panel A the production function S shifts upward to the position S' after a new labor-saving device is introduced. Panel B represents the effect of intensive farming innovations by a shift of the production function to the right, that is, from S to S''.

As Boserup points out, the two types of innovations differ in three important ways. First, innovations of labor-saving technology tend to raise the returns per unit of labor, whereas the opposite is true with new labor-using technology. Panel B shows the reduced returns per unit of labor after a labor-using innovation is adopted, but the innovation is able to provide a higher peak output, point A'' as compared with point A, by absorbing more labor than was possible before.

Second, only after a certain point does the benefit of absorbing more labor for producing a larger total output offset the disadvantage of reduced returns per unit of labor under the new labor-using technology. This is point B in panel B. Before this point, both the average product

21

and the total product are lower for S'' than for S at any given level of L. But after B, the total product of S'' is higher than that of S even though its average product remains lower.

Third, new labor-saving instruments and technology usually entail a long process of invention and accumulation of engineering skills. In contrast, intensive farming techniques can come into being with relative ease. Intensification in farming sometimes involves no more than using existing implements in a different way or rearranging existing crops. In an area where the growing season is sufficiently long for two crops, double cropping merely requires repeating the same operation needed for a single crop. Since the benefits of labor-saving devices are obvious and immediate, they will be applied at once and widely diffused as soon as they are made available at a reasonable cost. Labor-using technologies, however, may be first invented in a few pockets of high population density long before they become widely adopted in a country. As mentioned before, such inventions are useful only in areas with sufficient density to enable them to go beyond the critical point B.

As far as land use is concerned, virtually every country has experienced a long history of gradual intensification. Boserup breaks up this long, continuous process into five stages: forest-fallow cultivation, bush-fallow cultivation, short-fallow cultivation, annual cropping, and multicropping. Here, however, I adopt a two-stage classification, with the multiple-cropping index (sown area divided by cultivated area) equal to unity as the demarcation point. Written records exist describing deliberate forest burning during the Shang dynasty, but historians are uncertain whether this was done for purposes of hunting or land clearing before cultivation or both. At any rate, this period is too remote to constitute a main concern for the present study.

Historical data suggest that short-fallow cultivation on lands divided by permanent boundary marks began in China no later than the tenth century B.C. Probably beginning in the fourth century B.C., the Chinese gradually shortened the average fallow time and raised the multiple-cropping index. For the country as a whole, the index probably reached unity by the twelfth century. The same process took place in Europe much later. According to Boserup, the average fallow time in Europe was shortened during and after the Middle Ages, and the index did not reach unity until the latter half of the eighteenth century.

A multiple-cropping index equal to unity represents a significant turning point in agriculture. Before it was attained, the typical farmer grew one crop and worked approximately the same number of working days in a year regardless of the average fallow time. He could raise the total output either by promoting the unit yield or by plowing more land with more efficient implements. Shortening of fallow is, therefore, accompanied by rising returns per unit of labor. After this point, the farmer can attempt to get more output by growing more than one crop a year. He has to work more days in a year but does not necessarily need more efficient implements because the same set of implements can be used for both crops. The rising index then ceases to be an indicator of labor productivity.

These changes did not take place at the same speed in every region in China. Although many intensive farming techniques are known to have been devised in Han times (206 B.C.-A.D. 220), most of them had not become widespread until after the twelfth century. The variation in population density in different regions is believed to have been responsible, to a large extent, for their uneven tempos of technological development. As late as the eleventh century, certain areas in Szechwan and Hupei still practiced bush-fallow and grass-fallow cultivation even while neighboring districts had employed highly intensified methods (involving weeding and the use of the hoe) for quite some time. It is unlikely that this divergence was the consequence of a poor state of technological transmission, but rather that in areas of labor shortage (where point B of Figure 1.4 was unattainable) the newer, intensive methods would not lead to an increase in total output and were therefore not economically justified.

The Chinese methods of fertilization and multicropping are so labor consuming that they yield a considerably lower average output per man-hour than other, simpler methods of fertilization and annual cropping. Many other countries simply cannot afford the amount of labor required. Chinese intensive farming brings high yields per crop hectare at the expense of a much heavier input of labor per crop hectare. Indeed, labor input per crop hectare in China in the 1930's was in some districts as high as 600 working days, ten to twenty times the usual labor input for dry crops of cereals under the type of extensive plow cultivation applied in many other underdeveloped countries.[9]

The theoretical premises developed in this chapter will be tested in subsequent chapters against Chinese historical data. Specifically, Chapters 2 through 4 will be devoted to the measurement of population and arable land in traditional China so that we can obtain a fairly clear notion about the relative growth of the two most important economic variables. Population pressure may be detected directly from man-land ratios and indirectly from ratios of urban population to total population; with fairly high urban-rural mobility, as was the case in China, the size of the urban sector is ultimately determined by the rate of surplus grain production in the rural sector. Chapters 5 and 6 will examine land fragmentation and land distribution to ascertain to what degree the factor markets were atomistic with a large number of participants on both the demand and the supply side.

Chapters 7 and 8 will survey the evolution of tenure systems in China to determine if my postulated adjustments in the face of increasing population pressure are borne out by facts. In this connection, other relevant aspects of Chinese agricultural institutions will be discussed.

The problem of agricultural technology will be discussed in Chapter 9. Since the development of farming technology in China has already been carefully investigated by numerous studies, there is no need for repetition. Our discussion will accordingly be confined to the measurement of changes in the returns to labor and in the general standard of living that have resulted from intensified farming.

Throughout this book, my theoretical hypotheses are to be tested primarily against data from the agricultural sector, since this is by far the most important sector of a premodern economy. As I have pointed out earlier, ruralization of nonagricultural production was part of an institutional adjustment by rural households undertaken to cope with rising population pressure during later Chinese history. Because of the complexity of the process of ruralization of nonagricultural production and limitations of space, this issue and its ramifications will be treated in detail in a future study. It should be noted here, however, that the question of ruralization of nonagricultural production is by no means unique to Chinese history. A great deal of recent literature by Western historians is devoted to the subject of proto-industrialization, a phenomenon found in some European rural communities before industrialization.[10] In such areas overpopulation compelled rural households to engage in the production of nonagricultural goods for market. The difference between proto-industrialization in these European rural villages and the ruralization of nonagricultural production in China is only one of degree. Proto-industrialization in Europe took place only in a few rural pockets where population growth was unusually fast or where land was unusually poor in quality. Ruralization of nonagricultural production in China, by contrast, was as universal as the overpopulation that caused it.

2

Population Growth

A New Interpretation

One of the great controversies among students of Chinese economic history has focused on whether population growth in China was a dependent or independent variable of production technology, especially of agricultural production. Early modern scholars, accepting the basic assumptions of Malthus, often regarded population as a dependent and endogenous variable, viewing improvements in land use and discoveries of higher-yield crops as the stimulus of, and precondition for, further population expansion. This view has been challenged by new studies by Boserup, Perkins, and Hsu, as cited in Chapter 1.

It is interesting to note that Marxist economic historians in China hold a "neutral" view on this issue. Built on the theory of a one-factor (labor) production model, which inherently rejects the law of diminishing returns, and on the theory of surplus value, which asserts that laborers, by their very nature, can always produce more than they need for subsistence consumption, Marxist economics has never incorporated the Malthusian theory of population. As faithful Marxists see it, a country's population cannot impose a problem on its economy unless laborers are overexploited by greedy capitalists or feudal lords. On the other hand, Marxist theoreticians assert that technology and productivity changes are the independent and fundamental variables that determine the "mode" of production and superstructures in society; that is to say, technology and labor productivity dictate—and are not dictated by—superstructures, including the family system and demographic characteristics. Thus, regardless of the level of technology, the so-called population problem is nothing but a matter of poor distribution. Marxist historians, however, are also perplexed by the failure of technology as an independent and automatic force in premodern China.

Newly available historical data strongly indicate that, at least in traditional China, population growth was an independent and exogenous variable to which the people responded by adjusting their production technologies and economic institutions.

China has a long history of recording national, regional, and local population data, but the statistics are often erroneous. There are unexplainable variations, conflicts between numbers of persons and numbers of households, contradictory figures from different sources, and numerous possible errors caused by repeated transcriptions and printings. Although counting heads was a much easier task than measuring land, the general quality of population data from historical documents is poorer than that of land data, not only because population vicissitudes occurred more rapidly than land changes but also because historically the Chinese people were geographically highly mobile. Land returns obtained from a land survey might remain valid for a relatively long period of time, whereas population counts required frequent revision or they would quickly become obsolete.

Many excellent studies in Chinese, Japanese, and English have assessed demographical data from Chinese historical materials.[1] These studies have attempted to determine where and to what extent such data are useful and whether a general trend of Chinese demographic development can be detected; none is designed to reconstruct a reliable series consistent with modern standards. Generally, these works have employed two different approaches to evaluating the credibility of historical demographical data. One approach has been to study the institutional and political conditions of various time periods to ascertain when and where specific Chinese governments had the necessary instruments, capabilities, and determination to obtain reasonably reliable results. This type of study would provide at least some circumstantial evidence about the quality of such data.

The other approach has been to conduct consistency tests on the data by comparing regional and provincial returns compiled from different time periods. This type of study is less fruitful because of some inherent limitations. First, though the absence of consistency among data from different time periods may indicate unreliability, the existence of consistency may not necessarily prove its opposite. If the population data under comparison were biased by more or less the same degree, they would still pass the consistency test. Second, except in the Ming and Ch'ing periods, when most of the provincial boundaries were stabilized, political subdivisions changed drastically from one dynastic period to the next. Unless the investigator selects a set of subdivisions from a given dynasty as a basis and then regroups the population data of individual localities from other dynasties, a consistency test can hardly be conclusive. Third, such a study requires absolute knowledge of regional hostilities, migrations, and resettlement programs, to list only some of the factors that might have affected interregional population movements in various periods.

Since I am primarily concerned with the general historical trends of population and man-land ratios, I shall rely on the previous institutional analyses to select a few relatively accurate figures as benchmarks in the long history of China. I am less concerned here with regional demographic patterns or movements than with overall population trends. While fully aware of the substantial changes in the delimitations of national boundaries at various times and of the serious underregistration of non-Han peoples in the border areas, I feel no need to make any major adjustment, for the simple reason that total acreage of farmland and total population were presumably affected by the same factors and in the same directions.

I would, however, like to offer some new interpretations of the findings presented in previous studies. The first point to emphasize is that a high degree of stability of demographic characteristics prevailed during peaceful times. The second point concerns the relation between the recurrence of large-scale wars and population cycles.

Recent studies of historical populations have greatly benefited from new techniques of demographic analysis based on the notion of a stable population. In such an analysis, reproduction rate and age-specific mortality rates of a population are assumed to be fairly stable. Thus, the population will increase (or decrease) indefinitely in a regular manner and its age structure will remain the same. A stable population is, of course, only a theoretical model that may not often be found in the real world. Mortality rates are affected by major wars, epidemics, and serious crop failures; fertility rates, in some cases, tend to vary as the average marriage age fluctuates in response to vicissitudes of economic conditions. In addition, migration upsets the stability of a population that otherwise qualifies as stable. During relative peaceful times in history, the Chinese population appears to have fit the definition of a stable population quite well, or at least better than most European populations.

Historically, to the extent that it could do so, a country was most likely to control its population by regulation of fertility rather than mortality. Fertility, moreover, is decisively influenced by nuptiality. Before the advent of modern birth control devices, a person who found supporting a family too burdensome might wish to postpone marriage. Therefore, the degree of population stability in premodern times was largely determined by the relative strength of the institution of the family and its concomitant value system in a given society.

The population of China in the early part of the twentieth century has been called a "stable population" as defined by modern demographers.[2] A more recent study based on genealogical materials of some clans in the lower Yangtze region also reveals fairly stable characteristics for the period 1400-1900.[3] Because the institution of the family and its social value system existed in China long before 1400, I am inclined to believe that the Chinese population may have experienced a high degree of stability even long before 1400.

Historically (or at least after the fifteenth century), deriving from the tradition of individualism, most young men in European societies were very cautious in making matrimonial decisions. Because supporting a family and raising children were considered personal responsibilities that should not be transferred to anyone else, marriage could be considered only when adequate financial means were available. As a result, the marriage rate, the average marriage age, and the crude birth rate in those societies after the fifteenth century all tended to vary in accordance with prevailing economic conditions.

Numerous studies have confirmed significant variations in nuptiality among European countries. The mean age of first marriage in Ireland was about only 17 for women before the Great Famine of 1847 but it jumped to nearly 30 for women and 35 for men after 1850.[4] A French study shows that after a severe plague in Boulay, France in 1635-36, when roughly 23 percent of the population died within four months, the average marriage rate changed drastically.[5] Other investigators have discovered that marital fertility as well as nuptiality in many European countries in preindustrial times were closely correlated with either the harvest cycle or the variation of real wages.[6] Even in prewar Japan, where the institution of family was characterized by primogeniture as well as other factors, cyclical fluctuations in marriage rates are found to have occurred as direct responses to business cycles.[7]

In sharp contrast, the Chinese family structure, the tradition of ancestor worship, and the concept of filial piety meant that matrimonial decisions in China could not be a matter of personal choice. Instead, getting married as early as possible and raising as many sons as possible became a man's inalienable obligation to his ancestors and family. A man had to do his best to fulfill this obligation regardless of his economic circumstances; failure to do so was considered by the person himself, his parents and family, and even the whole community as a grave and inexcusable sin. In many cases, parents or other relatives would assume the financial burden of supporting the family if the person was very young or destitute. Consequently, unless constrained by extraordinary circumstances, the average marriage age was customarily young and the birth rate firmly determined by biological factors. (Naturally, however, it is unnecessary to assume 100 percent universal marriage, which would have been unlikely even in traditional China.) Under such circumstances, the percentage of people who preferred to remain unmarried or who could not get married was low, and moderate fluctuations of this low percentage would not significantly upset the characteristics of the stable population. Moreover, migration as a disturbing factor was minimal in Chinese history.

If the Chinese population has indeed remained fairly stable since, say, the Han period, what would be the plausible range of average growth rates during peaceful periods relatively free of wars, epidemics, and natural calamities? In discussing population data from the Han dynasties, Durand has assumed a mortality rate capable of yielding a life expectancy of 30 years or less and a gross reproduction rate of 3.[8] A stable population with such rates would imply a birth rate near 50, a death rate near 35, and an annual rate of natural increase approximating 15 per 1,000. Durand has taken this as the upper limit for accepting historical population data. Although a death rate of 35 per 1,000 is not too unreasonable as compared with the findings of local population surveys done in the 1930's,[9] a birth rate of 50 per 1,000 seems too high; to maintain such a high birth rate would entail not only early marriage but also practically universal marriage. Tsui-jung Liu has found that the average growth rates of the clans she studied fall within a range of 7 to 14 per 1,000. If we include families who had lower incomes and resided on less productive land, the acceptable range of average growth rates may be lowered to 5 to 10 per 1,000. Any historical data implying an average rate of population growth considerably exceeding 10 per 1,000 over a period of several decades or longer are implausible and should be rejected.

Apparently the major large-scale warfare recurrent in China interrupted what otherwise would have been stable population growth. Contrary to the Malthusian postulate, however, the major hostile activities of Chinese history were not a positive check internally generated by overpopulation. Most conflicts began with foreign invasions that occurred when neither the invading regimes nor the ruling Chinese governments were faced by any serious overpopulation problems. In the fourth century, for example, the northern tribes launched an attack on the Chin when the Chinese government was handicapped by a severe shortage of manpower. On the other hand, few of the civil disorders that erupted during periods of relatively strong population pressure were of long duration. Wars of attrition constituted an exogenous, independent variable in Chinese history that had enormous impact on the pattern of population growth.

Because of a lack of established codes of conduct governing warfare, Chinese wars and conflicts were extraordinarily destructive. Direct casualties were never confined to combat soldiers, and it was not unusual for the population of an entire city to be slaughtered by an invading force. The "scorched-earth policy" might be practiced by either side, whether government troops or indigenous rebellious forces, and it rendered vast regions uninhabitable. Besides the death toll directly related to belligerence, the remaining population would be sharply reduced by food shortages and widespread epidemic diseases. Shocked by a reported loss of 15 million lives in the Taiping Rebellion (1851-64), some Western observers have called it the greatest civil war in human history. In reality, many wars in China before the Taiping Rebellion were more pronounced in scope, duration, intensity, and degree of devastation.

The effects of war on China's population growth depended on two parameters. First, given the total death toll and a stable population growth rate determined largely by biological factors during postwar years, is the speed with which wartime loss could be recovered, and this is related to the population base. Thus, given a 1 percent growth rate determined by normal biological factors, the loss of 25 million people, or half, of a base population of 50 million would require seventy years to recover. The same number of casualties from a base population of 400 million, however, could be fully recovered in six years. Therefore, despite its immense devastation, the Taiping Rebellion caused merely a tiny ripple in the rising tide of Chinese population—a ripple, moreover, completely incapable of functioning as a Malthusian positive check.

The second crucial parameter is the frequency of large-scale devastating wars. Because Chinese wars were exogenous in nature and were not caused by overpopulation, their occurrences formed a random pattern. Given a relatively small population base—say, 50 million—and a stable growth rate of 1 percent in peaceful times, in the long run the population could not grow without a peaceful interval between two major wars long enough to allow for full recovery. Otherwise, major wars would only lead to a cyclical movement of population, with each new peak no higher than the previous one. If wars broke out at infrequent intervals that were long enough to enable each peaceful period to exceed the amount of time necessary for full recovery, the population would grow in a pattern of cyclical movements revolving around a rising trend line, with each new peak surpassing the preceding one.

These two parameters jointly produce a turning point that converts the first pattern of cyclical movements into the second pattern. That is, if a government managed to maintain peace considerably beyond the time period required for full recovery, the new peak population would surpass the previous peak. The enlarged population base would in turn determine a relative reduction in the degree of destruction caused by the next major war. Recovery would subsequently require less time, the population would stand an increasingly improved chance of expanding, and the rising population base would continue to reduce the relative destructive power of future wars. Once this phase was entered, scarcely any positive check would be powerful enough to reverse or stop the rising trend. Thus, after the Chinese population broke, say, the 300 million mark, no war with conventional weapons could be sufficiently destructive to wipe out half of the population. The degree of depopulation would consistently decrease and a shorter time period would be required for recovery. Eventually, the cycles would be obscured, leaving only the rising trend line visible.

Historical Data on the Chinese Population

The earliest population data in Chinese history that Durand and Bielenstein regard as worthy of consideration are statistics of persons and households for certain years during the Han. The first set of data comes from the year A.D. 2 (see Appendix A), in which a total of 59.6 million persons was recorded for the empire as a whole. This was seven years before Wang Mang usurped the throne of the Western Han, and the figure probably represents a peak after a long period of peace and prosperity.[10] The next four population returns

A.D. 57	20 million
A.D. 75	34.1 million
A.D. 88	43.3 million
A.D. 105	53.2 million

supposedly reflect the recovery phase that took place after the serious depopulation between the two Han dynasties.

Some of these returns, however, are obviously defective. The implied annual rates of growth—27.3 per 1,000 between A.D. 57 and 75, and 19 per 1,000 between A.D. 75 and 88—both appear to be too high. The increments probably include both natural population growth and the repatriation of displaced people who had failed to register previously during the period of disorder. The recorded annual rate of growth fell to 11 per 1,000 in the period A.D. 88-105, suggesting that by this time the household registration work had largely returned to normal. In other words, we suspect that the two totals for A.D. 57 and 75 excluded considerable numbers of displaced persons. If the 43.3 million figure in A.D. 88 is taken as a base for backward projection, a growth rate of 10 per 1,000 would imply a total population of 31 million in A.D. 57.

The next population peak of 56.4 million was recorded in A.D. 156. Shortly after that date, the empire virtually disintegrated as it entered a phase of almost 400 years of civil wars and foreign invasions with occasional short spells of relative peace. Few of the population returns published in this period, especially national totals, can be of high quality. The next viable population figure—46 million— was compiled in 606 by the Sui government after the empire was once again reunited. During the T'ang dynasty, statistics are available for 27 dates, among which eight totals compiled between 705-55 are judged by Durand as more or less meaningful. Over these 50 years, the Chinese population rose from 37.1

to 52.9 million, exhibiting a reasonable growth rate of 8 per 1,000 per annum. The year 755 marked the beginning of another long era of turmoil and hostile activities, in which the census system undoubtedly broke down.

Although population returns were more frequent during the Sung than in any previous dynasty, these data are highly controversial. The area reunited under the effective rule of the Sung was much smaller than in both the Han and T'ang empires. Moreover, the Sung census data consistently manifest an unusually small average size of households— slightly over 2 persons, in contrast to the average of 5.7 to 6 persons during the T'ang.

There are two different explanations for these incredibly low ratios. One group of historians posits that the Sung government divided households with land property into several classes but selected only upper-class families with more than one male adult to fill public service offices in local government. Those positions were not only compulsory and nonpaying but also extremely time consuming, so that large wealthy families had strong incentives to break up their original households. Thus a "parent" household might be split into several smaller ones, each having no more than one male adult and a fraction of the family property. In the opinion of these scholars, population enumerations might be close to the truth whereas the number of households was probably exaggerated.

This argument, however, suffers from several fatal weaknesses. Both the number of such public service positions and the number of wealthy families originally designated as upper class were not large enough even for the whole country to have created such a tremendous distortion in the household counts. If only 10 percent, say, of total households qualified as upper-class families, how many units of smaller households would each of the "parent" households have to create to reduce the national average ratio of persons per household from about 6 to slightly over 2? More important, if household splitting motivated by the desire to avoid compulsory public service were indeed the cause, the average household size should be unusually small only among *chu hu* (resident households) who owned land and hence might be selected to fill in such positions, but not among *k'e hu* (nonresident households) who owned no land and hence were not qualified for such works. Yet the average number of persons per household in the latter group, about 1.5, was far smaller than in the former.[11]

34

The other theory contends that the average number of persons per household was uniformly small during Sung times simply because the Sung census was limited, as a rule, to male adults or what was called *ting*. An imperial mandate issued at the beginning of the regime (963) stipulated that the annual household registration in each locality must count the number of male adults between 20 and 60 years of age, but the inclusion of females and males outside this age range was optional.[12] The high degree of stability in the ratios of persons per household and the identical rates (9 per 1,000) by which both the population and number of households had increased throughout the period seem to imply that a stable institutional relationship existed between the two variables.

If such a relationship did in fact exist, the totals of households should be more or less valid. One way to estimate population size in a given year, then, is to multiply the number of households by a reasonable ratio of persons per household. If the average ratio of the T'ang dynasty (5.8 persons) is carried over to Sung times, the population around A.D. 1109 may be estimated as 121 million. Using this number as a base for reverse projection and a growth rate of 9 per 1,000, the estimated population around 961 would be 32 million. In other words, the Chinese population had increased nearly four times in a period of 150 peaceful years.

As a rule, whenever natural calamities occurred, the Sung government would either dispatch special missions or instruct the local authorities within whose jurisdiction the disasters took place to provide relief food, shelter, or other necessities for the refugees. Occasionally, the special missions or local relief agencies later published detailed accounts of the numbers of families and persons who had received relief provision. Such accounts were supposed to cover all members in each family rather than male adults only. In Table 2.1, records reported by various localities in different years are assembled. They indicate an average of 5.61 persons per household.

Such relief registrations are suspected to contain two potential types of biases. First, unless the relief agency had some effective control over the distribution of relief goods, such as actually counting heads, there might be a tendency for the recipient families to exaggerate their family size. Second, in the case of certain types of calamities, such as severe floods, or in the case of unduly delayed relief, abnormal or premature deaths might have reduced the average size of refugee families below the normal level.[13] If the two biases in opposite directions offset each other to a large

TABLE 2.1

Refugee Registrations in Southern Sung Disaster Areas, 1132–1210

Year	Area	Number of households	Number of persons
1132	Kao-yu	1,080	6,000
1169	Chen-chiang	269	1,346
1171	Ho-fei	344	1,996
1171	Chi-an	341	2,112
1181	Nan-kang chün	29,578	217,883
1191	Hsing-chou	3,492	19,209
1191	Ch'ang-chü	179	1,063
1190-94	Lin-an	50,000	300,000
1201	Lin-an	1,321	5,345
1204	Fu-chou	39,000	185,690
1208	Lin-an	560	2,081
1209	Lin-an	850	3,676
1210	T'ai-p'ing-chou	67,504	415,071
1210	Kuang-te-chün	55,073	237,221
TOTAL		249,591	1,400,693

SOURCES: Liang Keng-yao 1978, p. 149; Mu, p. 157. I am grateful to Liang Keng-yao for notifying me about the misprinted figures in his original article. The figures have been corrected accordingly.

extent, the average number of persons per household revealed by those relief records would still be relevant and hence may be used to calculate the total population of the Sung period. If we use the ratio of 5.61 persons per household, the resulting population size in 1109 is 117 million, a figure practically identical with the estimate given earlier.

The country was soon partitioned by the Jürchen Chin in the north and the Southern Sung on the opposite side of the Huai River. While the Southern Sung maintained the same household registration system, which resulted in an equally small ratio of persons per household, the Chin enumerations called for full coverage. The Chin census of 1195 recorded a total population of 48.5 million and a ratio of 6.7 persons per household. Although the territory of the Chin included parts of Manchuria and Mongolia, population in those areas was sparse. The number of households in the Southern Sung in 1193 was 12.3 million, which, if multiplied by a ratio of 5.8 persons per household, would yield a population figure of 71.3 million. The sum of the two figures is about 120 million, comparable to the estimated total population at the end of the Northern Sung. Apparently, the hostilities of the two rival states along a more or less stationary battlefront were less destructive than a war with changing front lines, permitting the size of the overall population to remain the same.

Five censuses were taken by the ruling Mongols during the Yüan dynasty for the areas inside the Great Wall, but Durand and other demographers have discovered that those enumerations were incomplete. What seems certain is the continuous decline in population throughout the dynasty. The population must have reached its nadir during the years immediately before the Ming troops drove the Mongols out of China and reunited the empire. There is no need, however, to adjust the Yüan population statistics, since we have no viable acreage data for that period to complement them in computing man-land ratios.

More interesting are the population returns of the Ming dynasty, which present two extreme cases. On one hand, the new system of household registration and the determination of Emperor T'ai Tsu to obtain accurate census data produced two sets (for 1381 and 1391) of demographic data that are generally considered the best in Chinese history.[14] On the other hand, population returns after 1402, published almost annually until 1522 and decennially thereafter, are virtually worthless. In some decades, the figures show an incredible constancy, suggesting that most local officials responsible for population enumerations merely repeated the same figures year after year. In many other cases, however, the changes are too abrupt to be true and cannot be attributed to such events as the wars against the Tartars, the invasion of Japanese pirates, the Korean expedition, and campaigns against the rebellious southwestern tribes, all of which occurred after those abrupt changes in population count. Most experts share the view of Ping-ti Ho that the Ming population grew steadily from the base figure of 60.5 million in 1391. Perkins estimates that the total population at the end of the sixteenth century was somewhere between 120 million and 200 million.[15] We are inclined to believe that the peak was reached around 1590, with a total approaching 200 million. There is certainly no circumstantial evidence to suggest an average population growth rate below 6 per 1,000 during the relatively peaceful years between 1391 and 1590.

The process of political disintegration and economic deterioration began in the early seventeenth century under the reign of Wan-li. The central government was weakened by in-fighting between opposing factions, and the country was ravaged by numerous revolts, especially the rebellious forces led by Li Tz'u-ch'eng and Chang Hsien-chung. These were immediately followed by the invasion of the Manchus, who finally established the Ch'ing dynasty to replace the Ming. This chaotic period also witnessed two epidemics, the worst ever recorded in Chinese history (1586-89 and 1939-42), that devastated the population of northern China and parts of the lower Yangtze Valley.

Official population returns for the Ch'ing dynasty have been compiled in a recent research paper.[16] The figures for the early years of the period, however, are not directly usable. Up to 1740, the census data compiled by the Manchu government referred to adult males, known as *ting*, for the purpose of poll tax and labor conscription. Beginning in 1740, the *pao-chia* system instituted at the local level, in which a certain number of households in the same neighborhood were organized as a *chia* and a certain number of *chia* as a *pao*, was charged with the function of reporting population counts, and coverage was extended from taxable male adults to all people. This complete coverage, along with the separation of census from tax-collecting files, helped greatly to improve the quality of population data. Allowing an adequate period of time for the initiation and refinement of the new methods, population data recorded after 1775 are believed to be of a fairly high quality. A total of 268 million people were registered in 1776.

Several previous studies attempted to reconstruct the population counts of the early Ch'ing by multiplying the *ting* figures by an assumed ratio of total population to male adults.[17] Although this approach is generally sound, both the *ting* figures and the population-*ting* ratios selected by these studies are highly questionable. Not all *ting* returns are suitable for this type of projection.

The first national total of *ting* for China was reported in 1651. At the beginning, a *ting* was strictly defined as a male adult between the Chinese age of 16 and 60. Furthermore, local household registers, known as *pien shen t'se*, recorded the numbers of other population groups in addition to *ting*. For instance, the register of the first *chia*, fourth *t'u*, sixteenth *t'u*, Sui-an county, Yen-chou prefecture, Chekiang, for the year 1712[18] gives the following population counts in the *chia*:

ch'eng ting (male adults)	14
ta kou (female adults)	19
pu ch'eng ting (presumably persons below 16 and over 60)	27

Another household register for a single family headed by Fang Tseng-nien in the 3rd *chia*, 45th *t'u* of Sui-an county in the year 1692 shows the following:

ch'eng ting	10
ta kou	9
pu ch'eng ting	7

Registers for two other individual households, Fang Chen-lung and Fang Li-yu, with unknown location and time, display the same three categories. Obviously, the local household registration kept the records of all three, but only the *ting* returns were aggregated and published.

This system of household registration was marred, however, by two factors that render the *ting* figures for some years unusable in estimating total population. First, the registration was revised every five years (1652, 1657, 1662, and so on) so that the number of *ting* remained relatively constant during the intermittent years but displayed abrupt jumps in registration years. This irregular movement was particularly conspicuous in the early years, as evidenced by sharp increases in *ting* returns for 1652 and 1657. It naturally follows that returns for registration years are better in quality than those for interim years.

Second, beginning in the K'ang-hsi reign, many local officials proposed to simplify tax collection by merging the poll tax on male adults with the land tax; some localities quickly made this change even without sanction from the central government. For example, in 1667 T'ai-kang county of Honan adopted a new policy by which every 33.3 *mou* of farmland was assessed as one *ting* for the purpose of taxation.[19] Similar methods of tax assessment were introduced in other localities in later years. This practice became even more widespread after the K'ang-hsi Emperor declared in 1712 that *ting* taxes for all districts in the country were fixed permanently on the basis of the 1711 *ting* returns. The merging of the *ting* tax and the land tax was officially declared a nationwide system in 1724. Although the number of localities that had changed the definition of *ting* to cope with the new tax system between 1667 and 1724 and measurement of the *ting* unit under the new definition are difficult to ascertain, it is, nevertheless, quite clear that not all *ting* returns from various localities during this period were intended to measure the numbers of male adults.

I have chosen the return of 1657, with a total of 18,611,996 *ting*, as the

TABLE 2.2

Population and Ting *Returns from Selected Localities During the Ch'ing Dynasty*

Locality	Total population	Ting
Wan-chüan, Shansi	18,776	5,395
Chung-mo, Honan	84,460	12,826
T'ai-hu, Anhwei	47,379	9,923
Tung-ling, Anhwei	14,953	3,498
Shan-yang, Chekiang	115,210	23,432
Wu-i, Chekiang	9,486	2,408
Fu-liang, Kiangsi	100,192	29,911
Yuan-chou, Kiangsi	175,841	36,338
Kuang-chi, Hupei	54,176	11,714
Chi-chou, Hopei	68,050	15,571
Ling-ling, Hunan	56,027	15,563
Hsün-chou, Kwangsi	865,387	260,598
TOTAL	1,609,937	427,177

SOURCE: Kuo, p. 58.

benchmark number for my estimate of total population because the underlying data were collected after the household registration operation had been improved by the new regime but before the definition of *ting* was altered in any locality. Furthermore, 1657 was a year for household registration revision, in which population data were updated.

The next problem is to determine a reasonable population-*ting* ratio. In his recent study, Kuo Sung-i has canvassed a large number of local gazetteers published during the Ch'ing dynasty and found 22 counties and prefectures that reported both total population figures and *ting* returns for the same years or periods.[20] Out of the 22 cases, ten must be eliminated because they exhibit a population-*ting* ratio below 3.20. Such a low ratio implies that either the death rate or the birth rate was extremely abnormal,[21] a situation that may be possible in some households under extreme circumstances but would be highly unlikely for a large sample of population. In these ten cases either the *ting* unit meant something other than the number of male adults or the returns were utterly unreliable. The remaining twelve cases are reproduced in Table 2.2.

The combined totals from the twelve localities yield an average population-*ting* ratio of 3.77. By multiplying this ratio to the *ting* figure of 1657, a total population of 70.2 million is obtained for that year. If the total population of 1776 (268 million) is taken as another benchmark, the implied annual growth rate over this period is 11.3 per 1,000, which is

TABLE 2.3

Official Data and Estimates of China's Population, Selected Years, A.D. 2-1848

(million)

Year	High	Low	Year	High	Low
2	59.6		1109	(121.0)	
57		(31.0)	1193	(120.0)	
105	53.2		1381		59.8
156	56.4		1391		60.5
280		16.2	1592	(200.0)	
606	46.0		1657		70.2
705		37.1	1776	268.2	
755	52.9		1800	295.2	
961		(32.0)	1848	426.7	

SOURCES: Numbers without parentheses are official data, taken from Durand, "Population Statistics." Numbers in parentheses are estimates; see the text.

barely outside the reasonable range of population growth rates in peaceful times as determined earlier.

There is a way to check the validity of the estimate. The thorough survey of 22 provinces conducted by John Buck and his associates in the late 1920's and early 1930's reveals an average birth rate of 38.3 per 1,000, an average death rate of 27.1 per 1,000, and a growth rate of 11.2 per 1,000.[22] These statistics fit best the Model West of stable population.[23]

Mortality level	8
Gross reproduction rate	2.50
Birth rate	40.40 per 1,000
Death rate	27.85 per 1,000
Growth rate	12.55 per 1,000
Life expectancy	34.892 years

This model suggests a population-*ting* ratio of 3.52, which is very close to the 3.77 estimated earlier. The resulting estimate of total population for 1657 will then be 65.5 million, which, when compared with the 268 million of 1776, produces an average growth rate of 11.9 per 1,000 over this period. That all these estimates appear consistent with each other to such a surprising degree suggests that the reconstructed total population of 70.2 million for 1657 is likely to have a tolerably small margin of error.

To sum up, the population data for the benchmark years selected earlier are tabulated in Table 2.3. The cyclical movements are clearly visible. Moreover, the durations of the rising phases of these cycles may be approximately calculated as follows:

45 years	(A.D. 60–A.D. 105)	in the Eastern Han
38 years	(580–618)	in the Sui
50 years	(705–755)	in the T'ang
150 years	(960–1110)	in the Northern Sung
220 years	(1380–1600)	in the Ming
190 years	(1660–1850)	in the Ch'ing

Clearly, before the Northern Sung wartime years outnumbered peaceful years, and even the peaceful intervals were comparatively short. None was sufficiently long to permit the population at its trough point to double itself, unless the natural rate of growth could be raised substantially higher than 15 per 1,000. As a result, the population fluctuated in a cyclical pattern below the 60 million mark, which was the first peak reached in A.D. 2.

The crucial turning point finally occurred when, after steady growth for 150 years during the Northern Sung, the population surpassed previous peaks by a sizeable margin so that major wars and natural disasters became relatively less destructive. The only reason China survived the onslaught of the Mongols in the thirteenth century was, as Perkins points out, that the Mongol armies were too small and the Chinese population too large.[24] Consequently, demographic development began to show cyclical movements upward around a rising trend line.

Even longer in duration, the two peaceful intervals after the Northern Sung made this rising population trend more definite. As the population base continued to expand, the recovery phase after each major war or disaster became shorter. After 1820 or thereabouts, the demographic data reveal a smooth rising trend line, with a few almost indiscernible drops. In the face of such a large population the so-called positive checks became virtually powerless to halt its growth. The Chinese population would continue to expand, though somewhat less rapidly, as the weight of the population gradually depressed the natural growth rate.

3
Urban Population

THE CITIES—sometimes called urban centers—of traditional China differed from medieval European cities in two crucial respects. First, unlike European cities, which were created by craftsmen, merchants, and escapees from nearby feudal manors and which performed primarily economic functions, traditional Chinese cities were multifunctional: politically, they served as gridpoints of the nationwide administrative network, militarily as strategic posts, and economically as concentrated markets and centers of manufacturing production. Second, in contrast to the clear rural-urban dichotomy in medieval Europe, Chinese cities were to some extent integrated with the countryside. People enjoyed a high degree of freedom in choosing between agricultural and nonagricultural occupations and could move fairly freely between the two sectors.

For these reasons, the Chinese urban sector grew much faster than Western cities. On one hand, the city's multifunctional role created a larger urban population; on the other hand, with high intersectoral mobility the rural sector served as a vast reservoir of manpower for the urban sector to draw on as necessary. As will be shown later, the capital city of China reached the enormous size of about 2.5 million by the thirteenth century; a substantial number of other large cities had developed by then as well. During roughly the same period, Europe had only a handful of medium-sized cities, none of which reached the 100,000 population mark. The largest, all in Italy, were Florence (90,000), Milan (75,000), and Venice (90,000).[1] In fact, outside China no city reached 2.5 million in population before London in the late nineteenth century.

Even with favorable factors, however, the growth of China's urban sector was still subject to a natural constraint. In a preindustrial and more or less closed economy, the total population of cities, regardless of the function they were built for, was ultimately limited by the productivity of the rural sector. Unless grain was imported, the nonagricultural population was obliged to depend on the agricultural sector for foods. Thus, if the rural population had to consume 90 percent of their grain output (i.e., a rate of surplus grain equal to 10 percent), the proportion of urban population in the total population could never surpass 10 percent even with an efficient mechanism to extract and transfer the rural surpluses.

Moreover, the rate of surplus grain in the rural sector also sets a ceiling on degree of concentration of urban conglomerations, that is, on how large they can be. With a 10 percent rate of surplus grain, a city of 1 million would have to receive its food supply from a rural population of 10 million, a city of 2 million would have to collect grain from a rural population of 20 million, which would naturally require a larger supply area. Conceivably, some size limit exists for large cities beyond which the transportation cost of shipping grain would be prohibitively high.

Since the rate of surplus grain sets the necessary condition (not the sufficient condition) for urbanization, changes in the proportion of urban population within the total population shed important light on changes in agricultural productivity. Furthermore, to the extent that surplus population occur, changes in urban-rural population distribution can indicate where this surplus population is harbored.

First, however, we must define the statistical manner by which Chinese urban population will be determined. Given the fairly high intersectoral mobility of premodern China, it is obviously impossible to measure the urban sector by occupations; cities or urban centers may only be defined by the number of residents they contain. To compare early data with the 1953 census data, then, I will follow the definition used by the Chinese government in the 1953 census: namely, urban areas (cities and towns) are those with 2,000 or more inhabitants.[2]

Pre-Sung Cities

Almost from their inception, one of the important functions performed by Chinese cities was that of seats of administrative offices. Thus, they formed a hierarchy of several levels consisting of the national capital, state or provincial capitals, prefectural capitals, and county capitals (see Appendix B). This hierarchical structure became entrenched after the Ch'in unification in 220 B.C. organized the whole country under a huge bureaucracy.

Moreover, because cities were built by governments, a more or less standard layout obtained for them. They were first built in the Chou as capitals from which various vassals could govern their fiefs, with city size regulated according to the vassal's rank. The city was usually surrounded by an inner and an outer wall. Within the walled area, the locations of palace, government offices, residential wards, temples, and market were predetermined in accordance with the standard city plan; residential wards were also divided by a standard gridiron of streets. Except for minor local variations, this general pattern was followed by ensuing dynasties down to the Northern Sung.

The planned features of Chinese cities during this long period lasting until the Northern Sung make estimation of urban population relatively easy. According to the standard layout, the area inside the inner wall of a city was divided into square blocks, called *li*, of equal size. Each block measured 300 double steps on each side, equivalent to 405 by 405 meters, or a total area of 0.164 square kilometers.[3] Most of the square blocks were designated as residential wards. During the Chou, all lands, rural or urban, belonged to the government, which distributed them to individual families according to certain simple formulas. In cities, two criteria for allotting residential land for dwellings are known to have been enforced. Each common family of standard size (five members) was entitled to 1 *chan*, or about 273 square meters. For aristocratic families (known as *shih* and *taifu*), the allotment per household was 3,280 square meters. Thus, each residential ward contained either 600 households of commoners or 50 aristocratic households. It was a rule that urban dwellers were assigned to the residential wards closest to their workplaces. In other words, inhabitants were grouped by occupation.

Because no information survives about what proportion of the area surrounded by the inner wall was normally designated as residential, the population density of Chinese cities cannot be calculated directly from land allotments. If we assume two-thirds of the walled area for residential use and an average size of families as five persons in the Eastern Chou period, the population density would have been 2,400 households, or 12,000 persons, per square kilometer (or 120 persons per hectare).

For medieval Europe, the distribution of gross density for 92 cities dating from 1348 to 1550 has been estimated as follows:[4]

45

Gross density (persons/hectare)	Number of cities
Under 80	27
81-125	44
126-75	13
Over 175	8

The assumed density of 120 persons per hectare appears to be very close to the average figure for those European cities. This density seems in most cases to have provided adequate space for comfortable urban living.

Because of the planned nature of urban land use in ancient China, the range of variation for urban population density was relatively narrow: the figure of 120 persons per hectare is not only a good estimate of average density but also very close to the upper limit. Another important factor as compared with medieval Europe, was the less popular use of horses as a means of transportation. Thus, except in the national capital, streets in Chinese cities were generally narrower, an observation frequently made by foreign visitors in the nineteenth century.

The standard size of residential wards remained approximately the same in Han and T'ang times, and probably in the Northern Sung as well, although the term *li* was changed into *fang*.[5] At some time during the period 350-220 B.C., however, the country turned from the public land system to private land ownership, and individual households gained the freedom to determine the size of the land on which they were to build their residences. Consequently, the number of households in each residential ward was no longer so uniform. And the general trend was a rising one. During the latter part of the fifth century, the number of households in each *fang* in the capital city Lo-yang varied from 500 to 1,000.[6] Hino Kaisaburo has estimated that the average number of households in each ward in Ch'ang-an during the T'ang was about 2,000.[7] The official records of the Northern Sung for the year 1021 show that the number of households in each ward in the capital city Pien-ching varied from 327 to 2,978, with an average of 810 households per ward.[8]

This rising trend of household density inside residential wards was reinforced by the fact that the average size of households had increased from a level of slightly below five persons to about six persons during the same time span. On the other hand, palaces, administrative offices, and markets seem to have occupied a progressively larger proportion of urban lands. Although this tendency offset, to some extent, the rising trend of population density inside residential wards, the average gross density in Chinese cities is likely to have shown a rising trend after the Chou.

It is possible to estimate, in very approximate terms, the peak urban populations during the Warring States period and the Western Han. For the Warring States period, useful information includes (1) statutory sizes of walled cities ruled by vassals of various ranks, (2) measurements of the sites of ancient cities recently excavated, and (3) names of cities recorded in historical documents. Paul Wheatley has identified 466 cities existing in the period 722-481 B.C., whereas Li Chi counted 585 identifiable cities and 233 cities for which exact dates could not be determined.[9]

Most of these cities are assumed to have survived the Warring States period. After the first Emperor of Ch'in conquered all the rival states and unified the country in 220 B.C., cities were integrated into a nationwide hierarchic administration system. Altogether 36 large cities were designated as the provincial capitals of Chun, a political division containing several counties. The remaining cities were designated as county seats, but the exact number of those second-level cities was not given. Based on this information, we may assume that around 300 B.C. there were at least 36 large cities and 500 smaller ones with a population of over 2,000. In other words, each of the seven rival states controlled on the average slightly over 70 cities.

Using the size of the walled (inner) area as an indicator of population, we can identify at least nine cities containing more than 100,000 people each. It would not be too far off the mark, therefore, to assume an average population of 50,000 for the 36 large cities. For the 500 secondary cities, an average of 5,000 people is assumed. Thus, the total Chinese urban population around 300 B.C. is estimated to have been 4.3 million. Estimates of the peak population around 300 B.C. vary from 25 to 40 million;[10] the generally accepted figure is 30 million. The estimated proportion of urban population is thus 14.3 percent.

The peak urban population of Han China can be estimated with somewhat better certainty. According to a Japanese study, there were altogether 26,635 *t'ing*, the basic subdivision in rural areas during the Western Han, with an average size of 320 households or 1,660 persons.[11] The implied size of the rural population would thus be 49,194,000 persons. To this number we must add the population of some very small county seats that probably numbered below 2,000, for even though those people did not live in the rural *t'ing*, their cities do not qualify as urban centers by our definition. The Han census taken in A.D. 2 gives eight frontier *chun* containing 100 counties,[12] for which the size of the county seat population is suspected to be less than 2,000 persons. The total population in the 100 tiny county seats is estimated to have been about 150,000. Thus, the total rural population in A.D. 2 is estimated to have been 49,344,000.

China's total population in that year is given as 59,600,000 persons. Thus, the estimated composition would be 82.8 percent rural and 17.2 percent urban. A slightly higher percentage for the urban population has been derived through a different approach, namely, by directly estimating the populations in cities at various levels. In fact, the 17.2 percent is the lower limit of urban population in the Western Han; to accept a larger size of rural population would mean an average size of *t'ing* above the level of 1,660 persons, which would mean some *t'ing* would have had 2,000 inhabitants, thereby making them urban centers according to our definition.

This period of roughly two thousand years also saw a rising degree of urban concentration, as measured by the size of the largest city. Lin-tzu, capital of the state of Chi, was the largest city in the Warring States period with a reported total of 70,000 households.[13] Surviving documents describe the city as surrounded by a wall 50 *li* long with 13 gates. If the city was square in shape, the total walled area would be 25.6 square kilometers. Using the estimated gross density of 120 persons per hectare, the city could house 307,200 dwellers, a figure fairly consistent with the reported number of households. The actual site of the city recovered from excavations, however, indicates a substantially smaller area of 17 square kilometers, but even this size could contain 204,000 people or more.

The Western Han capital of Ch'ang-an reached an official size of approximately 250,000 people.[14] Ch'ang-an may not even have been the largest city of that time, for a comparable population was registered in Cheng-tu. Furthermore, these figures refer to civilian households registered with local authorities; the total population of Ch'ang-an would have been much larger if military personnel and other categories of people who were not required to register locally had been counted.

Ch'ang-an was considerably enlarged during the T'ang, when it was once again made the national capital. The walled area was now 8.33 by 7 kilometers, or about 58.31 square kilometers.[15] This size could easily accommodate 700,000 people on the basis of a gross density of 120 per hectare. With the addition of armies and other unregistered persons, the total population of Ch'ang-an during the T'ang may be estimated as between 800,000 and 1 million.

Sung Cities

Urban China underwent significant changes shortly before or during Sung times.[16] First, economic development stimulated the country's urban sector to an unprecedented degree. Second, many of the previous restrictions and regulations concerning urban dwellers and market activities had been relaxed or removed. Third, unlike the T'ang period, when the government prohibited the establishment of marketplaces outside *fu* or prefectural seats and county seats, small market towns below the rank of county seats mushroomed. Some of the towns had been formed just outside large cities as satellite markets to facilitate the great increase in commercial activities; some were converted from the sites of garrison headquarters, known as *chen*, under the T'ang military system; some were the expanded nodes of land or water transportation lines; and some were the result of the natural growth of small commercial communities.

These changes had a profound impact on the urban sector. I am concerned here, however, only with their effect on urban population density and the new structure of the urban sector. Other consequences, such as the development of nighttime activities and other aspects of urban lifestyle, will not be examined.

Removal of the zoning law, which had formerly enforced a strict separation of residential wards from wards designated as markets or commercial districts, now permitted merchants and workshop owners to select locations for their business anywhere in the city. Moreover, the fact that storeowners and their families were now permitted to stay in the stores at night allowed a given area of urban land to accommodate more people than before.

During the T'ang dynasty, each residential ward, known as a *fang*, was surrounded by a wall; only a few gates served as entrances into the ward and were closed at night. Except in special cases, individual houses had no doors leading to the main streets. After such ward walls were removed in the Sung, house owners were not only able to open up private doors directly facing the streets, but some of them also attempted to extend their houses by occupying part of the street. This phenomenon, called "invading the streets," was frequently reported in many Sung cit-

49

ies. The traffic situation was further worsened by those families who built temporary houses in the streets and other reserved open space or on riverbanks; some streets became virtually impassable.

In Sung times the area confined by the inner wall of most large cities became so crowded that people gradually filled up the area surrounded by the outer wall, called the *lo-cheng*, and finally moved to suburbs outside the outer wall. City authorities were compelled to establish suburban wards as new urban administrative units, and thus suburbanization became a well-established phenomenon in Sung China.

According to records from 1021, Pien-ching, capital of the Northern Sung, had 121 *fang* in the area surrounded by both the new and old walls, plus 14 *fang* outside the city walls. For the 121 inner wards, the average density was 810 households, which may be converted into 4,700 persons at a rate of 5.8 persons per household. The total 135 wards, inside and outside the city walls, would then have nearly 110,000 registered civilian households.[17] We are also told that the perimeter of the combined walls was 50.6 Sung *li*, or a total of 34.6 square kilometers for the walled area.[18] The walled area contained 568,700 inhabitants, yielding an actual gross density of 164 persons per hectare.[19] Obviously, this figure is considerably higher than the estimated gross density of 120 persons per hectare in the capital cities of previous dynasties, probably for the reasons explained earlier, namely, economic development, lifting of the zoning law, removal of ward walls, and occupation of streets and reserved space.

As Pien-ching continued to expand, the number of registered civilian households in the entire urban area is estimated to have increased to 160,000 by 1080 and to 180,000 by 1100.[20] The peak population in Pien-ching may be broken down as follows:

Registered civilians	
(180,000 households × 5.8 persons)	1,050,000
Armies	200,000
Other unregistered population	150,000
TOTAL	1,400,000

The most magnificent city in Chinese history was Lin-an—the present-day Hang-chou in Chekiang—during the thirteenth century. After being designated the "temporary capital" of the Southern Sung government in 1132, Lin-an experienced an unusually fast period of growth. The officially registered population of Chien-t'ang county, the seat of the prefecture, grew at a rate of 1.2 percent between 1170 and 1225,[21] whereas the suburban communities surrounding Lin-an expanded even faster—2 percent a year—during the comparable period. The size of the peak population in metropolitan Lin-an, however, has been the subject of heated debate among scholars for several decades.

The conservative estimate made by Shigeru Kato, mainly on the basis of the official household counts of Ch'ien-t'ang and Jen-ho counties, was later supported by Etienne Balazs and Liang Keng-yao. This estimate consists of the following components:[22]

Population	Number of households	Number of persons
Inside the city wall	180,000	900,000
Southern suburbs	80,000	400,000
Northern suburbs	40,000	200,000
TOTAL	300,000	1,500,000

Using the estimated grain consumption and one official report of the suburban population in 1218, Hino Kaizaburo and T. H. Hollingsworth arrived at a much higher figure, broken down as follows:[23]

Population	Number of households	Number of persons
Inside the city wall	300,000	1,500,000
Southern suburbs	400,000	2,000,000
Northern suburbs	200,000	1,000,000
TOTAL	900,000	4,500,000

To ascertain the peak population of Lin-an, it would be helpful to estimate the peak size of the urban area. Even though the size of the urban area cannot indicate the population size of a declining city in which an unknown amount of space has been vacated, the peak area may still indicate population size when all existing space is fully utilized and residential and commercial areas are in a process of expansion caused by mounting population pressure. Despite the fact that most of Marco Polo's reports about Lin-an's extravagant prosperity are exaggerated, some of his information about the city is useful and can be confirmed by other sources. Both he and Odericus da Pordenone, a Catholic priest from Italy traveling in China about the same time, mentioned that Lin-an boasted numerous buildings several stories high for commercial and residential purposes.[24] The fact that Meng Yuan-lou made no similar observation in his famous book about Pien-ching during the Northern Sung[25] suggests that population density in Lin-an was probably higher than in Pien-ching.

51

Most important, according to Marco Polo, Lin-an had a straight main thoroughfare along which ten marketplaces were evenly spaced 4 miles apart.[26] This suggests the thoroughfare had a total length of no less than 36 miles, or 58 kilometers. Both Marco Polo and Ibn Batuta explicitly mentioned that it took more than one day to traverse the long street of Lin-an. This observation was fully confirmed by two Chinese writers of the late 13th century, who said that it took several days to go through the city.[27]

Lin-an's wall was reconstructed and extended several times before the city was made the national capital of the Southern Sung. The final city wall, perhaps the longest ever built in China, had a circumference of 70 *li*. The walled area was rectangular rather than square because it was confined by West Lake on the west side and by the river on the east side. Judging from the numbers of city gates on the four sides and the locations of these gates, some of which are identifiable on today's map of Hangchou, the measurements of the walled area were probably 15 *li* east-west and 20 *li* north-south. The urban area, however, gradually developed outward from both the south and north ends, turning the rectangle into a long belt. It was this belt that was traversed by the long thoroughfare seen by Marco Polo.

A report from the mayor of Lin-an to the Emperor in 1141 stated that the urban area had extended rapidly beyond the city wall into the southern and northern suburbs and that the two suburban communities, each one already as large as an ordinary county, were 30 *li* apart.[28] He requested, therefore, permission to establish two suburban administrative units, called *hsiang*, under the jurisdiction of the metropolitan government of Lin-an. The administration office of the southern suburb inaugurated in that year was 1 *li* from the south gate of the city and that of the northern suburb was 6 *li* from the north gate,[29] implying that by 1141 the two city gates were about 20 to 23 *li* apart and the thoroughfare was at least 30 *li* long.

The two suburban communities continued to expand at a rapid rate. An official document dated 1226 mentioned that each suburban administration covered a territory with a circumference of 60-70 *li*. In other words, each suburban community was as large in area as the city proper. The total length of the thoroughfare at that time was probably 60-65 *li*; Lin-an had almost reached its maximum size by then. According to the two Chinese writers cited earlier, who described Lin-an in great detail during the last years of the Southern Sung, or shortly after the occupation of the city by the Mongols in 1275, each suburban community had finally extended to several tens of *li* from the city wall, with a population comparable to an ordinary prefecture (larger than a county). The final length of the thoroughfare passing through the city proper and the two suburban communities we may estimate to have been 75 *li*, or 35 kilometers.

This estimate is confirmed by a report of Odericus da Pordenone[30] that the suburbs outside each city gate of Lin-an extended 8 miles with networks of prosperous streets. Eight miles is equivalent to 28 *li*, so the three sections of the thoroughfare would add up to about 75 *li*, or 35 kilometers, in length. While this distance falls short of the exaggerated figure provided by Marco Polo, it would nevertheless have required more than one day to walk.

The firmer and more interesting evidence is that many of the landmarks of Lin-an's suburban communities mentioned by the two thirteenth-century writers are still identifiable on today's map of Hang-chou. For instance, Pai-ta-ling and Mei-cheng-chiao in the territory of the southern suburban administration are close to the present railway bridge crossing Chien-t'ang river. The famous rice market mentioned in Wu Chih-mu's *Meng-liang-lu*, which is said to be connected with the fish market by a bridge called Hei-chiao, is far north of the present city of Hang-chou. There is no doubt that the urban area of Lin-an in its maximum size did span such an enormous distance.

This long belt was not of a uniform width. The northern suburb, which jurisdictionally also covered the western suburb, was much wider than the city proper. Perhaps 15 *li*, or 7 kilometers, is a good estimate for the average width of the belt. The estimated total acreage for the whole urban area of Lin-an would then be 245 kilometers (35 × 7). In view of the strong pressure for expansion, the gross density of inhabitants could hardly fall short of 100 persons per hectare. Therefore, the peak population of metropolitan Lin-an around 1220 is estimated to be 2.5 million.

Despite the enormous variation in the estimates of Lin-an's total population, scholars do not differ too widely in judging the population in the walled area. There is no reason to believe that the gross density of population in the walled area of Lin-an could have fallen substantially below the estimated rate of 164 persons per hectare for the inner wards of Pien-ching in 1021. If the same gross density is applied, the 65 square kilometers of walled area in Lin-an could have contained 1.07 million. Even if a density of 120 persons per hectare—at the least—is used for calculation, a population of 780,000 would be obtained.

It is Lin-an's suburban population, rather, that has been the main subject of debate. Regarding population counts in Lin-an's suburbs, an official document dated 1218 said: "Now . . . the household counts have increased, 400,000 in the southern *hsiang* [suburb], about double that of the northern *hsiang*."[31] Thus, the total count in the two suburban communities added up to about 600,000. Unfortunately, the original statement failed to give the unit of the counts—600,000 of what? Some scholars have interpreted this account to mean 600,000 households. This figure seems inconceivably large, as it would imply a suburban population of over 3 million. The other interpretation, identifying the figure as 600,000 persons, is likewise not acceptable, because the unit "person" was never used for either household registrations or censuses in Sung times. My own speculation is that the unknown unit in the official document was the standard unit used in all Sung censuses—*kou*, or male adults. The ratio of *kou* to persons was roughly 1 to 2.5, hence the suburban population given in the report was 1.5 million. When added to the population in the city proper, it yields 2.5 million as the total population in the urban area of Lin-an.

The new estimate of 2.5 million is happily consistent with many other pieces of information. Odericus da Pordenone observed that more people lived in the suburbs than in the city proper. This statement sounds reasonable, because two suburban communities would probably have a total territory of 180 square kilometers, more than double that of the walled area; even with a lower density, the suburban population should be larger than that in the walled area.

Reporting on the total population inside and outside the city wall of Lin-an, Wu mentioned that there were "several hundreds of thousands of households or 1.1 million *kou*."[32] Using the same 2.5 to 1 ratio, the implied number of persons would be 2.7 million. Our new estimate of Lin-an's population around 1220 may be broken down as:

Population	Number of households	Number of persons
Inside the city wall	180,000	1,000,000
Southern suburbs	180,000	1,000,000
Northern suburbs	90,000	500,000
TOTAL	450,000	2,500,000

Obviously, this is a compromise of the earlier estimates by Kato and Hino. The household return for the whole Southern Sung was officially given as 12,670,801 in 1223. Lin-an's urban households as a percentage of the national total would then be:

Estimate by	Estimated Lin-an urban households	Percentage of national total
Kato	300,000	2.37%
Hino	900,000	7.10%
Chao	450,000	3.55%

At the bottom of the urban structure in Sung China there were numerous small market towns below the county seat level which mushroomed recently, but it is difficult to gauge the total population in those small conglomerations. From historical materials of Sung times, Yoshiyuki Sudo has identified the names of 227 *shih* in south China.[33] For some, the sizes are known; they range from 328 to 639 households. In addition, he can identify 44 *chen* and *pu*, though the list is certainly far from complete. On the other hand, some of the *shih* identified by Sudo, such as those outside the city wall of Lin-an, are known to have been annexed by large cities as their suburban units.

There is no way to determine the total number of *shih* and *chen* in the Southern Sung. In view of the fact that the official records of the Jürchen Chin, who occupied north China, listed 513 *chen* as subdivisions below the county seat but above the village level,[34] there were probably more than 500 comparable subdivisions in south China, whose economy was more prosperous. Here we take 500 as the number of small market towns and 2,200 as their average population. The total population in those market towns is thus estimated at 1.1 million, or about 200,000 households.

Even though the margin of error in estimation may be quite large in this case, it is relatively unimportant. To miss by 50 percent would create a difference of only about a half million in population, a figure barely enough to match one or two large cities. In fact, there were quite a few large cities in the Southern Sung. For instance, judging from the perimeters of city walls, Ping-chiang (Su-chou) and Hu-chou probably had more than 350,000 persons each, Shao-hsing and Ch'ang-chou more than 100,000 each.[35]

Yoshinobu Shiba has calculated the percentage of urban population for the following localities during the Southern Sung period:[36]

Yin county	13%	T'ing-chou prefecture	33%
She county	7%	Han-yang prefecture	13%
Tan-t'u county (1208-24)	37%	Ching-men prefecture	17%
Tan-t'u county (1265-74)	38%		

Liang Keng-yao has compiled similar data for a larger sample of thirteen localities, and the weighted average of these urban population ratios is 16.8 percent.[37]

If the national total (for the Southern Sung only) of households in 1223 and our new estimate of Lin-an's population are taken as the basis, the distribution of urban population would be:

Lin-an	3.55%
Market towns (200,000 ÷ 12,670,000)	1.58%
Other cities [(100 − 3.55 − 1.58) × 16.8)]	15.93%
TOTAL	21.06%

Depending on whether Kato's or Hino's estimate of Lin-an's population is used, the resulting urban population would be either 20.08 percent or 24.02 percent.

Northern China under the Jürchen Chin had a lower ratio of urban population than southern China; my estimate is 19.3 percent.[38]

The Post-Sung Cities

Few students of Chinese economic history fail to notice a distinct pattern of development in urban China after Sung times—the multiplication of market towns, large and small, all over the country. This change was particularly striking in the Yangtze delta during the late Ming and the early Ch'ing. Most historians believe that the emergence of these commercial conglomerations is nothing more than a sign of accelerated economic development and part of the natural process of urbanization. It seems to me, however, a reversed trend of urbanization—diversification and decentralization of the urban sector—because the increase in the number of market towns was accompanied by another interesting trend. Although the populations of many cities rose and fell and a few cities, like Su-chou, even grew to an impressive scale, none had reached 1 million before 1850. Nor had any city ever reached the size of metropolitan Lin-an until Shanghai surpassed the 2.5 million mark after 1925.

Equally worth noting is the background against which many of the market towns in Kiangnan came into existence. Increasing population pressure in Ming-Ch'ing times compelled rural households to undertake various activities in subsidiary production to accommodate the ever-increasing labor inputs that could no longer be absorbed in agriculture. Cotton textiles were probably the most popular item among rural households in Kiangnan, and silk products came next. Facing the new pattern of production for these items and many other handicraft products, merchants began to cluster in convenient points close to villages so that they could collect cotton and silk products from rural families scattered in those villages. Those centers eventually developed into market towns. The newly emerged towns usually had two important features—a minimum total distance to a maximum number of villages and proximity to a major transportation line.

In other words, some commercial activities had moved from large cities to rural areas, where an increasing portion of nonagricultural production was carried out. The frequently cited case of Sheng-tse *chen* in the prefecture of Su-chou makes a good example. A small village of 50 to 60 families in the 1490's, Sheng-tse had developed into a large town with 20,000 households and 73 streets by the nineteenth century. According to the town's official history in the *Wu-chiang hsien-chih* (Wu-chiang Gazeteer), production of silk fabrics was confined to the city of Su-chou during the Sung and Yuan dynasties but began to spread among rural dwellers after the 1420's. By the early eighteenth century, virtually all rural households in an area about 40 to 50 *li* wide between Sheng-tse and Huang-hsi were engaged in this work. Thus, Sheng-tse served conveniently as a collection point.

In sum, it was the ruralization of nonagricultural production in China that induced the diversification of the urban sector. Gilbert Rozman has used a diagram to demonstrate the contrast patterns of urban networks in Ch'ing China and Tokugawa Japan.[39] The drastic difference in degree of decentralization between the two urban sectors demonstrates that the Chinese pattern was by no means normal.

Let us now turn to the measurement of urban population in China after Sung times. Rozman and G. William Skinner provide ready access to population figures for Chinese cities in the 19th century.[40] From a large quantity of local gazetteers, Rozman has compiled population data for urban centers around 1820. His findings, however, require a few adjustments to be consistent with my definition of urban population.

Among the seven levels of centers Rozman has classified, the seventh

TABLE 3.1
Population of Urban Centers, ca. 1820

Level of urban center and range of population	Number of centers	Total population (millions)
1 (1,000,000 and over)	1	1.0
2 (300,000-1,000,000)	9	5.0
3 (30,000-300,000)	100	6.0
4 (10,000-30,000)	200	3.0
5 (3,000-10,000)	1,100	5.5
6 (2,000-3,000)	1,500	3.7
TOTAL		24.2

SOURCE: Rozman, pp. 218, 273.

consists of small units with a population of less than 500. These are too small to qualify as urban centers by our definition and should be eliminated. Even for his sixth level, which includes centers with a population of between 500 and 3,000, those under 2,000 in population should also be excluded. We assume that, out of his 6,000 centers at the sixth level, 1,500 had a population of between 2,000 and 3,000 and that the average population for the 1,500 centers was 2,500. Thus, Rozman's data may be rearranged as shown in Table 3.1. The official figure for the total population of China in 1820 was 353 million. Thus, urban population was 6.9 percent of the national total.

The other set of data have been compiled by Skinner for the year 1893. Among his eight classes of urban centers, the seventh and eighth levels are below the minimum population I have used to define the urban sector; hence they should be excluded. The remaining six classes are presented in Table 3.2. If the national total of 426 million (the official figure for 1901) is used, an urban population ratio of 6 percent will result.

Skinner's estimate appears to be an understatement. Although his data for large and medium cities are believed to be quite reliable, the data for small cities may be incomplete. Fortunately, the census data of 1953 provide some information enabling us to make a reasonable adjustment to Skinner's estimate. Only 60 years elapsed between 1893 and 1953, a span sufficiently short for us to speculate on the development pattern of a certain segment of population.

The 1953 census shows that there were 4,226 urban centers in that year, with populations ranging from 2,000 to 20,000. The total population for that class was 24,699,000, or 4.24 percent of the national total in 1953. This population range covers the fifth and sixth levels plus the peripheral cities and towns of the fourth level, whose average population was 17,200.

TABLE 3.2
Population of Urban Centers, 1893

Level	Number of centers		Average population (000)		Total population (000)
	Central	Peripheral	Central	Peripheral	
1	6	0	667.0	0	4,002
2	18	2	217.0	80.0	4,066
3	38	25	73.5	39.4	3,778
4	108	92	25.5	17.2	4,336
5	360	309	7.8	5.8	4,600
6	1,163	1,156	2.3	1.8	4,756
TOTAL					25,538

SOURCE: Skinner, p. 287.

Based on Skinner's estimates, the population sum for the three groups of urban places may be calculated as:

Level	(000)	
Sixth	4,756	
Fifth	4,600	
Fourth (peripheral)	1,582	(= 92 × 17,200)
TOTAL	10,938	

This sum accounts for only 2.57 percent of the national total. It is hardly conceivable that this segment of the urban sector had gained so much (from 2.57 to 4.24 percent) in relative importance in such a short period of time.

We must, then, assume that the trend of multiplication of market towns had come to a halt by the end of the nineteenth century and the new pattern of urban development had become the expansion of treaty ports. That is, we assume that very few new market towns emerged during this short period, and that the existing ones at best had grown at the natural rate of population growth. Therefore, the proportion of the three groups combined could not have been too different from 4.24 percent in 1893. The distribution of urban population in 1893 may be reestimated as:

Level	(000)	
First	4,002	
Second	4,066	
Third	3,778	
Fourth (central)	2,754	(= 4336 − 1582)
Fourth (peripheral), Fifth, and Sixth	18,062	(= 4.24% × 426,000)
TOTAL	32,662	

A new urban population percentage of 7.67 is then obtained.

TABLE 3.3

Population of Urban Centers, 1953

Population range	Number of centers	Total population (000)	Average population
3,000,000 and over	1	6,204	6,204,417
1,000,000-2,999,999	8	14,815	1,851,897
500,000-999,999	16	11,405	712,831
200,000-499,999	34		
100,000-199,999	51	20,134	42,840
50,000-99,999	78		
20,000-49,999	307		
2,000-19,999	4,226	24,699	5,845
TOTAL		77,257	

SOURCE: Nai-ruenn Chen, pp. 128-30.

Of course, the most reliable set of urban population data thus far is that obtained from the 1953 census.[41] With a few minor inconsistencies among data from different Chinese sources reconciled, the census statistics are reproduced in Table 3.3. Given a total population of 582.6 million for that year, the urban population percentage was 13.2. In addition, Chinese official sources have provided the urban population percentage before and after the census year·

1949	10.6%	1954	13.6%
1950	11.2%	1955	13.5%
1951	11.8%	1956	14.2%
1953	13.2%	1957	15.4%

One may conjecture that the percentage of urban population in the 1930's was probably no different from that in 1949, about 10 percent.

Implications

I will now assemble all the urban percentages derived in the previous sections.

300 B.C.	14.3%	1893	7.7%
A.D. 2	17.2%	1930	10.0%
1220 (South		1949	10.6%
China only)	21.0%	1953	13.2%
1820	6.9%	1957	15.4%

The results are amazing. Three stages of urbanization, with three separate trends of movement, seem to have occurred in Chinese history.

No one can quarrel with the general validity of the 1953 census data and the urban percentages immediately before and after that year. Roz-man's estimate and the adjusted figures of Skinner are also generally ac-ceptable in view of their perfect consistency with the rising trend demon-strated by the statistics of the 1940's and 1950's.

On the other hand, no one can deny the crude nature of the pre-Ch'ing estimates. The gap is too large, however, to be explained away by any assumed statistical discrepancy. If we insist, for example, that ur-banization is an ongoing process in one direction and that urban popula-tion percentages must show a rising trend, however slowly, over time, we must be prepared to demonstrate a very low urban population percentage for 1220, let alone 300 B.C. By reversing the rising trend shown by the data from the nineteenth and twentieth centuries, the backward projected urban population around 1220 would have been as low as 4 percent of the national total, or even lower. It is much more difficult to defend a low percentage than our high estimates; the 4 percent can be nearly ac-counted for by the single city of Lin-an. Even if the lowest estimate of Lin-an's population is taken, we still can easily account for the 4 percent simply by adding two or three large cities like Su-chou and Hu-chou. On the other hand, it is relatively easy to defend the high estimates. In fact, I am willing to allow a 50 percent margin of possible errors for the pre-Ch'ing percentages, because, even after being cut by half, they are all still higher than the percentage for 1820.

A plausible conclusion is that the shocking figures presented here are not merely statistical; they reflect, at least in part, the true situation. The development of Chinese cities and towns did undergo three distinct stages. In the first stage, which terminated at the end of the thirteenth century or shortly thereafter, China's urban population grew not only in absolute number but also in relative terms; the proportion of urban popu-lation was slowly climbing. This increase was accompanied by a rising degree of concentration, as evidenced by the ever-expanding size of the largest city in the country. I believe the most crucial factor underlying this pattern of development to be the gradual increase in the output per unit of agricultural labor inputs. With an enhanced rate of surplus grain, the rural sector could support a larger and larger urban sector. Moreover, large cities could continue to grow without having to collect grain from an expanded supporting area so that the shipping cost could remain at a reasonable margin. The Southern Sung's Lin-an is a good example of this relationship. A large number of wealthy farmers in the North fled to the South after the Jürchen invasion; they became landless and emigrated into cities, especially Lin-an.[42] It was the changed economic foundation, as a necessary condition, that enabled the capital city to accommodate such a large population. Had it not been for the high rice yield boosted by the new strain in that period and the low shipping cost due to the excellent water transportation in the region,[43] Lin-an could not have supported 2.5 million people.

The second stage of Chinese urban development terminated in the first half of the nineteenth century. Again, the changes originated mainly in the rural sector rather than the urban sector. Since rural families were the only economic institution that was perfectly flexible in using labor inputs, the increase in the man-land ratio during the second stage induced rural families to employ more labor-intensive farming techniques on one hand and to increase subsidiary production for nonagricultural goods on the other hand. The reduction in grain output per unit of labor input under intensive farming naturally depressed the rate of surplus grain in the rural sector. While this circumstance might not lead to a decrease in the total number of city dwellers, it tended to slow down the relative growth of the urban sector and led to a decline in the proportion of urban population within the total population. The degree of concentration tended to descend as well, because the same city population of 1 million would now have to collect grain from a much larger supporting area with a rising margin of shipping cost. The other outcome was that the expansion of rural subsidiary production lured merchants to centers near rural clusters as collection points.

The 7 percent urban population measured by Rozman for 1820 was probably the lowest point the descending trend reached. In absolute terms, the number of urban dwellers around 1820 was not much larger than that in the mid-thirteenth century for China as a whole. In other words, the enormous increment in population over this long period of time was absorbed primarily by the rural sector.

The third stage of development, in which the proportion of urban population again ascended and at an unprecedented fast rate, began sometime in the mid-nineteenth century. In a century the percentage more than doubled. For this stage, there is a generally agreed explanation: urbanization was stimulated by the introduction and establishment of modern industry and commerce in treaty ports after China's contact with foreign powers. This trend can best be illustrated by the growth of the two largest cities, Shanghai and Tientsin, during this period.[44]

Year	Shanghai	Tientsin	Year	Shanghai	Tientsin
1852	544,413	—	1910	1,289,353	—
1860	—	60,000	1922	—	838,629
1865	691,919	—	1927	2,641,220	—
1900	1,000,000	320,000	1935	3,529,120	1,348,905

In short, China's third stage of urbanization largely followed the pattern experienced by many European cities in the eighteenth and nineteenth centuries but bore little resemblance to urbanization in pre-Sung China.

4

Measuring the Area of Cultivated Land

Traditional Units of Measure

The official histories of various Chinese dynasties provide some national land statistics that are occasionally broken down into individual provinces or subdivisions. To compare these statistics, however, is by no means a straightforward task. Besides physical expansion and reduction in areas of cultivated acreage, there are a number of other distorting factors: first, the measuring units were changed drastically in different periods; second, unsatisfactory cadastral techniques generated a systematic bias in the reported data; third, the size of the national territory varied considerably over time, hence the cadasters were not really comparable in coverage; and finally, because land surveys were intended to determine local tax bases, taxpayers had a strong incentive to underreport or avoid reporting landholdings. The degree of underreporting and omission was further related to the tax system itself and each government's administrative efficiency.

Although it is possible to improve the quality of these statistics by making partial adjustments, it is impossible to reconstruct a set of data capable of meeting modern standards. We can assert, however, that the adjusted data are probably sufficient to show the magnitude of cultivated land areas and broad trends of development.

The Chinese empire's cultural and political influence traditionally determined the scope of its territory without artificially drawn border lines. Consequently, the size of China's territory was always in a state of flux. Fortunately, the effect of territorial changes upon the total acreage of cultivated land was far smaller than might be imagined. As any topographical map of China clearly demonstrates, except in Manchuria, which remained undeveloped despite its large plains until the nineteenth century, the country's arable land is concentrated in the inland areas south of the Ch'in Ling mountains. Dictated by natural factors, the geographical distribution of agricultural activities has remained fairly stable in northern China, where territorial variations have usually taken place. The distribution of population followed the same pattern simply because, before industrialization, only those regions conducive to food production were inhabited. Therefore, any large territorial variation in the peripheral areas would not affect cultivated acreage and population figures by a significant margin—that is, higher than 10 percent. Moreover, territorial changes affected both population and cultivated acreage in the same direction. To the extent that the ultimate objective of this study is to determine not land size per se but the man-land ratio, the distortion caused by territorial variation is minimal.

The measurement of land area in China began with the lineal measure *ch'ih*, the Chinese foot. Above this was the *pu*, which at different times meant either a lineal length of a double step or a double step squared. The higher levels were the *mou* (Chinese acre) and the *ch'ing* (= 100 *mou*). (For convenience, these measures are listed in Appendix A.) The length of the basic lineal measure, *ch'ih*, changed in virtually every dynasty, and the relation between any two levels of measuring units—for example, the number of *ch'ih* in each *pu*—did not remain constant. Fortunately, these measuring units are described in official histories, and actual samples of measuring instruments survive.[1]

Table 4.1 shows the number of measuring devices preserved from various dynasties. In spite of possible shrinkage or deterioration of the sur-

TABLE 4.1
Sample Historical Measuring Rods (Ch'ih)

Dynasty	Number of sample measuring rods	Maximum length (cm)	Minimum length (cm)
Warring States	8	23.1	22.5
	165 writing tablets	22.5	22.0
Western Han	13	23.75	22.85
Eastern Han	8	24.0	23.0
	158 writing tablets	24.1	22.5
Three Kingdoms and Ch'in	9	25.13	24.0
T'ang	37	31.2	28.0
Sung	8	32.84	28.06
Ch'ing	4 construction measuring rods	32.0	31.0
	2 tailor's measuring rods	35.18	34.88
	1 land survey measuring rod	34.23	

SOURCE: Tseng, pp. 162-82.

TABLE 4.2

Changes in Standard Measures of Land from the Chou Dynasty to the Republic

Dynasty	Time period	Cm per ch'ih	Ch'ih per pu	Cm per pu	Square pu per mou	Square meters per mou	Shih-mou equivalent
Chou	1121-221 B.C.	22.50	6	135.00	100	182.25	0.273
Ch'in	220-206 B.C.	23.10	6	138.60	240	461.04	0.691
Western Han	205 B.C.-A.D. 8	23.10	6	138.60	240	461.04	0.691
Eastern Han	9-220	23.75	6	142.50	240	487.34	0.731
Wei	221-265	24.12	6	144.72	240	502.65	0.754
Western Chin	266-316	24.12	6	144.72	240	502.65	0.754
Eastern Chin	317-420	24.45	6	146.70	240	516.50	0.774
Southern and North- ern Dynasties	421-580	29.51	6	177.06	240	752.40	1.128
Sui	581-618	29.60	6	177.60	240	757.00	1.135
T'ang	619-906	30.00	5	150.00	240	540.00	0.810
Five Dynasties	907-960	31.00	5	155.00	240	576.60	0.865
Sung	961-1279	31.00	5	155.00	240	576.60	0.865
Yuan	1280-1368	34.00	5	170.00	240	693.60	1.040
Ming	1369-1644	34.00	5	170.00	240	693.60	1.040
Ch'ing	1645-1911	34.00	5	170.00	240	693.60	1.040
Republic	1912-	33.33	5	166.65	240	666.53	1.000

SOURCE: Chao and Chen, 1982, p. 70.

NOTE: The new Han gauges were introduced by Emperor Wu (140-86 B.C.); the Chou gauges were used in earlier years of the Han.

viving measuring rods over long periods of time, in most cases the difference between the longest and the shortest in each dynasty is negligible. This circumstance suggests that some effort was made by the ruling governments in each dynasty to standardize the measuring units used in different parts of the country. There are two exceptions, however. First, based on historical documentation, measuring rods used by the Northern Dynasties during the fifth and sixth centuries were not standardized and were substantially longer than those used in the Southern Dynasties. Unfortunately, no sample measuring rods from the Northern Dynasties survive to validate this data. Second, the Manchu government during the Ch'ing dynasty failed to standardize lineal measures, which consequently varied both geographically and functionally (as, for example, in tailoring, construction, and land measurement). This chaotic situation, further aggravated by the introduction of Western measures and weights in the nineteenth century, reached its peak at the end of the Ch'ing and the early Republic. Therefore, in terms of distortion stemming from the lack of standardization of measuring units, earlier statistics are more reliable than Ch'ing data.

Historical data clearly demonstrate a steady increase in the length of the *ch'ih* (see Appendix C). The number of *ch'ih* in each *pu* and the number of square *pu* in each *mou* also changed over time, and the variation in the size of the *mou* embodies these changes. Table 4.2 lists the measures relevant to land acreage during different periods in Chinese history along with the coefficients for conversion into present-day *shih mou*.

Cadastral Surveys and Registration

Given the vastness of China's territory and the technical difficulties involved in surveying land, large-scale cadastral activities could not be frequently conducted. Moreover, because cadastral surveys were generally used to determine tax liabilities for landowners, they were not considered popular government actions. Consequently, only a few nationwide cadastral studies are known to have taken place in the history of China.

The Han histories have provided total acreages of cultivated land (in million *mou*) in the whole of China for six years:

A.D. 2	8,270	A.D. 144	6,896
105	7,320	145	6,957
125	6,942	146	6,930

The data for four years were released in the inauguratory years of four new emperors, and the data for one year were released in the second year of a new emperor. Apparently it was a common Han practice to review existing land and population registers immediately after the inauguration of a new emperor and to release the tabulated sums. These data could not have been the result of actual land studies because a nationwide cadastral survey would have taken at least four years to complete. It is unclear whether the land acreage for the year A.D. 125, the fourth year of Emperor An of the Eastern Han, was the outcome of a new land analysis. Han histories do not indicate any land measurement during the first few years of An's reign.

A reference does exist, however, to a survey made during the reign of Kuang Wu, the first emperor of the Eastern Han. In A.D. 40, Kuang Wu sentenced more than ten local officials to death for their failure to present accurate statistics from land surveys conducted in their jurisdictions.[2] Unfortunately, the figures for this survey were not cited.

The next officially documented imperial mandate to conduct a cadastral survey was the edict of the Eastern Ch'in emperor in 330, when the government decided to abolish the *k'o t'ien fa* (lump sum agricultural tax). This land survey was intended to assist collection of a newly designed land tax that imposed three *sheng* of grain per *mou* of farmland. The results of this attempt were not reported.

Although reliable data on population and land were indispensable for implementing the equitable field system, this system applied to the allocatable public lands only; there was no corresponding need for the government to know the exact sizes of private estates. This is perhaps the reason why no aggregate land acreage has been reported by any of the dynasties adopting the equitable field system. Shortly after 780, when private ownership of land was fully restored, a countrywide land survey was ordered by the T'ang emperor for the purpose of enforcing the new double-tax law.

In the Sung dynasty rulers paid greater attention to land measurement, and large-scale land surveys took place more frequently, than in any other dynasty in Chinese history. A thorough survey of the entire country was conducted by the first Sung emperor, T'ai Tsu, who personally selected emissaries in 961 to carry out this special mission. The sentence of banishment he imposed on one regional magistrate who did not accurately report his district's land survey results served as a cautionary punishment for the rest and ensured a reasonably accurate outcome.[3] A similar action was taken in 992 by the succeeding emperor.

Eighty years later, another effort was made by Wang An-shih, the great reformer of Sung times. His square field law, which was part of a sweeping economic reform program, involved not only surveying lands but also rearranging them into large squares measuring 1000 *pu* per side. All fields had to be further classified into five grades according to the quality of their soil. Partly because the task of rearranging lands was extremely time consuming, and partly because the entire reform program met with strong objections from conservative elements at various levels of government, Wang An-shih could only complete the survey and rearrangement of farmland in the heartland of China, or in about 30 percent of Sung territory, over a period of thirteen years.

Even the much weaker government of the Southern Sung managed to carry out a large-scale land survey within its territory. It took six years (1143-49) and covered all but a few prefectures in the border regions, which were excluded by a special imperial decree because of their remoteness. This cadastral effort deserves special attention because a new cadastral format, known as the *ch'en chi pu* (literally, cutting-board registers), was used.

As a prototype of the famous fish-scale register, the *ch'en chi pu* recorded the following mandatory information for each plot of farmland: a small map showing the shape and location of the plot; measured lengths of its boundary lines; and its size, history of ownership (such as inherited or purchased), and type of operation (such as self-cultivation or leasing).[4] The owner, any tenants, and the local official in charge of the survey were required to sign the map and the data sheet, guaranteeing the accuracy of its information. The cadasters were then checked by inspectors from higher levels of government; any falsified reporting constituted a punishable offence.[5] After its accuracy was substantiated, a copy of the data sheet was issued to the owner as an official certification of ownership. Thereafter, any land purchase, mortgage, or other type of land transfer was not considered legal unless the private deed was supported by this official certification.[6] Obviously, this new format of land registration greatly enhanced the quality of acreage statistics.

Two national land studies are known to have taken place during the Ming dynasty. Notwithstanding a few recording errors, these two land surveys, which will later be discussed in detail, yielded the best acreage statistics ever produced in traditional China. According to surviving documents, the initial Ming survey began in the first year of the new regime (1368). It took nearly two decades to improve cadastral techniques and revise the registration format several times; the survey, using the revised procedures, was concluded in 1393.

A number of salient features in this first Ming survey are worth citing. First, because it was conducted simultaneously with a population census, mutual checks could be made between the two sets of statistics. Second, the Ming emperor T'ai Tsu mobilized not only civilian administrators and their employees but also a large number of military personnel to assist in the operation. Third, both the cadasters (known as the fish-scale registers) and the household registers (known as the yellow registers) were the most elaborately designed in Chinese history. Fourth, the penalty against falsification or inaccurate reporting was so severe that even trivial irregularities were punishable by death.[7]

The second Ming land survey was begun in 1578 and concluded four years later. It was also the final countrywide land survey before the twentieth century, since no comparable effort was attempted by the Manchu government during the Ch'ing period. The most striking feature of the 1578 study was a new and more satisfactory surveying technique for determining land area.

Before examining this technique, a brief review of Chinese surveying methods may be helpful. It was fairly simple to determine the size of a plot during the period of the well field system in the Chou dynasty because farmland was commonly arranged in square blocks and grids, and perhaps in rectangles, during the latter part of this period. Even after the well field system was replaced by private land ownership, farmland was probably still demarcated in the same manner, for the easiest way to integrate or partition lands would be to follow the same rectangular divisions.

The *Chiu Chang Suan Shu* (Nine Chapters of Arithmetic), the earliest Chinese work on geometry, presumably published about 100 B.C. contains a chapter on land measurement that presents methods for measuring fields in various shapes. Except for square and rectangular divisions, its measuring formulas are of academic interest only because obviously no farmland could have been partitioned into round, ring, and oval shapes during the Han or any other period. On the other hand, this tract fails to present a formula for measuring quadrilaterals, a shape into which square and rectangular fields could have easily been converted

70

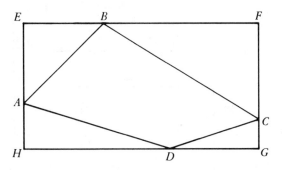

Fig. 4.1. Land-measuring technique used in the second Ming land survey, 1578.

through gradual distortions of the original rectangular boundary   lines.

Based on a surviving land deed from A.D. 81, which indicates the lengths of the four sides and the area of the land in question, we know that peasants by this time had improvised the following formula for measuring quadrilaterals:[8] Suppose *a* and *c* represent one pair of a quadrilateral's opposite sides, and *b* and *d* the other pair of opposite sides. The area may be approximated as

$$\frac{a+c}{2} \times \frac{b+d}{2}$$

In other words, this formula measures a quadrilateral as if it were a rectangle. Mathematically, it creates an upward bias because the area measured is always larger than the true size. The degree of distortion depends on the degree to which the four angles of the quadrilateral depart from 90 degrees (rectangular angles).

Despite the unsatisfactory distortion inherent in this method, it was adopted by all ensuing mathematical works and land area conversion tables in China up to the 1578 land survey. Possibly even before this time, some people may have been aware of the formula's bias but were unable to offer a better substitute. By his insistence on dividing farmland into squares, it is suspected that Wang An-shih, for example, may have been partially motivated by the desire to eliminate such distortions.

Consequently, a correct method for surveying quadrilateral lands was employed for the first and only time in the 1578 survey.[9] Although the original verbal description of the measuring technique is not totally clear, it may be illustrated in Figure 4.1. If the quadrilateral field in question is *ABCD*, to obtain its exact size a rectangle *EFGH* is drawn to contain it.

71

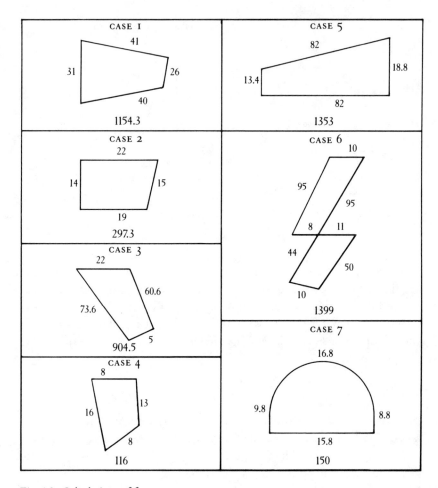

Fig. 4.2. Calculations of farm area:

CASE 1
(26 + 31) ÷ 2 = 28.5
(41 + 40) ÷ 2 = 40.5
28.5 × 40.5 = 1154

CASE 2
(22 + 19) ÷ 2 = 20.5
(14 + 15) ÷ 2 = 14.5
20.5 × 14.5 = 297.3

CASE 3
(22 + 5) ÷ 2 = 13.5
(66.6 + 73.6) ÷ 2 = 67.1
13.5 × 67.1 = 905.8

CASE 4
(8 + 8) ÷ 2 = 8
(16 + 13) ÷ 2 = 14.5
8 × 14.5 = 116

CASE 5
(18.8 + 13.4) ÷ 2 = 16.1
(82 + 82) ÷ 2 = 82
16.1 × 82 = 1320

CASE 6
(10 + 8 + 11 + 10) ÷ 4 = 9.75
(95 + 95 + 50 + 44) ÷ 2 = 142
9.75 × 142 = 1385

CASE 7
(8.8 + 9.8) ÷ 2 = 9.3
(16.8 + 15.8) ÷ 2 = 16.3
9.3 × 16.3 = 151

The sizes of both the rectangle and the four rectangular triangles *AEB*, *BFC*, *CGD*, and *DHA* can then be easily determined. The exact area of the quadrilateral is thus the difference between the area of the rectangle *EFGH* and the combined area of the four rectangular triangles.

Probably because of the multiple steps necessary for this calculation, however, which were more complicated and time consuming than previous survey techniques, the correct formula was never used again after the 1578 survey. Seven actual cases taken from various fish-scale registers of the Ch'ing dynasty are presented in Figure 4.2 to illustrate the process. All numbers are measured in *pu* (the Chinese double step). The length of each line is indicated by the number beside it; the number at the bottom denotes the measured area of the plot as actually recorded in the cadaster.[10] Computational procedures have been reconstructed based on the traditional approximation method. Except for a few small discrepancies obviously caused by the original surveyors' practice of rounding off, our figures are identical to the registered sizes.

Unfortunately, there is no way to determine quantitatively the extent of the bias deriving from faulty mathematical procedures as embodied in various historical surveys other than the one taken in 1578. The most we can conjecture is the following: First, until the Northern Sung, the bias was unlikely to be substantial because both the equitable field system and the square field system required the partition of farmland into units of regular shapes. This upward bias, however, could have occurred slowly after the original pattern of partition was gradually distorted during intermittent periods. Second, this bias would have been more pronounced in the south than in the north because, even without government regulations, peasants themselves tended to divide their farms in more or less regular shapes (there was no need for them to do otherwise), and topographical conditions in the south would not always permit the regular partition of land. Third, this bias tended to increase after the Sung, partly because no additional land legislation stipulating regular partition of farmland was announced, and partly because the center of China's agricultural production gradually shifted to the south. Farming then increasingly utilized hilly land and fields in small valleys or along riverbanks, which could hardly be arranged into regular shapes. In fact, an inspection of Ming and Ch'ing land registers reveals that the quadrilateral was by far the predominant field shape in the southern provinces.

The Fish-Scale Register

It is impossible to make a reliable assessment of Ming and Ch'ing land returns without first understanding some details of the fish-scale register, a revolutionary system that significantly improved the quality of these statistics. In fact, a number of misapprehensions about the land returns of this period persist among scholars who have not seen these materials. Fortunately, I have had the opportunity to examine a total of sixteen fish-scale registers and thirteen household registers of various types, in addition to other relevant documents surviving from the two dynasties.[11] Based on the information derived from these archives, I will try to clarify this system of measurement.

The use of fish-scale registers was likely to generate highly accurate data for a number of reasons we will explore here.

1. The Ming government designed two parallel registration systems for land and households, respectively, to separate land ownership records from those relating to tax assessment; these were the fish-scale and yellow registers. The fish-scale register was a complete list of all plots in a given village or subdivision. Although the document provided the owner's name and land size for each plot, the tax collector still could not determine the total tax liability of a household in the village on this basis because the fish-scale register did not indicate whether the family owned lands in other villages. The function of determining tax liabilities was performed by the yellow register and other household registers that replaced it in the late Ming and the Ch'ing. Under the yellow registers system, a household was required to report the total amount of landholdings regardless of location and was thus further subject to verification by the government. The separation of land measurement from tax collection greatly weakened a landowner's incentives to underreport or conceal his landholdings. Moreover, unlike the yellow register, which relied on self-reporting, the original fish-scale registers contained data from actual land surveys. All tax evasion tricks widespread at the time occurred only under the yellow register system.

2. The fish-scale registers were also meant to supply official certifications of land ownership to landholders. Because this certification constituted legal protection should any disagreements over land titles or transfer arise, few could afford to ignore it. I have reviewed thousands of land deeds from the Ming-Ch'ing era but do not recall any that failed to mention the number assigned to the plot in the local fish-scale registration.

According to one study, after the official fish-scale registers of Nanch'ang, Kiangsi were destroyed during the T'aip'ing Rebellion, people wishing to sell or transfer their lands had to pay high prices to obtain unofficial title certifications from those families in possession of the draft volumes of fish-scale registers.

3. Since the fish-scale registers included survey maps for individual plots and a general map for all plots in the subdivision, it would have been difficult for any family to underreport its land area by bribing official surveyors. To underreport would have involved changing the lengths of land boundary lines, which would have rendered them inconsistent with those recorded for the adjacent plots. Omitting a plot entirely would have been even more difficult because a gap would have appeared on the general survey map for the whole subdivision. The only plots that could possibly have been disguised were newly reclaimed fields that were not adjacent to other farms on all sides. After the 1368-93 land measurement, the Ming emperor T'ai Tsu announced that all newly reclaimed farmland in the country was to be tax exempt for an indefinite time in order to encourage land reclamation. Tantamount to an official sanction for concealing new lands, this decree eventually became the main loophole in the land registration system. The problem eventually became so widespread that Emperor Shen Tsung was compelled to conduct a new countrywide land survey in 1578-81 to recover the disguised land.

Another disputed issue involves the type of land that owners were required to register. The Japanese historian Taiji Shimizu first raised the question by contending that Ming land returns were distinguished by two separate reporting systems, one including hilly land the other omitting it.[12] Judging from the surviving samples of fish-scale registers I have examined, Shimizu's theory appears to be unfounded. Both the Ming and Ch'ing governments adopted a standard four-way classification of land as follows: *t'ien* (paddy land or irrigated land), *ti* (dry land), *shan* (hilly land), and *t'ang* (marshland).

Although some registers added a few more categories to accord with local conditions, none eliminated any item from the standard classification. Specifically:

1. Four fish-scale registers from the Ming used the four-way standard classification with no further breakdown.

2. One fish-scale register from the Ming used the four-way classification with a further breakdown of seven grades.

3. Four fish-scale registers from the Ming listed only paddy land and

dry land. Hilly land and marshland were missing not because the two categories had been eliminated, however, but because, as the maps given in the four registers show, there was no hilly land and marshland in their respective territories. Three of the registers had further breakdowns.

4. Two fish-scale registers from the Ch'ing used the standard classification.

5. Four fish-scale registers from the Ch'ing showed no hilly land or marshland, again because none existed in the territories under inspection. Various grading systems were used, however; in one case, unused lands were listed as a separate category, which was further classified into four grades.

6. Thirteen household registers from the Ming and Ch'ing all used the standard classification.

7. Seven landholding lists for individual households also used standard classification.

In sum, not a single instance verifies that hilly land in a specific territory was excluded from the land registration. The real problem we have detected, however, is that, unlike the other three categories, hilly land was never clearly defined. It seems to have included all private lands located on hills that could provide the owners some economic gains. There was no clear qualitative distinction made among hilly fields, paddy fields, and dry fields located on hills; the three categories were sometimes used interchangeably. Thus, one Ming fish-scale register created two categories: "irrigated land converted from hilly land" and "dry land converted from hilly land." Even though the lack of unequivocal definition can be a source of confusion, it need not overly concern us as long as our primary interest lies in the aggregate land returns.

A more serious misunderstanding is the so-called *mou* conversion problem stressed by Ping-ti Ho.[13] The strong influence of this theory on scholars is demonstrated by Dwight Perkins, who has attempted to adjust the Ch'ing land acreages to remove the downward bias supposedly introduced by the *mou* conversion practice.[14] Ho argues that low-grade lands in the Ming and Ch'ing were converted to high-grade lands at substantial discounts to achieve equitable taxation. This widespread practice, he believes, created a serious downward bias in contemporary land statistics because numbers of units in land tax payment, or the so-called fiscal *mou*, were reported rather than actual *mou*. Obviously, his failure to realize that there were two separate registration systems serving different functions led him to this conclusion. The fish-scale registers recorded the true sizes of farmlands, along with survey maps, for the purpose of compiling land returns and supplying legal certification and identification of ownerships. The household registration files, including yellow registers, *pien-shen ts'e* (Book of Compilation and Verification of Households), *shih-cheng ts'e* (Book of Tax Collection), and *fu-i ch'üan-shu* (A Comprehensive Book of Taxation and Labor Conscription) primarily served the function of determining tax liabilities for households or localities.

To substantiate his contention, Ho cites a number of passages and cases from Ming-Ch'ing works on the subject of *mou* conversion. None of these examples, however, was gathered from the fish-scale registration files. This is all perfectly understandable because discounting the size of poor land was merely a fiscal operation to achieve equitable taxation. *Mou* conversion was never intended to be a formula for measuring land areas.

According to Ho, these examples from various provinces indicate that mou conversion was extensively practiced in most parts of China, particularly in the regions north of the Huai River as well as in Anhwei."[15] While this statement is perfectly true, it does not follow at all that land returns suffered a downward bias. *Mou* conversion was irrelevant to the calculation of total acreage. Fortunately, considerable data surviving from the province of Anhwei provide the true picture. One survey made in the early part of the twentieth century found that all 57 counties in Anhwei province used *mou* conversion in the calculation of land taxes;[16] the investigator tabulated all the conversion ratios, which varied from locality to locality. It was also revealed, however, that 55 out of the 57 counties in Anwhei used the standard gauges of 240 *pu* per *mou* to measure land areas.[17] Obviously, land measurement and tax determination were two separate matters, and only the latter involved *mou* conversion.

The two atypical counties were Hsiu-ning and She, in which lands of different grades were measured by differential gauges and the measured acreages were then converted into fiscal acreages, as was the practice in other counties, for purposes of taxation. These two special counties may be called cases of double conversion. The relevant ratios used in the two counties are given in Table 4.3.

The Ming and Ch'ing archives I have examined fully confirm this information. Among the sixteen fish-scale registers from the two dynasties, seven used 240 *pu* per *mou* as the uniform gauge for all grades and all

77

TABLE 4.3

Land-Measuring Gauges and Mou *Conversion Ratios*
for Taxation in Two Anhwei Counties in the
Early Twentieth Century

Category	Hsiu-ning county	She county
Land-measuring gauge (*pu* per *mou*):		
Paddy:		
Upper grade	190	240
Medium grade	220	260
Lower grade	250	280
Dry land:		
Upper grade	200	240
Medium grade	250	260
Lower grade	350	280
Mou conversion ratio for taxation (fiscal *mou* equivalent of 1 measured *mou*):		
Paddy	1.000	1.000
Dry land	0.738	0.561
Hilly land	0.221	0.434
Marshland	1.000	1.191

SOURCE: Fu Kwang-chi, pp. 8235-51; Chen Pao-chung, pp. 10037-42.

types of land. In nine, all from Hsiu-ning and She, differential measuring gauges were used. For instance, the Wan-li fish-scale register from Hsiu-ning employed six differential measuring gauges, five of which are identical to the Hsiu-ning land measuring gauges given in Table 4.3.

Among the thirteen household registration files (*pien-shen ts'e* and *shih-cheng ts'e*), three were from counties in Chekiang that did not follow the *mou* conversion practice but simply applied differential tax rates on actual acreages. Ten converted actual acreages into fiscal units in a standard format: "*x mou* of land in a certain category (such as dryland) is converted into *y mou* of *shui tien* [taxable land]". Obviously, all lands were measured originally in standard *mou* and were then converted into fiscal units for the purpose of determining tax payments. In other words, *mou* conversion was merely a substitute for differential tax rates. On what grounds can one assert that the whole set of actual acreages was first measured and then discarded after *mou* conversion? The same question may also be posed in a different way: When two sets of land data were available, one set measured in more or less standardized units and the other in widely varying local units (228 ratios in Anhwei alone), which set should be used to arrive at national totals?

A comparison of the usage of terms may also help answer the question. The standard unit (240 *pu*) was normally called *mou* with no adjective attached; occasionally it was referred to as *min mou* (civic acre). The converted fiscal unit was called *shui mou* (taxable acre), *che mou* (converted acre), or *ts'e mou* (acreage unit in the book of grain tax). All total acreage figures I have seen published in official documents and thousands of private deeds from the Ming and Ch'ing have used the term *mou*.

National Acreage Data

As indicated earlier, national statistics are available for total acreages of Chinese farmland for six years during the Han. Unfortunately, no similar data have been released for A.D. 40, the year in which a country-wide land survey is known to have taken place. The total acreage statistics for A.D. 2, however, appear to be consistent with the five figures after A.D. 104. They show a reduction of farmland from the time of the Western Han to the Eastern Han, presumably because of the enlargement of the measurement unit *ch'ih* between the two periods. These figures, converted into standard *shih mou*, are slightly over 500 million *mou*, with some negligible variation. The fact that no substantial revision was made in the years after the land survey in A.D. 40, suggests a general reliability for the Han acreage figures. The population during the Eastern Han had declined somewhat from its peak in the Western Han because of increased civil disorders. The per capita acreage of farmland, on the other hand, showed a mild increase, reflecting the rising ability of peasants to cultivate more land.

The next trustworthy national acreage account appeared in 976, or 830 years after the last available Han figure. Since this set of data was published only fifteen years after Emperor T'ai Tsu of the Northern Sung ordered a countrywide land survey, it probably represents results compiled from actual cadasters. The total amount of farmland was about half that recorded during the Han, primarily because the land survey took place immediately after Emperor T'ai Tsu reunited the nation, when much of the land had been laid to waste by prolonged wars and before the Sung government had time to promote reclamation and agricultural rehabilitation. To a lesser degree, the reduction in acreage was caused by the loss of some northern plains to foreign tribes.

The quality of land returns during the Northern Sung quickly deteriorated thereafter as more and more land was reclaimed and brought under cultivation without being properly registered. In addition, powerful families and local magnates found new ways to avoid reporting their landholdings in part or in full. The official figure of registered farmland rose from 295 million Sung *mou* in 976 to 462 million by 1072. But there are indications that a large proportion of farmland was still not incorporated into the 1072 return.

Part of the economic reform program initiated by Wang An-shih in 1072 involved measuring farmland and rearranging it in large square blocks. This scheme, which lasted thirteen years, was accomplished in four provinces plus the capital prefecture of Kaifeng. A new total acreage of 248 million Sung *mou* was obtained for the combined five districts. A comparison of the new acreage with the land returns originally registered in these districts (132 million Sung *mou*)[18] implies that about 47 percent of farmland there had escaped land registration but was recovered in this new land survey. Given the possibility that these districts might have harbored a relatively large number of powerful families because of their proximity to the national capital, the proportion of unreported farmland might have been somewhat higher here than in other parts of the country. If we assume the national average of unreported land to be 40 percent, the total cultivated area should be raised to 770 million Sung *mou*, or about 666 million *shih mou*. This figure is about 17 percent higher than the maximum amount registered during the Han.

The two national land measurements made during the Ming dynasty produced more reliable results, but they contain a number of obvious recording or transcription errors. Fortunately, the data were published in sufficient detail to enable us to make credible adjustments. During the reign of Emperor T'ai Tsu, the national land survey and population census were conducted simultaneously and their results were compiled in the 1393 fish-scale and yellow registers. Thus, questionable figures can be detected by comparing the two sets of data.

Except for the periods when China was divided into two or more independent states, there was usually a single region characterized by the most extensive economic activities and the highest population density in terms of farmland (or the lowest per capita acreage of farmland). This

TABLE 4.4
Land and Population Returns, 1393

Prefecture	Cultivated acreage (million *mou*)	Population (000)	Per capita acreage (*mou*)	Adjusted cultivated acreage (million *mou*)	Adjusted per capita acreage (*mou*)
North Chihli	58.2	1,926	30.2		
South Chihli	126.9	10,755	11.8	79.9	7.4
Chekiang	51.7	10,487	4.9		
Kiangsi	43.1	8,982	4.8		
Hukwang	220.2	4,702	46.8	36.4	7.7
Fukien	14.6	3,916	3.7		
Shantung	72.4	5,255	13.7		
Shansi	41.8	4,072	10.2		
Honan	144.9	1,912	75.8	27.5	14.3
Shensi	31.5	2,316	13.6		
Szechwan	11.2	1,466	7.6		
Kwangtung	23.7	3,007	7.8		
Kwangsi	10.2	1,482	6.9		
Yunnan	—	259			
Kweichow	—	—			
TOTAL	850.4	60,537	14.0	502.5	8.3

SOURCE: See Chao 1980, p. 52.

was particularly true during the reign of the Ming emperor Hung Wu, when both the economic and the political centers of gravity coincided. We would expect the population density per unit of arable land gradually to decline, or the per capita acreage to rise, as we move away from the economic center. This effect should hold true in interprovince as well as intraprovince comparisons.

Table 4.4 shows the officially published returns of the land survey and the population census conducted during the reign of Hung Wu. Column 4 computes the per capita acreage for various provinces. The economic center was located in Chekiang, Kiangsi, and Fukien, the three provinces that were least devastated by the invading Mongols. Per capita acreage was lowest (between 3.7 and 4.9 *mou*) in the center and gradually rose moving away from the center so that population densities formed a radiating pattern. This regular pattern of radiation, however, is interrupted by three figures that consequently seem questionable: (1) South Chihli (the present Kiangsu and Anhwei), (2) Hukwang (the present Hunan and Hupei), and (3) Honan. The discrepancies between these figures and those from their neighboring provinces are too abrupt to be explained by any real factor.

81

TABLE 4.5
Land and Population Returns of South Chihli, 1393

Prefecture	Cultivated acreage (000 *mou*)	Population (000)	Per capita acreage (*mou*)	Adjusted cultivated acreage (000 *mou*)	Adjusted per capita acreage (*mou*)
Ying-t'ien	7,270	1,193	6.0		
Su-chou	9,850	2,355	4.1		
Sung-chiang	5,132	1,219	4.2		
Ch'ang-chou	7,973	775	10.2		
Chen-chiang	3,845	522	7.3		
Lu-chou	1,622	367	4.4		
Feng-yang	41,749	427	97.7	4,749	11.1
Huai-an	19,333	631	30.6	9,333	14.7
Yang-chou	4,276	736	5.8		
Hui-chou	3,534	592	5.9		
Ning-kuo	7,751	532	14.5		
Ch'ih-chou	2,284	198	11.5		
T'ai-p'ing	3,621	259	13.9		
An-ch'ing	2,102	422	4.9		
Kwang-te	3,004	247	12.1		
Hsü-chou	2,834	180	15.7		
Chu-chou	315	24	13.1		
Ho-chou	425	66	6.4		
TOTAL	126,920	10,745	11.8	79,920	7.4

SOURCE: See Chao 1980, p. 54.

Let us consider South Chihli first, for which we must examine land and population distribution by prefecture to identify the sources of error. This is done in Table 4.5. Here we can easily observe the same radiating pattern of population diffusion. Prefectures in the lower Yangtze valley such as Sung-chiang and Su-chou had per capita acreage figures similar to Chekiang's, whereas Hsü-chou and T'ai-ping in the northern part of the province had figures almost identical to Shantung's. The only two figures that appear questionable are those for Feng-yang (97.7 *mou* per person) and Huai-an (30.5 *mou* per person).

Alternatively, we may compare total acreages of the two prefectures as recorded in 1393 with the data from some later years:

Year	Feng-yang (00 *mou*)	Huai-an (00 *mou*)
1393	417,493	193,330
1502	61,262	101,072
1578	60,191	130,826

Because the two prefectures were well-publicized destinations of resettlement during the first few decades of the Ming dynasty, the statistical decline shown here is absolutely counterfactual. One of the commonest types of errors in numerical transcription found by historians in Chinese historical documents is the copier's inadvertent insertion of a single horizontal bar (–) into a long number. These two cases seem to be of this sort. Therefore, if the two figures for 1393 are corrected as 47,493 and 93,330, they not only accord with the later data but also yield two per capita acreages completely consistent with all other prefectures in the province for the year 1393. The corrected provincial total also fits the diffusion pattern perfectly; that is, the resulting per capita acreage of 7.7 *mou* is higher than that shown by its southern neighbor, Chekiang, but lower than that shown by its northern neighbor, Shantung.

The total acreage of Hukwang—2,202 million *mou*—was too large to be credible. This figure yields a per capita acreage of 46.8 *mou*, nearly ten times the figure of its neighboring province, Kiangsi. Several theories have been advanced to explain the possible source of error and suggesting adjustments. Taiji Shimizu contends that the acreage of Hukwang appears large because it included hilly land whereas other land returns did not.[19] Hiroshi Fujii rejects Shimizu's theory on the grounds that the amount of hilly lands was too small to account for such a huge discrepancy.[20] He has summed up the land returns for individual districts in Hukwang and concluded that the correct acreage for that province in the early Ming was approximately 24 million *mou*. This amount, however, seems too small because it leads to a per capita acreage (5.1 *mou*) comparable only to that of Chekiang. Another theory suggests that the exceedingly large figure was probably the result of an inadvertent repetition of the number 2 in the recording or transcription. In other words, instead of 220.2 million *mou*, it should be 20.2 million *mou*. Again, the difficulty of accepting this new figure is that it is too small to yield a reasonable per capita acreage compatible with the general pattern of population diffusion. It would imply a per capita acreage of 4.2 *mou*, which, by virtue of being even smaller than that in either Kiangsi or Chekiang, would qualify Hukwang as the center of farming activities in that period. In his memorial reporting the land survey of 1578-81, the governor of Hukwang cited the "original acreage" as 36.4 million *mou*. This figure is acceptable because the resulting per capita acreage (7.7 *mou*) is in line with that of Kwangtung and Szechwan.

The total acreage of farmland in Honan was recorded as 144.9 million *mou*. This produces per capita acreage of 75.8 *mou*, an amount far ex-

TABLE 4.6
Land Returns, 1581
(000 *mou*)

Province	Original acreage	Reduction in acreage	Increase in acreage	New total acreage
North Chihli	(58,249)		3,297	(61,546)
South Chihli	(81,018)	2,024	6,105	(87,123)
Chekiang	(51,705)		4,589	(56,294)
Kiangsi	(43,118)		6,145	(49,264)
Hukwang	36,437	956	55,190	91,628
Fukien	(14,625)			(13,422)
Shantung	80,077		36,575	116,652
Shansi	(41,864)		2,250	44,114
Honan	100,732		4,440	105,173
Shensi	47,259		3,098	50,357
Szechwan	(13,482)		27,452	(40,934)
Kwangtung	26,635		7,121	33,756
Kwangsi	(10,240)		76	(10,317)
Yunnan	(1,799)			(1,799)
Kweichow	752	51	159	911
TOTAL				(763,290)

SOURCE: The numbers without parenthesis are from *Ming shih lu*, various months from the eighth to the tenth year of the Wan Li reign. The numbers in parentheses are estimates provided by the author.

ceeding what an ordinary peasant could possibly till at that time. The adjustment for the Honan return is relatively easy. The provincial gazetteer for Honan explicitly gives 27.5 million *mou* as the correct land area of that province during Hung Wu's reign. The adjusted per capita acreage would then be 14.3 *mou*, comparable to that in Shantung and Shensi, which had similar economic conditions. All the adjusted provincial figures and the new national total are presented in Table 4.4.

To induce settlers to reclaim land in the less densely populated provinces, the first few Ming emperors reiterated the mandate of Emperor T'ai Tsu that newly reclaimed land need not be measured and could be exempted from land taxes indefinitely. This led to an ever-widening discrepancy between total acreage originally measured under the fish-scale registration and actual cultivated land. This tendency was checked by Emperor Shen Tsung, who ordered another national land survey to make all land accountable under a new tax system—the *i t'iao pien fa* or single whip tax. This survey, as discussed in Chapter 3, began in 1578. In the next few years, governors of various provinces submitted their memorials reporting the results of land surveys in their jurisdictions. These reports consisted of the following items: (1) original acreage, the amount of farmland previously registered; (2) reduction in acreage, if the acreage

TABLE 4.7
Comparison of Land Returns, 1393 and 1581
(000 *mou*)

Province	1393 returns	1581 returns	Increase
North Chihli	58,249	61,546	3,297
South Chihli	79,927	87,123	7,196
Chekiang	51,705	56,294	4,589
Kiangsi	43,118	49,264	6,146
Hukwang	36,437	91,628	55,191
Fukien	14,625	13,422	−1,203
Shantung	72,403	116,652	44,249
Shansi	41,864	44,114	2,250
Honan	27,537	105,173	77,636
Shensi	31,525	50,357	18,832
Szechwan	11,203	40,934	29,731
Kwangtung	23,734	33,756	10,022
Kwangsi	10,240	10,317	77
Yunnan	—	1,799	—
Kweichow	—	911	—

SOURCES: Tables 4.4 and 4.6.

registered immediately before the new land survey was less than the original acreage; (3) increase in acreage, if the total area measured in the new survey exceeded the original acreage; and (4) new acreage: the total area measured in the new survey.

The data from those memorials are presented in Table 4.6 without parentheses. In cases where the governor failed to provide the full information for his province, we have derived the unknowns from the items he did supply or from other sources;[21] these estimates are in parentheses.

The national total acreage obtained from the new land survey was 763 million *mou*, representing an increase of 51.9 percent from the 1393 returns. The changes were primarily the results of reclamation activities performed by the settlers who had moved from the lower Yangtze river valley to sparsely populated provinces. As can be seen from Table 4.7, during this period the cultivated areas were enlarged in all provinces but Fukien. The most sizeable increments occurred in Honan, Hukwang, Shantung, and Szechwan. This effect is fully confirmed by the resettlement policies announced by various Ming governments.[22] The early resettlement programs during the reign of T'ai Tsu quickly populated the areas of Feng-yang, Huai-an, and other prefectures along the Huai river. Thereafter, Honan, Hukwang, Shantung, and Szechwan were designated as the main destinations of large-scale resettlement programs with special tax incentives. Generally, settlers tended to migrate to areas where

85

the cropping system was already familiar to them. Thus, settlers from the areas north of the Yangtze river moved to Honan and Shantung, where wheat was the staple crop; settlers from Chekiang and Kiangsi tended to go to Hukwang and Szechwan, where the climate permitted them to continue growing rice.

Special attention should be paid to the column of acreage increases in Table 4.6. These numbers represent the amounts of unregistered lands that were recovered in the new survey and accounted for 20.5 percent of the total acreage of farmland in the country.

During the Ch'ing dynasty, many prefectures and counties conducted local land surveys in different years, but there was no synchronized measurement for the nation as a whole. Every 20 years or so, the central government compiled local land statistics to arrive at a national total; the quality of such land data is undoubtedly inferior to the land returns of the Ming. On the other hand, the continued use of fish-scale registers, some of which were updated periodically at the local level, presumably should have prevented rampant underreporting. Consequently, the quality of the Ch'ing data is believed to be better than that of the Sung.

In the 1930's, John Buck embarked on a large-scale agricultural survey at Nanking University by selecting more than 16,000 farming households from 148 counties in the 22 inland provinces.[23] He and his field workers discovered that the areas registered at the seats of local governments were only about 77 percent to 80 percent of the acreages they themselves estimated. The implied rate of underreporting was surprisingly close to the 20.5 percent manifested by the 1581 land returns. Assuming that, under the control of the fish-scale register, the degree of underreporting could rise to a maximum level of 20 percent, I have raised the land acreages of the Ch'ing dynasty by a sliding percent. Specifically, it is assumed that in 1662, when land was relatively abundant and reclamation activities had not begun, land was not concealed, but for the subsequent benchmark years, when large-scale reclamation activities were under way and some of the newly reclaimed land was not added to the existing land registers, the official acreage figures were raised by the following rates:

Year	Official acreage (million *mou*)	Adjustment ratio	Adjusted acreage (million *mou*)
1784	761	1.12	852
1812	789	1.15	907
1887	925	1.20	1110

The adjusted acreages are then converted into *shih mou.*

TABLE 4.8
China's Cultivated Acreage, A.D. 2-1930

Dynasty and year	Original data (million *mou*)	Adjusted acreage (million *shih mou*)
Western Han, 2	827	571
Eastern Han, 105	732	535
Eastern Han, 146	694	507
Northern Sung, 976	295	255
Northern Sung, 1072	462	666
Ming, 1393	850	522
Ming, 1581	701	793
Ch'ing, 1662	549	570
Ch'ing, 1784	761	886
Ch'ing, 1812	789	943
Ch'ing, 1887	925	1,154
Republic, 22 provinces, 1930	1,143	1,143

SOURCE: Original data from Buck, p. 164. Data adjusted for underreporting by author.

All the historical data from land returns we have examined in this chapter are presented in Table 4.8, along with the results of our adjustments. For easy comparison, the adjusted figures are given in *shih mou*. The last figure in the table is the total acreage of cultivated land in the 22 inland provinces, as estimated by Buck on the basis of his 1930 sample study. As the table clearly shows, a succession of serious efforts to enlarge the amount of cultivated land in China began in the Sung Dynasty. Probably by the mid-nineteenth century, this endeavor reached its physical limits in the inland territory, since all land that could be possibly used for agricultural production had been brought under cultivation. The adjusted acreage for 1887 represents the total cultivated area in the 22 inland provinces plus a small amount in the southern part of Liaoning. Since that time and until the 1930's there was virtually no increase in cultivated acreage in the 22 provinces; reclamation activities after 1850 have been concentrated in the virgin territory of Manchuria.

5

Man-Land Ratios and Land Fragmentation

Man-Land Ratios

We are now ready to combine acreage data and population data for the benchmark years A.D. 2-1887. Although the measures are not exact, they should still be able to indicate significant historical changes. The resulting per capita cultivated acreages are presented in Table 5.1. Based on these ratios and other related data, we may divide China's history into three distinct stages reflecting the changing ratio between available land and labor input in agricultural production. This classification is meant only to highlight some of the major characteristics in each period for China as a whole at the risk of ignoring the considerable regional variations in tempo and pattern of development.

In the first stage, labor was clearly the constraining factor because total agricultural output was determined primarily by the amount of available labor and that labor's productivity. Because of its relative abundance, land had not yet become a constraint in agricultural production. The amount of land brought under cultivation was largely determined by how much the average farmer could effectively till; conceivably the marginal product of land could have changed to a negative value if the limited amount of labor were spread over too large a area.

The two Han periods undoubtedly belong to this initial stage, as evidenced by the gradual increase in per capita cultivated acreage. Judging from the farming technology known to have been prevalent in the first century, it would have been difficult for a standard farm household with five members to manage a field substantially larger than 50 *shih mou*. The gradual increase in per capita acreage was, presumably, the consequence of slow improvement in both labor productivity and farming implements. Of course, part of this improvement was embodied in the rising multiple cropping index; the average farmer in the latter part of the

TABLE 5.1
Per Capita Acreages of Cultivated Land, A.D. 2-1887

Cultivated land		Population		Per capita acreage (*shih mou*)
Year	Amount (million *shih mou*)	Year	Number (million)	
2	571	2	59	9.67
105	535	105	53	10.09
146	507	146	47	10.78
976	255	961	32	7.96
1072	666	1109	121	5.50
1393	522	1391	60	8.70
1581	793	1592	200	3.96
1662	570	1657	72	7.92
1784	886	1776	268	3.30
1812	943	1800	295	3.19
1887	1,154	1848	426	2.70

SOURCES: Tables 2.3 and 4.8.

Han was able to enlarge his farm as well as reduce the percentage of land for fallowing. For China as a whole, however, the average index was unlikely to be greater than unity since the fallow system was still necessary in many regions. Highly intensive farming was practiced only in a few pockets in which population density was abnormally high.

No aggregate data of this type are available for the period between the third and the seventh centuries. Nevertheless, land legislation from that period may help us understand factor endowments as they existed at that time, provided we accept the assumption that such land regulations were not formulated without some reference to existing man-land ratios and to labor productivity. There are signs that the four hundred years or so after the Eastern Han also belonged to this first stage, with labor continuing to be the constraining factor in agricultural production.

In fact, labor shortages were substantial during the Western Chin, when the country was slowly recovering from a severe depletion of its population. The official history of the Western Chin documents that peasants tended to overextend their labor to unduly large tracts of land, thereby causing the unit yield to fall to a level so low it was barely sufficient to compensate for the seeds used.[1] To correct this bias, the Chin government promulgated the law of land possession (*chan t'ien fa*), which set limits on landholdings for small cultivators who had no sources of labor other than family members.

Taking a family with two adult laborers, husband and wife, as a hypo-

TABLE 5.2
Equitable Field System Allotment Quotas, by Dynasty

Dynasty	Quotas (*mou*)		Converted to *shih mou*	
	Cropland	Hereditary land	Excluding hereditary land	Including hereditary land
Northern Wei	60	20	67.5	90.2
Northern Chi	120	20	135.3	157.9
Sui	120	20	136.2	158.9
T'ang	80	20	64.8	81.0

SOURCE: See Chao and Chen 1982, pp. 35-40.

thetical unit, the law allowed a total of 100 *mou* (70 for the husband and 30 for the wife) as the ceiling on the amount of land they could jointly own. Presumably, the Chin legislators considered this amount as the upper limit for efficient farming, beyond which total output was likely to be reduced. One hundred Chin *mou* is equivalent to 75.4 *shih mou*, an amount substantially larger than a similar family could have obtained during the Han. Given the large amounts of unused land in this period, it is quite possible that the Chin government allowed a rather generous maximum. This new prescription, however, reflected more fundamentally the increase in peasants' productivity between the two periods. Thus, the maximum amount of land that could be efficiently farmed had naturally increased.

The trend of development became even clearer after the introduction of the equitable field system (*chün ti'en fa*) by the Northern Wei (Toba) in 485. The law of land possession was meant to dictate ceilings for individual landholdings without actually distributing land to peasants according to the announced formula. The equitable field system formulated quotas according to which farmland was actually allotted to tillers. The designer of the equitable field system, Li An-shih, stated explicitly that the quotas had been determined in such a way as to achieve a reasonable match between labor and land.[2] The quotas were revised in subsequent dynasties to cope with changed factor endowments in agricultural production. For the same hypothetical peasant household, the total areas of land to be allotted in accordance with the quotas stipulated in various dynasties are compared in Table 5.2.

The Northern Wei quotas were those areas actually to be tilled by their recipients in each year, or what are now called "sown areas." Fallow lands would be distributed in addition to these quotas if conditions necessitated the implementation of this measure. The Northern Ch'i and Sui quotas were cultivated areas inclusive of fallow land. Hereditary lands were assigned to the planting of perennials; hence, no fallowing was necessary. Compared to the landholding ceilings of the Western Chin, which included both fallow lands and fields devoted to perennials, quotas under the equitable field system were larger. It is unclear, however, whether the Northern Ch'i and Sui quotas represented an enlargement or reduction from those of the Northern Wei. If the average index of multiple cropping during that time period was higher than 0.50—that is, less than half the cropland was set aside for fallowing each year—the new quotas may be regarded as an enlarged per capita acreage. The fact that the Sui government did not make any significant adjustment in land allotment quotas after the north and the south were reunited suggests that the man-land ratio in the south was not drastically different from that in the north.

The obvious quota reduction in the T'ang dynasty marks the beginning of the second stage of agricultural development.[3] By now, land had emerged as the constraining factor. The previously ascendent trend of per capita acreage was basically a result of the rising productivity of peasants, thanks to the introduction of increasingly improved implements and farming methods. This trend could no longer be sustained in the second stage, because by this time the amount of available land had become a limiting factor in and of itself.

As Table 5.1 shows, the peak T'ang population was no larger than that in the Han, suggesting that the per capita acreage of farmland in the T'ang should be at least as large as that in the Han. Yet the average farmer living in the seventh and eighth centuries was undoubtedly more productive and able to manage a larger tract of land than he actually tilled. The scarcity of farmland in T'ang times, therefore, should be understood in this relative sense.

Even the smaller quotas of land allotment announced by the T'ang government became impractical within a short time. By 730, or about a century after the establishment of the dynasty, nearly 80 percent of the districts had been declared "narrow areas" in which standard allotment quotas were reduced by 50 percent.[4] In fact, shortage of land was one of the major reasons contributing to the eventual collapse of the land allotment system. The increasing population pressure was somewhat alleviated after the rebellion (755-63) of An Lu-shan and Shih Ssu-ming, two frontier generals during the reign of Hsüan Tsung. Based on the observations of a high-ranking official, the average farmland per standard household around 786 seemed to be 50 T'ang *mou* or about 40 *shih mou*,[5] which was comparable to the level indicated by the A.D. 2 surveys. An incomplete census undertaken by Emperor Shih Tsung of the late Chou in 958 revealed that a total of 2.3 million households occupied 108.5 million *mou* of farmland, or approximately 47 *mou* (40 *shih mou*) per household.[6] This was not significantly different from the estimated 7.96 *shih mou* per person at the beginning of the Northern Sung.

Beginning in the eleventh century, man-land proportions in China clearly entered their third stage, which has continued to modern times. The third stage differs from the second in that per capita acreage of farmland began to decline in absolute terms. Since population growth in this stage formed a cyclical pattern around a rising trend line, the deteriorating process of per capita acreage took the opposite pattern and oscillated around a descending trend line. During periods of large-scale turmoil, such as the invasion and occupation of China by the Mongols in the thirteenth and fourteenth centuries and the last few decades of the Ming dynasty, the drastically reduced population granted the land shortage problem a temporary respite. But the increase in the man-land ratio was to resume as soon as the recovery phase began.

Of course, there was wide regional variation in man-land ratios. Surviving rental records of the offices managing the so-called school lands in six districts in Chekiang and Kiangsu, dating from sometime during the twelfth century, show that the 1,060 tenant households renting the school lands were classified as follows according to the amount of land rented:[7]

Amount of land rented	Number of tenants	Percent of total tenants
1-10 *mou*	756	71.3%
10-30 *mou*	152	14.4%
30-100 *mou*	115	10.8%
over 100 *mou*	37	3.5%

More than 85 percent of the tenants had farms smaller than 30 *mou* each; most owned less than 10 *mou* of farmland. The few who had rented more than 100 *mou* of land were actually not peasants themselves. They took large amounts of lands from the schools, re-rented them in smaller pieces to true farmers, and then received the rental differentials as incomes.[8] It is safe to say that the average farm size in these two provinces had fallen below 30 *mou* by this time.

TABLE 5.3
Average Size of Farm by Province, 1936
(*shih mou*)

Province	Per farm household	Per farmer	Province	Per farm household	Per farmer
Kiangsu	14.3	3.8	Shansi	34.5	7.4
Chekiang	14.3	3.7	Shensi	28.5	5.0
Anhwei	15.9	2.5	Kansu	28.8	5.4
Kiangsi	19.8	3.5	Fukien	13.0	2.4
Hunan	13.8	2.7	Kwangtung	8.2	1.1
Hupei	12.6	2.5	Kwangsi	13.1	2.8
Szechwan	11.3	2.8	Yunnan	13.8	2.8
Hopei	22.7	4.2	Kweichow	39.5	9.1
Shantung	19.3	3.7	National		
Honan	23.1	4.2	average	18.4	3.6

SOURCE: Land Commission, p. 25.

In the north, however, the average farm size was generally larger. Similar rental records of school lands in seven districts in Shensi province under the rule of the Chin Tartars around the year 1194 revealed the following average sizes of tenant farms:[9]

District	Average size (*mou*)	District	Average size (*mou*)
Hsien-ming	69	Hu-hsien	30
Ch'ang-an	36	Yun-yang	5
Lin-tung	53	Ching-yang	7
Hsing-p'ing	54		

The last two districts appear to be exceptional cases.

As Table 5.1 shows, the per capita acreage of farmland for China as a whole dropped to a nadir of about 4 *shih mou* toward the end of the Ming dynasty and again to a new record low in the nineteenth century—even below the 3 *shih mou* mark. A nationwide survey conducted by the Republic of China in the 1930's (see Table 5.3) gives a national average acreage in 1936 of 3.6 *mou* per farmer. Assuming 20 percent as the proportion of nonagricultural population, the per capita farm size in 1936 would be approximately 2.8 *mou*.

Land Fragmentation

In his monumental study of Chinese land utilization, Buck noted land fragmentation, that is, each farmer's ownership of widely scattered plots of land, as one of the salient characteristics of Chinese agriculture in the 1920's and 1930's.[10] He defines a "parcel" as an independent piece of land, bounded by the land of other owners, that may contain one or more "fields" depending on its size. Buck's study shows that two-thirds of the farms surveyed had one to five parcels per farm, and more than one-fifth had six to ten parcels per farm. The average parcel size was 1.16 acres in the wheat region but only 0.79 acres in the rice region. A parcel often contained more than one field, so that the average farm had 5.6 parcels but 11.6 fields. The average distance of all parcels from the farmstead was 0.4 mile—0.5 for the wheat region and 0.3 for the rice region.

Up to now, two theories have been commonly used to explain the historical rise of land fragmentation in China: (1) the Chinese system of *fen chia*, that is, dividing the family property, and (2) the emergence of absentee landlords. It is implausible, however, to attribute land fragmentation, a phenomenon that occurred only after the eleventh century, to institutions that existed for more than two thousand years. The number of absentee landlords, mostly rich merchants, was very significant as early as the period of Emperor Wu during the Western Han, and they became a major target of criticism from such Confucian scholars as Tung Chung-shu. More important, these two theories contradict the empirical data currently available. A new explanation is obviously needed that is consistent with existing data.

The Chinese custom of *fen chia*, under which a household's property is divided among all heirs in equal shares after the death of the head of household, is often given as the main reason for the extreme degree of land fragmentation in traditional China. This theory is questionable, however. Even though *fen chia* reduces the average size of farms, it does not necessarily fragment them into scattered fields and parcels. If the original estate of the household is a large piece of land—say, 500 *mou*— and is to be inherited by five sons, it is easily divided into five small farms of 100 *mou* each without further partition. Even if the 500 *mou* are of varying quality, the lands do not have to be divided up to achieve complete fairness among the heirs because the five shares may be allocated in such a way that they provide equal amounts of yield or income. In fact, this is exactly the system recorded in all the *fen chia* documents I have seen—landed property is divided into equal shares in terms of normal yield rather than sheer acreage. None of these documents mentioned that a parcel of farmland was to be partitioned among several heirs.

Some scholars believe land fragmentation in China to be the result of the migration of landowners into cities. They argue that, in buying lands,

94

absentee landlords no longer cared where the plots were located and whether they were adjacent. This explanation, however, is not supported by the findings of Buck, who reported that the holdings of owner farmers likewise consisted of scattered parcels.

A new and more plausible explanation is that land fragmentation was a result of tremendous population pressure and shortage of farmland, which became pronounced after the eleventh century. This theory, moreover, is supported by empirical evidence. Partition occurred not in the process of land inheritance, but in the process of buying and selling land. Given the serious shortages of land, demand for it was immensely strong relative to the supply, resulting in what may be called a sellers' market in China.

First, a person who once acquired land would be very reluctant to alienate it. When he was forced by hardship or other extraordinary circumstances to sell, he would try to sell no more than absolutely necessary. Thus a landowner would customarily partition a relatively large piece of land and sell only parts of it. Over time, this piece of land might be sold to several buyers in small parcels. This behavior is substantiated in actual land transaction documents I have seen.

Second, as Chapter 6 will show, the rate of land accumulation was so low in traditional China that a landowner could add only a small piece to his holding every few years. By the time he was ready to buy, he had little choice in terms of location and had to settle for the size of plot he could afford. As a consequence, a typical landowner ended up holding small plots scattered not only throughout the same village but sometimes throughout the neighboring region.

Third, price differentials existed between large and small plots because of the unbalanced market demands. In other words, only one segment of the land market was especially active—the market for small parcels. Since most buyers could afford only small plots, those who wanted to sell large pieces of land might not always find buyers. Thus, large plots were usually sold at a discount whereas small plots were sold at the premium price. These differentials in land price can be easily detected in the land purchase records of private households.

To exclude the effect of price fluctuations over time, let us compare land prices for plots purchased by a given family in a period no longer than two years. The following examples are illustrative:

1. Land records of the Chen family (1486-1554), four plots bought in

1553 (price per *mou* is given in taels, one tael being equivalent to about one ounce of silver):

Plot size (*mou*)	Price per *mou*	Plot size (*mou*)	Price per *mou*
1.2	7.0	1.0	7.5
1.0	7.5	0.5	8.0

While the differences in price are quite clear in this example, we are not sure whether they reflect different grades of land. In some cases it is possible to calculate the land price per unit of "normal rent." The results are land prices adjusted for variation in unit yield, which is taken as the indicator of land quality.

2. Land records of the Wang family (1563-83), plots bought in 1567 and 1568 (converted price in this and the next two examples is given in taels per 25 catties of rent):

Plot size (*mou*)	Converted price	Plot size (*mou*)	Converted price
2.853	0.49	1.100	1.01
2.600	0.95	0.990	1.12
1.730	0.93	0.375	1.30
1.670	0.93		

3. Land records of the Yu family, plots bought in 1675:

Plot size (*mou*)	Converted price	Plot size (*mou*)	Converted price
3.323	0.34	0.920	0.70
1.642	0.70	0.620	0.62
1.294	0.70		

4. Land records of the Wang family (1717-52), plots bought in 1743:

Plot size (*mou*)	Converted price	Plot size (*mou*)	Converted price
1.80	1.27	1.20	1.50
1.68	1.33	0.62	1.50

It is evident that even plots larger than 2 *mou* would have to suffer a substantial discount in their selling price, for only a small percentage of buyers could afford to buy lands of that size. Facing such an unbalanced land market, potential sellers would naturally cut up their lands into smaller plots so that they could sell them at premium prices.

The process of land fragmentation in China may be traced from the

Sung dynasty, when the country began to feel the dual pressures of population and land shortage. Surviving records of some public school systems in various localities of Chekiang and Kiangsu provide detailed information about the sources from which public schools acquired their lands during the Southern Sung. The following cases, in which, because of crimes committed, lands were confiscated by the government from their original owners and then transferred to the public school systems, are especially revealing because they clearly show the fragmentation of land ownership when the lands were in the hands of their original owners.

1. Lands confiscated from Chuang Ju-jui, in Wu-hsien, 1196.[11] The holding, totaling 43.72 *mou* (see Appendix A), consisted of six plots scattered in three *po* of two counties. The average size of the six plots was 7.29 *mou*.

2. Lands confiscated from Chen Chien, in P'ing-chiang, 1209[12] A total of 92.53 *mou* scattered in three *po* of two *hsiang*.

3. Lands confiscated from Hsi Chi, in P'ing-chiang, 1209.[13] Twenty plots totaling 258.25 *mou*, scattered in three *tu*. The average size of the plots was 12.91 *mou*.

4. Lands confiscated from Yu Ju-hsien, in Shan-yin county, 1263.[14] A total of 203 *mou* were divided into 101 plots, with an average size of two *mou* per plot; these were located in nine *hsiang*.

5. Lands confiscated from Chang Hung, in P'ing-chiang, 1242.[15] A total of 165.83 *mou* were divided into 34 plots, or 4.88 *mou* each, located in nine *hsiang* of three counties.

The process of land fragmentation is also evident in the changes in the average size of plots. The earliest extant landholding records were for the estates owned by the Kuang Ts'i temple located in the Ch'un-ming gate, Wan-nien county (the present Hsien-ning county, Shensi province) around the year 993.[16] These records were made before the adoption of the *chen chi pu* system of land registration, and no registration numbers were assigned to various plots. Using Buck's definition of parcel (a piece of land bounded by the land of other owners), let us identify each parcel on the landholding records by determining whether the piece of land was adjacent to another piece of land owned by the temple. Temple lands were in two general locations, north and east. Temple holdings on the north side consisted of the following seven parcels:

Parcel	No. of fields	Total *mou*	Parcel	No. of fields	Total *mou*
1	26	346	5	20	772
2	18	406	6	8	407
3	34	1,634	7	2	119
4	27	752			

The average size of parcels was as large as 634 *mou*; the largest parcel exceeded 1,600 *mou*. The average size of fields was 33 *mou*.

Temple holdings on the east side consisted of a single large parcel of 1,734 *mou*, which was divided into twelve adjacent fields. The average size of fields on the east side, 144 *mou*, was larger than that of fields on the north side. Out of the twelve fields, the five central fields were arranged in a rectangular form; the other seven fields, which were located along the sides of the parcel, had somewhat irregular shapes. The largest rectangular field had an area as large as 702 *mou*.

The land records of another temple (Ch'ung Chen) in the same general region (Fu-feng county, Shensi province), but at a later time (1003), show that the temple had 418 *mou* divided into eleven adjacent fields.[17] The largest field was 81 *mou* and the smallest 7 *mou*, with an average size of 38 *mou*. Obviously, fields (or plots) of over 30 *mou* and parcels of several hundred *mou* each were not unusual in the northern provinces during the early part of the eleventh century.

In the southern provinces, however, the situation during the twelfth and thirteenth centuries appeared strikingly different. By the year 1149, virtually all farmlands within the jurisdiction of the Southern Sung were registered under the new system of *chen chi pu*. Each plot, comparable to what Buck calls a "field," was assigned a registration number for the purpose of identification. In addition to the five cases of confiscated estates cited earlier, we can compute the average size of plots for the following cases:

1. Lands purchased by the public school of Canton in 1184:[18] (a) purchased from Chen Shao-chu, eighteen plots totaling 339.91 *mou*, averaging 18.9 *mou* per plot; (b) purchased from Chen Sung-ying, four plots totaling 65.88 *mou*, averaging 16.5 *mou* per plot; (c) purchased from Li Er-shih, eight plots totaling 129.96 *mou*, averaging 16.2 *mou* each.

2. School lands in Wu-hsien in 1196. No average size of plots can be calculated because of incomplete records. There were still some large plots between 20 and 43.35 *mou*.[19]

3. Land records for the same Wu-hsien school system in 1204:[20]

(a) Purchased in the fourth month of 1204, totaling 136.81 *mou*. The most interesting feature to note is that the lands were originally registered as nine separate plots, averaging 15.2 *mou* per plot, on the *chen chi pu*; but they were further divided into seventeen plots by the original owners, averaging 8.05 *mou* each.

(b) Lands totaling 86.23 *mou* were purchased in the seventh month of the same year. They were originally registered as thirteen plots averaging 6.63 *mou* each, but became fourteen plots in 1204, average size 6.16 *mou*.

(c) A transaction involving 58.72 *mou* located in Ju-Chiao *hsiang* was made in the same month. This land was divided into fourteen plots, average size 4.19 *mou*.

(d) Another transaction involving 64.98 *mou* located in Wu-chu *hsiang* was carried out in the same month. There were eighteen plots, average size 3.61 *mou*.

(e) Sometime later in the year, two plots located in I-ti *hsiang* were purchased, average size 3.63 *mou*.

(f) Lands totaling 43.72 *mou* were purchased from the neighboring county. They were divided into six plots, averaging 7.29 *mou* each.

4. Land acquisition records of the same school in 1205.[21] Four plots were purchased, with an average size of 9.22 *mou* per plot.

5. Seven land transactions by the same school in 1206:[22] (a) twelve plots, averaging 1.88 *mou* each; (b) twenty-seven plots, averaging 2.08 *mou* each; (c) thirteen plots, averaging 2.65 *mou* each; (d) the number of plots is not clear; (e) fourteen plots, averaging 1.61 *mou* each; (f) four plots, averaging 2.15 *mou* each; (g) fourteen plots, averaging 1.59 *mou* each.

6. The school system of Wu-hsi purchased 99 plots in 1243; average size 3.17 *mou*.[23] Again, judging by the registration numbers, these lands had been further partitioned by their original owners after registration.

7. Lands belonging to the Tung Yao Hsing Kung temple, Ch'ang-hsing Chou, recorded in 1313, showed an average size of 3.29 *mou* per plot.[24]

8. Land records recorded in 1344 for the Pao En Kuang Hsiao temple in Kuei-an, Hu-chou prefecture, showed an average size of 2.69 *mou*.[25]

Two relevant observations can be made from these land records for public schools and temples. First, there seems to be a declining trend in the average size of plots in this general area. Between 16 and 43 *mou* in the twelfth century, the average size had decreased to 2 to 15 *mou* in the thirteenth century. By the fourteenth century, virtually all plots were reduced to less than 5 *mou*. Second, there are indications that landowners divided up their lots before selling them. This practice was explicitly recorded in many cases. For instance, a compilation of artifacts found in the Liang-che area records the following transaction: "A part of a private plot, measuring 4.25 *mou*, was purchased. It was the western half of a plot originally measured 8.50 *mou*." And again: "A piece of high land located in Hsü-chun, measuring 2 *mou*, was alienated by the owner from a lot of 6 *mou*."[26] The fact that 26 out of the 99 plots purchased by the Wu-hsi public school in 1243 had been partitioned by the original owners from larger lots[27] is a clear indication of the popularity of this practice.

Ming-Ch'ing data also reveal a severe state of land fragmentation. On the survey map for each plot of land recorded in a fish-scale register, the owner was required to provide information about the lengths of borders and the owners of adjacent plots. If the plot was adjacent to another plot belonging to the same owner, the border was marked "adjacent to own land." Thus, most plots would be marked "adjacent to own land" if each landholder owned adjacent plots or if land in the locality belonged to only a few big landlords, but the percentage of plots with at least one side so marked is rather small. The following are a few examples:

Hsi county, 1573-1619: 42 percent. Another locality in Hsi county, 1573-1616, 20 percent.

An unidentified locality, 1651: paddy land, 21 percent; dry land, 30 percent.

Ch'ang-hua, Ming Dynasty: paddy land, 54 percent; dry land, 32 percent.

Hsiu-ning, 1573-1619: high-grade paddy land, 9 percent; medium-grade paddy land, 9 percent; lower-grade paddy land, 22 percent; high-grade dry land, 50 percent; medium-grade dry land, none; lower-grade dry land, 40 percent.

The problem was probably even more serious during the Ming-Ch'ing. Buck found in the 1930's that on the average each parcel had nearly two fields (11.6 : 5.6). That the Ming-Ch'ing data show more than half of the plots were not adjacent to land belonging to the same owner suggests that usually a parcel contained only one field. Thus, the average number of fields per parcel in the Ming-Ch'ing was close to one; virtually no farmer owned two adjacent fields.

Because it would have been uneconomical for a landowner to operate on so many scattered plots (he would have had to consume a great deal of energy and time in commuting every day), tenantry must have been extremely important under such conditions. Tenants could consolidate small fragmented plots into larger farms by leasing a number of adjacent plots belonging to different owners.

Private rent collection ledgers from Ming-Ch'ing times indicate that a landlord family had X plots usually leased to exactly X tenants, one plot to each tenant. A tenant's name seldom appears twice on the same ledger, which counted each plot as an entry. Yet the average size of plots barely exceeded 1 *mou*, far too small to provide the tenant with adequate income. This evidence seems to support my hypothesis that, because of the high degree of land fragmentation, a tenant tended to lease several adjacent plots from different landowners. It would have been uneconomical, hence undesirable, to rent several plots separated by great distances from the same family. Unfortunately, I found no rent ledgers belonging to different landlord families in the same locality during the same years, so that I am unable to demonstrate positively that some tenants' names appeared on a number of rent ledgers.

We have seen here how population pressure in China affected the labor markets, which in turn influenced the utilization of land in agricultural production. Chapter 6 will examine the relation between population pressure and land distribution.

6

Land Distribution

Factors Affecting Land Distribution

The status of land distribution in traditional China has been viewed in diverse ways. Whereas Western scholars do not see any clear-cut trend of deteriorating distribution, virtually all Chinese historians who adhere to the Marxist interpretation of economic development contend that land distribution in China became more unequal as a consequence of intensified class struggle over time and that the trend of deterioration was reversed only temporarily by a few major peasant rebellions that led to land redistribution at various levels. Adherents of the latter theory believe that the situation reached its nadir during the Ch'ing and attempt to substantiate this claim by identifying a handful of primary landlords, the most frequently mentioned being Kao Shih-ch'i, Hsu Ch'ien-hsueh, Li Wei, Ho Shen, and Po Ling. A modification of this standard contention states that even as the land distribution situation continued to worsen during the Ch'ing, more "commoner" landlords were present than in previous dynasties.

The only exception among the Marxists, so far as I am aware, is Chiang Tai-hsin, who criticizes the prevailing view:

> As for the state of land distribution during the early Ch'ing, most scholars previously thought that due to the extremely frequent annexation of land by landlords, most land was concentrated in the hands of the landlord class. . . . Some comrades even regard the state of land distribution during the reigns of Kang-hsi, Yung-cheng and Ch'ien-lung as 'given that one landlord occupied 1 million *mou* of land, the total farmland of 6 or 7 million *ch'ing* in the whole country would be owned outright by six or seven hundred major landlords.' We consider this judgment to be not entirely consistent with historical facts.[1]

By citing the records of land registration in several localities, Chiang concludes that most land was owned by peasants and that the general trend since the mid-Ming was actually diversification of ownership.[2]

This issue can only be clarified by meaningful quantitative measurement of the degree of concentration or unequal distribution of land. The conventional Gini coefficient and the extent of the landholdings of leading landlords will be used as indicators in this discussion. On the theoretical level, it is necessary to answer the question: What factors affected land distribution in China if the theory of intensified class struggle proves questionable?

Historically, one crucial factor was taxation. In virtually all dynasties after the Han, the chief source of government revenue was either a tax on agricultural output or a land tax of varying type. The tax burden relative to landholding was proportional, at least statutorily, in either case. On the other hand, every dynasty granted noblemen, high-ranking officials and generals, and certain other social categories the privilege of tax immunity. This made the actual structure of tax rates regressive at the upper end.

In addition to land or output taxes, governments usually imposed either a poll tax or labor corvée, known as the *ting*, on registered male adults. Land taxes and the poll tax or *ting* service were usually administered by the same agency working from the same set of household registers. Thus, as soon as a family was registered as a land tax-paying household because of their land property, it was automatically registered for the *ting* service. A lump-sum tax, the *ting* service rendered the actual rate structure highly regressive at the lower end as well. When a person owning only a tiny piece of land was registered as a taxable unit, his land tax payment might be light compared with that of a wealthier person, but he still had to contribute the same amount of *ting* service. Sometimes, if a person owned a very small amount of land, the combined levy of the land tax and the *ting* service might substantially exceed the gross yield of the land. In this case, the landowner would be disposed to relinquish his land, which had become in every practical sense a liability rather than an asset. Those in the best position to receive such lands were families enjoying the privilege of tax immunity. The history of China relates many tales of poor peasants seeking tax shelters in powerful households by donating their lands to the latter. This practice was a major factor in the concentration of land ownership.

There were a few exceptions to this rule, and the Sung period was one of them. As mentioned earlier, Sung governments regarded wealthy families as the most reliable agents for uncompensated public services and consequently conscripted only those families for such posts in local governments. Thus, households in possession of landed property during the Sung might either seek shelter by donating their lands to tax-immune families or try to avoid the obligation of public service by splitting their original households into smaller units that would consequently be ranked in a lower classification.

Under the equitable field system, at least during the early part of the T'ang, most farmland was owned by the government and distributed to peasants only for use in their lifetimes. The virtual absence of private ownership concentration, however, did not necessarily mean that the farms were of more or less equal size. Under the land legislation of the Toba Wei, for example, which permitted slaveowners to receive land allotments according to the number of slaves they owned, no real limit was placed on the size of farms.

For periods other than these exceptional times, there is no evidence to suggest that the inherently regressive nature of the tax rate structure became aggravated over time. In fact, the single whip tax introduced by the late Ming government and the efforts of the early Manchu rulers to integrate the land tax and the *ting* service were meant to remove these negative features from the overall rate structure. Therefore, taxation as a factor contributing to uneven distribution of land probably lost its significance after the fifteenth century.

Besides taxation, another causal factor in land distribution was economic development in general and commercialization in particular. This factor has captured the attention of many observers but has led to widely differing interpretations. Theoretically, economic development can influence land distribution in several ways.

First, although traditional China was a market economy, its factor markets were far from perfect in the early periods. Powerful families could forcibly detain people or deprive them of their rights to buy and own land. Over time, however, factor markets became freer as the influence of these noneconomic forces on the markets were gradually reduced and eventually removed. Moreover, when detained people regained their rights to buy and own land, the land market became more active, with an increasing number of participants on the demand side. In other words, concentrated land ownership is more likely to occur within an imperfect land market in which both economic and noneconomic forces operate than in a freer market in which land transactions are governed primarily by supply and demand. This effect of economic development on the land market was presumably extremely pronounced in the early, pre-Sung stages of Chinese history, but its importance tended to diminish when the factor market became highly competitive.

Second, as Ramon H. Myers has pointed out, commercialization of agriculture usually led to higher incomes for Chinese farming households.[3] In fact, this argument holds true not only for commercialization of farm products but also for commercialization of subsidiary products made by rural households. As Figure 1.2 demonstrated, commercialization tends to raise the marginal product schedule of farm goods, the marginal product schedule of subsidiary goods, or both. Theoretically, commercialization can affect the land market in two ways through its impact on farm incomes. On one hand, the demand function in the land market may be pushed (shifted) upward because farmers receive higher earnings, hence desire to expand their holdings and have the capability of doing so. On the other hand, the supply function may be pushed (shifted) downward because those marginal farmers who would otherwise be bankrupt and end up selling their lands can hold on now. In the extreme case, the land market can become a sellers' market, with few wanting to sell and many wanting to buy lands.

Third, a more controversial issue is the relation between commercialization and absentee landlords. Mark Elvin has suggested that, because of growing commercial activities during the Ming and Ch'ing, the amenities of urban living, and the relatively low returns in farm production, wealthy families became increasingly less inclined to invest in land.[4] Consequently, large landlords left the countryside for cities, so much so that "by the beginning of the nineteenth century, the Chinese countryside was becoming predominantly a world of smallholders, that is to say of peasant owners and of petty landlords who owned on average only a little more land than a well-off peasant."[5] While Elvin's description of land distribution in the nineteenth century is perfectly accurate, this situation probably existed long before the date he has given. Nor is the causal relationship as straightforward as he has suggested. The capital movement Elvin has depicted could have been true only if most major landlords, once enticed by the high rates of return in commerce, lost interest in investing in land forever.

China's powerful and durable tradition of agricultural fundamentalism dating from the time of the Western Han, is well known. Aside from the pragmatic view held by the common people that land as an object of investment was indestructible and hence safer than other types of property, Confucian philosophers further asserted that farming was the only productive endeavor among all economic activities and therefore should be especially encouraged. Consequently, one of the socioeconomic policies endorsed by all Chinese governments since the Western Han was to grant a high social status to peasants but to discriminate against merchants in many respects.

The typical reaction of merchants was, understandably, to adopt commerce and other nonagricultural enterprises, because of their comparatively high rates of returns, as a merely temporary means towards the accumulation of wealth. As soon as they had accumulated sufficient funds, merchants tended to withdraw their capital and invest it in land, a practice commonly referred to as "earning wealth through superficial occupations but preserving wealth through the fundamental occupation." Deeply influenced by this outlook, the Chinese economy has historically witnessed an incessant return flow of capital from the urban sector back to the countryside. This attitude was responsible for the persistently low rate of return in agricultural production as compared with alternative outlets for investment.[6] It is also a clear sign of misallocation of economic resources, for otherwise the supposed capital movement would have equalized the rates of return in the two sectors. In a sense, the low rate of return in agricultural production observed by Elvin is less a cause of the movement of capital into the urban sector than a result of the backward flow of capital into the rural sector. To some extent, this persistent backward flow of capital may be held responsible for the retarded development of the urban sector in later Chinese history.

Chinese historians from Han times on have been familiar with the backward flow of commercial capital, but they regard it rather as a major factor contributing to uneven land distribution. The purchase of farmland by merchants is described by these theoreticians as *chien pin*, or annexation of land. They tend to believe that the higher the degree of commercialization and the quicker the accumulation of commercial capital, the higher the degree of land concentration in a few hands. It was under the influence of this argument, advanced by such Han scholars as Tung Chung-shu, that Emperor Wu, during whose reign the inroads of commercial capital into the rural sector reached threatening heights, decided to confiscate lands owned by merchants.

How do we reconcile the two arguments? To understand the impact of the backward flow of capital generated by commercialization on land distribution, let us first consider a hypothetical agricultural sector that is completely isolated from other sectors. In such a sector the only group of people able to buy lands are the existing landowners, especially landlords, who own more land than they need for subsistence and can consequently accumulate surpluses. The sellers of land, on the other hand, are those small owners who fail to earn enough income from their lands. Thus, the sector will gradually be polarized when the small owners are forced to sell their lands tract by tract while the large owners expand their holdings with their surpluses year after year.

If commercial capital is injected into this previously isolated land market, the situation will be altered for a number of reasons. First, the presence of outside funds inevitably boosts demand in the land market, which in turn raises the bargaining power of land sellers as well as the price of land. Second, the intrusion of merchant capitalists into the land market tends to break the hegemony of existing landlords. There are now more buyers in the land market and very likely there will eventually be more landholders as well. Third, an alternative and better avenue is now open to poor landless farmers, who can first engage in other businesses promising higher rates of returns and then return to the countryside to buy land, if their ultimate preference is to remain a farmer. The plausible conclusion seems that commercialization and the inflow of commercial capital into the rural land market in traditional China tended to disperse what would otherwise have been highly concentrated ownership of land.

After Emperor Wu of the Western Han ordered an outright confiscation of all lands owned by merchants, no such drastic measures were enforced in subsequent dynasties, although social discrimination against merchants continued to exist. Although commercialization undoubtedly accelerated after the fourteenth century, there were no clear signs that Chinese merchants had shaken off their tendencies toward agricultural fundamentalism nor their ultimate preferences for becoming gentrified families with landed property. It may not be sheer coincidence, therefore, that the Ming and Ch'ing periods saw a continual process of land ownership dispersion in place of polarization. Instead of accumulating in the hands of a decreasing number of big landlords, farmland in the country was owned by an increasing proportion of small- and medium-sized holders.

107

Population growth was undeniably another factor that crucially affected the state of land distribution, though the relationship between the two phenomena appears to be even more complicated than that between land distribution and commercialization. First, as with the impact of economic development, the increase in the Chinese population tended to make factor markets freer. Historically, slavery has been a dominant system only in societies with a high scarcity of labor. The urge to enslave people tended to decline as the labor supply became more abundant and the cost of hiring free workers was cheapened by population growth. As will later be shown, the system of using slaves or compulsory labor vanishes naturally in an economy with substantial surplus labor. This in turn makes the land market more active because more people could participate in it, presumably on the demand side.

On the other hand, population growth beyond a certain point tended to have a negative impact on Chinese farmers' incomes—that is, it impoverished small landholders. This effect was demonstrated in Figure 1.2, in which the marginal product curve of agricultural labor shifted to a lower position. In Chinese history, however, this phenomenon was offset, to a large extent, by the adoption of more intensive farming and more subsidiary activities.

Moreover, the increasing size of the rural population relative to land supply, assisted by traditional inclinations toward agricultural fundamentalism, created a sense of scarcity among peasants about their landholdings. They became even more attached to land than ever, as evidenced by the quick spread of practices by which landsellers parceled their lands and sold a small piece at a time, or insisted on retaining the option to buy back the sold land wihtin an agreed time period, or preserved the so-called "surface rights of sold land." Even when it was absolutely necessary for them to sell their lands, they devised various means of avoiding alienating their entire ownership.

All the foregoing factors point in one direction, namely, the creation of the following net effects: The land market became freer and more competitive over time as fewer people could apply noneconomic forces to accumulate huge landholdings. More people entered the land market as demanders. And small landowners developed a stronger attachment to their land and an increasing reluctance to sell it. It became increasingly difficult for just a few wealthy families to dominate the land market and to purchase large amounts of land in a short period of time. All these effects will be illustrated with quantitative data in the following section of this chapter.

The Chinese inheritance system, under which parents bequeath their property equally among their sons, is a final relevant factor in land distribution. Unfortunately, however, most historians misunderstand its true impact. The Chinese inheritance system per se was rather neutral in terms of distribution; only differential reproduction rates might have produced an equalizing or disequalizing effect on land ownership distribution through the inheritance system. This effect may be illustrated by the following simple model.

To begin with, assume that n families own property and the same number of families are landless. The ratio of the two groups of families is thus $n:n$, or $1:1$. To simplify matters, let us further assume that the land is equally distributed among the propertied families. It is perfectly true that for individual households the equal inheritance system has the inevitable effect of breaking up large fortunes as long as the reproduction rate is higher than the replacement rate. Whether the state of land distribution measured in relative terms will change, however, depends on the relative reproduction rates between the propertied families and the landless families. There are three possible outcomes.

1. If the reproduction rate is the same for both groups of families—say, n becomes $2n$ in the second generation—the ratio of propertied families to landless families will then remain unchanged, or $2n:2n$, which is still $1:1$.

2. If the propertied families are generally more reproductive, yielding $3n$ as the number of propertied families and $2n$ as the landless families in the second generation, the ratio becomes $3:2$. Land distribution in relative terms tends to be increasingly equalized with every generation.

3. If the propertied families are generally less reproductive, yielding a ratio of $2:3$ for the two groups in the second generation, the relative distribution of land becomes more concentrated.

In contrast, under the primogeniture system adopted in feudal Japan and some European countries, the number of propertied households remained constant, whereas the number of landless families grew, as the total population expanded. In these societies a built-in factor tended to undermine equitable land distribution. In Chinese history, the reproduction rate of landless families is believed to have been lower than that of the propertied families for biological and economic reasons, and thus natural forces probably worked to equalize land distribution.[7]

Warfare is another relevant factor, but its impact on land distribution is not a matter for generalization. The so-called peasant rebellions throughout Chinese history certainly functioned to redistribute land. As for the invasions of foreign troops and power struggles between ruling cliques, their distributional effects are uncertain. During the third and fourth centuries, frequent wars drove peasants to powerful clans and local magnates for protection. Those clans who organized military forces and built fortifications for self defense usually assumed ownership of all lands within their spheres of protection; the result, of course, was further concentration of farmland. Interestingly, after the T'ang dynasty very few clans were powerful enough to organize similar self-defense units against invaders, whether from within or without. To some degree, redistribution of land would also take place immediately after each large-scale war, in which some landlords were killed or the documents of titles were destroyed.

It must be emphasized that distribution of land ownership and tenancy ratio, though they are related, are two different matters, in concept as well as in practice. Whether a person should buy land and how he should manage the land he has bought are two distinctly separate decisions influenced by two different sets of factors. Now that we have examined the important factors affecting land distribution in traditional China, we must turn to the actual management of this land. Whether an owner operated the farm by himself or leased it out to tenants or did both would depend on: (1) climatic conditions, terrain, type of crop, distance from houses, and many other factors that would determine the degree of risk and supervision costs, and (2) relative earning rates of alternate ways of managing the farm—that is, rental income as compared with net earnings from self-operation. As the next section will show, many landlords reserved some of their lands for self-operation and leased out the rest, but these proportions may have varied over time.

Our earlier discussion suggests that population pressure probably had a net effect of dispersing land ownership. Yet population pressure would also probably raise the tenancy ratio by altering relative rates of return in favor of leasing out land. Moreover, land ownership was sometimes so widely dispersed that a large number of owners possessing only a small quantity of land insufficient for subsistence were obliged to rent additional lands from others. Ratios of population density to tenancy may consequently be expected to show a positive correlation interregionally and over time. All these effects will be expounded in detail and tested against empirical data in Chapters 7 and 8.

Changes in Land Distribution

Confucian scholars during the Han were highly critical of what they regarded as the concentration of land ownership during that period, yet there are no concrete data enabling us to determine the degree of uneven distribution. Possibly these scholars exaggerated the situation to provide a theoretical foundation for reinstating the system of public ownership of land that had been highly praised by their teachers. Quantitative data are also lacking for the Wei and Chin, but circumstantial evidence suggests a deteriorating condition of unequal land distribution. Unlike during the Han, when there was still a high degree of social mobility, the social status of distinguished families during the Western and Eastern Chin became more or less fixed and their political privileges became hereditary. The chances for a commoner to climb to the top of the social ladder were limited. On the other hand, the availability of vast and as yet unused areas of arable land guaranteed the survival of a substantial proportion of small landholders who were themselves cultivators. This situation probably continued through the Southern Dynasties.

In the north, nationalization of land under the equitable field system during the period between 485 and the seventh century effectively removed the uneven distribution of private ownership. Nevertheless, as the equitable field system gradually collapsed after the ninth century, virtually all public lands fell into the hands of large wealthy families because only they were powerful enough to convert public lands into private estates in defiance of legislation. All indicators suggest that the status of land distribution reached a low point in the latter part of the eighth and ninth centuries. During that period the large estates, known as *chuang yuan*, were characterized by two features: they were usually very large in size, and each was an enclosed entity not intersected by other landowners' fields.

A long process soon began that witnessed the gradual disintegration of the large estates. The average size of landholdings decreased, and fields became scattered and interspersed. To some extent, these changes can be verified by quantitative data. Moreover, this dispersion process, which continued until the early twentieth century, I believe to be attributable to population growth and to the rising degree of commercialization in China.

We may begin our quantitative analysis of land distribution with the Northern Sung. As noted in Chapter 2, the Sung governments not only employed a dichotomous registration system dividing the population into resident households (*chu hu*) and nonresident households (*k'e hu*), but also published the returns periodically.

To understand the data, an explanation of the term *k'e hu* is in order. During the Han, *k'e* referred to those who were employed by others for various purposes regardless of whether they were from local communities or elsewhere and regardless of whether they themselves owned property or were landless. The meaning of the term changed during the T'ang, however, to indicate those who had moved from other places and had no local residence registration regardless of their current occupations. Since under the T'ang dynasty's equitable field law a household could receive a land allotment only when it had properly registered with the local government, most of these migrant households had no land allotments. This feature was later taken by the Sung government to define the *k'e hu*, namely, those who had no material goods, especially land. *K'e hu* households during the Sung had properly registered with the local government and might have resided in that locality for many generations, but they were still called *k'e hu* as long as they owned no land there. On the other hand, a *k'e hu* would be reclassified as a *chu hu* as soon as the household purchased a piece of land, however small.

The proportion of *k'e hu*, or nonresident households, in total households in the Sung times consequently represents the percentage of the landless population. It is a less perfect indicator of farmland distribution, however, because both categories, *k'e hu* and *chu hu*, included those living in the urban areas. The proportion of *k'e hu* should never be taken as a percentage of tenancy, however, for the landless *k'e hu* actually fell into several categories, such as tenants, hired farm laborers, and the so-called *she-t'ien-fu*,[8] laborers who were hired every few years for slash-and-burn cultivation of mountain fields.

Based on official records, the proportion of nonresident households was above 40 percent in the early years of the Northern Sung, and even

112

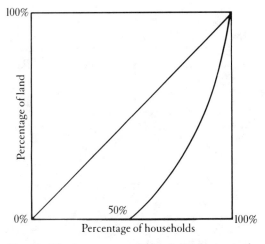

Fig. 6.1. The Lorenz curve for land distribution in the early Sung.

this figure may be a serious understatement. On one hand, the number of resident households registered in each year was an exaggeration, because wealthy people, as noted earlier, tended to split their natural families to avoid the obligation of public service. On the other hand, the nonresident households were likely to have been undercounted because of their high mobility, especially in the case of the *she-t'ien-fu* in the less developed, mountainous regions, where the land was utilized once in every few years and the landless workers, who would be disbanded after the harvest, had to move to other places the next year.

Both factors tended to create a downward bias in the proportion of nonresident households. Chao P'u, the famous minister, serving the first emperor of the Northern Sung, estimated the proportion of nonresident households in his time to be two-thirds.[9] While this estimate sounds too high, a figure of 50 percent was very likely. In other words, at least half of the households existing at the end of the tenth century did not possess land. This condition may be represented by the Lorenz curve in Figure 6.1, with the assumption that the land was not equally distributed even among resident households; it implies a Gini coefficient of about 0.75. This was the worst degree of unequal private distribution in Chinese history that we can quantify with some degree of certainty. On the other hand, the Gini coefficient here is probably far below that of the manorial systems in medieval Europe. To describe the type of land ownership

113

TABLE 6.1

*Ratio of Nonresident Households to Total Households
in the Northern Sung, 976-1099*

Year	Percent	Year	Percent	Year	Percent
976–87	41.2%	1048	35.7%	1078	32.7%
1023	38.0	1050	35.6	1080	32.7
1029	43.1	1053	35.7	1083	33.8
1031	36.2	1058	35.8	1086	33.7
1034	41.0	1061	34.9	1088	33.6
1037	41.6	1067	30.8	1091	33.3
1039	36.4	1072	30.4	1097	32.7
1042	35.3	1075	31.8	1099	32.6
1045	35.7				

SOURCE: Chen I-ping, p. 31.

prevalent in Sung China as manorialism thus contradicts the fact that about 50 percent of the population owned land.

Land distribution improved slowly but steadily throughout the Sung. Even official records (Table 6.1) showed a drop in the proportion of non-resident households from more than 40 percent to about one-third over a century's time. There is no evidence that the improvement was merely statistical because of any change in the household registration system.

As is well known, wide differences existed in the tempo of economic development among various parts of China. In some respects, regional differences at a given point in time may reflect the general path of development over time. Based on official returns of household registrations in 1080 for eighteen provinces plus the capital district, we can easily compute the regional proportions of nonresident households. Table 6.2 arranges these percentages in descending order. Anyone familiar with the economy and political geography of the Northern Sung can immediately recognize that this table roughly represents the varying degree of regional population density and commercialization in reverse order. Specifically, the areas of present-day Hupei, Hunan, and Kweichow were the least developed, with the lowest population densities, during the Sung; the proportion of nonresident households in those regions was accordingly the highest. In sharp contrast, the most commercialized areas, such as the Yangtze valley, the coastal area of Kwangtung, and the capital district, showed the lowest proportion of landless families.

Theoretically, if the factor markets were perfectly free, there would be little tenantry in a newly developed region where virgin land was still available and could be reclaimed by the landless. In reality, however,

114

TABLE 6.2

Ratio of Nonresident Households to Total Households in Various Provinces of the Northern Sung, 1080

Province	Percent	Province	Percent
K'uei-chou	70.3%	Chiang-nan-hsi	35.1%
Chin-hu-pei	57.4	Shan-fu-hsi	28.3
Tzu-chou	48.0	Ch'eng-tu-fu	28.2
Ching-hsi	47.6	Ho-pei	27.6
Chin-hu-nan	45.4	Kuang-nan-hsi	24.4
Fu-chien	44.4	K'ai-feng prefecture	21.9
Li-chou	43.7	Liang-che	20.2
Kuang-nan-tung	38.5	Ho-tung	19.2
Huai-nan	38.5	Chiang-nan-tung	17.8
Ching-tung	37.7		

SOURCE: *Yuan-feng chiu-yü chih*, various sections.

the scarcity of labor in such regions led powerful landowners to detain people by force as workers on their fields. Those workers were deprived of their right to acquire their own farms. This practice was documented by, for example, the following official source:

> In Pa-hsien, south Szechwan, the three clans of civilized aborigines, headed by Li Kuang-chi, Wang Yen, and Liang Ch'eng-hsiu, respectively, held several thousand households of farm laborers. From time to time the three clans coerced Han households into such services and killed those who resisted and took over their lands. Those Han people were compelled to be *k'e hu*, or what was called *na-shen* [offering their bodies].[10]

This is confirmed by several other sources and may be taken to account for the high proportion of *k'e hu* in these regions, but the distorting forces in both labor market and land market diminished in relatively developed provinces. As Chapter 8 will show, both the increased commercialization and the special efforts of the Sung government improved the factor markets over time.

The proportion of nonresident households in various regions as shown in Table 6.2 displays a pattern almost opposite to the interregional pattern of tenancy ratios found in later periods. This effect is consistent with our contention that land ownership distribution and tenancy distribution were governed by two different sets of factors. The Sung data also suggest that the effect of commercialization on land distribution was much more significant in earlier periods, when the imperfection of the factor markets was more pronounced.

More quantitative data are available from the Ming-Ch'ing period. Re-

TABLE 6.3

Land Distribution in Two Villages in Sui-an, 1862 and 1909

Size of landholding (*mou*)	Village I, 1862			Village II, 1909		
	Number of households	Percent of households	Percent of farmland	Number of households	Percent of households	Percent of farmland
0	50	13.3%	0%	445	34.6%	0%
0.01-0.99	89	23.7	3.3	147	11.5	14.5
1.00-2.99	122	32.5	17.8	304	23.6	12.0
3.00-4.99	36	9.6	10.6	151	11.7	11.9
5.00-6.99	24	6.5	10.6	75	5.8	8.9
7.00-9.99	24	6.5	14.9	60	4.7	10.1
10.00-14.99	8	2.2	7.3	48	3.7	11.8
15.00-19.99	13	3.4	16.4	23	1.8	7.9
20.00-24.99	3	0.8	4.9	12	0.9	5.3
25.00-29.99	2	0.5	4.0	5	0.4	2.7
30.00-39.99	4	1.0	10.2	7	0.5	4.8
40.00-49.99	0	0	0	5	0.4	4.4
50.00-69.99	0	0	0	2	0.2	2.4
70.00-99.99	0	0	0	2	0.2	3.3
100.00 or more	0	0	0	0	0	0
TOTAL	375	100.0%	100.0%	1,286	100.0%	100.0%

SOURCE: Reprinted from Chao and Chen 1982.

cently I gained access to a large amount of empirical material never before used by scholars that can throw light on important land issues during the period.[11] Four land registers (exact locations unknown) from this period state, for each plot of farmland registered, whether a plot was cultivated by the owner himself or leased out to a tenant, among other details. Based on these registers, I have calculated the proportion of owner-cultivated land in the four registers: 34.4 percent (1581, location unknown); 53.4 percent (sometime between 1645 and 1655, location unknown); 24.7 percent (1676, location unknown); and 37.5 percent (year and location unknown). Obviously, tenant farming was common in the sixteenth century.

The prevalence of tenantry, however, does not necessarily mean a high degree of land ownership concentration. The records of numerous local archives offer evidence not of major landlords, but of many small land-owners, each possessing a moderate amount of land beyond what he could operate by himself. This is especially clear in the household registers recording the size of land holdings for each household in the locality.

Table 6.3 gives the records of farmland distribution in two villages in Sui-an, Chekiang as of 1862 and 1909. The Gini coefficients computed for the two samples—0.63 and 0.71, respectively—are not substantially lower than those estimated for the Northern Sung. As a measure of distribution purely in relative terms, however, the Gini coefficients fail to indicate some of the drastic changes that had taken place between the two periods. Specifically, the number of large landholders as well as the differential between the largest and the smallest landholdings decreased sharply. From a practical viewpoint, the most crucial issue in examining land distribution in a country should be how large the major landowners are. It is a sign of improvement if the size of the largest amount of property owned by one landowner has been significantly reduced. When the largest property size becomes less than, say, 10 acres, no matter how much curvature the Lorenz curve shows, distribution ceases to be an important social concern.

In the 1862 sample, 13.4 percent of the households had no land; 56.7 percent had less than 3 *mou* and presumably had to rent some land in order to earn a subsistence income. About 25 percent of the families, who owned 3 to 15 *mou*, may be considered self-sufficient. Only 5.7 percent, with properties ranging from 15 to 40 *mou*, had surplus land for leasing; none had an estate exceeding 40 *mou*. Strictly speaking, none of the families in the territory qualified as a landlord. The 1909 records, though representing a larger sample, reveal a similar distribution pattern. About two-thirds of the households either owned no land or held less than 3 *mou*, a size too small for self-sufficiency. Only 56 families, or 4.4 percent of the total, owned more than 15 *mou* and were able to lease out their surplus land. No property reached the size of 100 *mou*.

Four sets of land tax collection records for four small villages in three counties[12] list the amount of land held by all owners in their jurisdiction: one in Ch'ang-chou, 1676; one in Hsiu-ning, 1711; another in Hsiu-ning, 1716; and one in Ch'i-men, 1850's. The land distribution data revealed by these records (Table 6.4) are incomplete because they do not indicate how many families were landless. Nevertheless, it is clear from the table that more than 90 percent of the landowners owned less than 30 *mou*.

Surviving land statistics from a few subdivisions in Chu-lu Hopei, as shown in Table 6.5, suggest that the state of land distribution in north China was no different. The computed Gini coefficients are 0.622, 0.604, and 0.672, respectively, and the proportion of landless households are 18.2 percent, 19.5 percent, and 25.5 percent, respectively.

Other local archives more or less confirm the same point. A household register of a village in Hsiu-ning (date unknown) gives the largest land holding in the jurisdiction as 31.3 *mou*. A tax collection book of a village

TABLE 6.4
Land Distribution in Four Villages, 1676-1850's

Size of landholding (*mou*)	Ch'ang-chou, 1676			Hsiu-ning, 1711		
	Number of households	Percent of households	Percent of farmland	Number of households	Percent of households	Percent of farmland
0.1-4.9	243	69.6%	20.1%	22	21.4%	5.1%
5.0-9.9	45	12.9	11.2	33	32.0	23.1
10.0-19.9	25	7.2	12.4	43	41.7	60.1
20.0-29.9	15	4.3	12.4	5	4.9	11.7
30.0-39.9	5	1.4	5.8	0	0	0
40.0-49.9	5	1.4	7.5	0	0	0
50.0-74.9	4	1.2	8.3	0	0	0
75.0-99.9	6	1.7	17.4	0	0	0
100.00 or more	1	0.3	4.9	0	0	0
TOTAL	349	100.0%	100.0%	103	100.0%	100.0%

Size of landholding (*mou*)	Hsui-ning, 1716			Ch'i-men, 1850's		
	Number of households	Percent of households	Percent of farmland	Number of households	Percent of households	Percent of farmland
0.1-4.9	30	26.3%	7.1%	46	65.7%	23.1%
5.0-9.9	43	37.7	30.7	14	20.0	21.1
10.0-19.9	37	32.5	52.7	4	5.7	12.1
20.9-29.9	4	3.5	9.5	2	2.9	10.0
30.0-39.9	0	0	0	3	4.3	21.1
40.0-49.9	0	0	0	0	0	0
50.0-74.9	0	0	0	1	1.4	12.6
75.0-99.9	0	0	0	0	0	0
100.00 or more	0	0	0	0	0	0
TOTAL	114	100.0%	100.0%	70	100.0%	100.0%

SOURCE: Reprinted from Chao and Chen 1982.

in Chi-hsi showed the largest landlord among the 520 households registered as of 1865 as having only 21.3 *mou*. The biggest landlord in all the local archives I have examined had an estate of 400 *mou* in 1675; the second largest owned 293.6 *mou* in 1647. In his study of the bursaries in the Kiangnan area during the late Ch'ing, Yuji Muramatsu discovered a similar situation.[13] According to the accounts of the Wu Yu-ching bursary in 1893, among the 34 landlords who entrusted it to collect rents, eight families had more than 200 *mou* each; five families had landholdings between 100 and 200 *mou*; and 21 families, or about two-thirds of the total, had less than 100 *mou* to lease.

Farmland in this region was divided into small plots. Each landowner was required by law to register his plots with the local government for tax assessment and ownership identification. In the land register, a regis-

TABLE 6.5

Land Distribution in Subdivisions of Chu-lu, Hopei, 1706-1736

Size of land holding (*mou*)	25 chia, 1706		4 chia, 1706		4 chia, 1736	
	Percent of households (N = 6,581)	Percent of farmland (N = 98,125 mou)	Percent of households (N = 1,071)	Percent of farmland (N = 15,053 mou)	Percent of households (N = 1,094)	Percent of farmland (N = 15,658 mou)
Landless	18.2%	0%	19.5%	0%	25.5%	0%
0-1	3.6	0.1	3.7	0.1	5.0	0.2
1-10	34.3	12.2	32.5	12.3	30.3	11.1
10-20	22.7	21.9	29.1	22.9	18.4	18.4
20-30	11.0	17.7	9.9	16.7	8.3	14.3
30-40	4.5	10.4	4.5	11.1	4.4	10.3
40-50	1.8	5.3	2.1	6.5	2.2	6.8
50-60	1.2	4.3	1.8	7.0	2.0	7.5
60-70	0.6	2.6	1.3	6.0	1.2	5.3
70-80	0.4	2.1	0.3	1.5	0.6	3.4
80-90	0.2	0.8	0.2	1.1	0.1	0.6
90-100	0.2	1.5	0.1	0.7	0.2	1.2
100-150	0.5	3.7	0.5	4.0	0.5	5.3
150-200	0.3	3.5	0.4	4.9	0.7	7.6
Over 200	0.5	14.0	0.3	5.4	0.5	8.0

SOURCE: Chiang Tai-shin, pp. 177-79.

tration serial number was assigned to each plot and a survey map was drawn to show its details. The average plot size, as computed from the fish-scale registers, was:

Wu-yuan (Ming): 1.42 *mou*.
Ch'ang-hua (Ming): 1.16 *mou*, paddy land; 0.63 *mou*, dry land.
Yi-hsien (Ming): 1.48 *mou*, paddy land; 0.51 *mou*, dry land.
Sui-an (Ming): 0.62 *mou*, paddy land; 0.69 *mou*, dry land.
Hsi-hsien (Ming): 0.68 *mou*. Another locality in Hsi-hsien, Ming dynasty: 0.89 *mou*.
Hsiu-ning (1573-1619): high-grade paddy land, 1.08 *mou*; medium-grade paddy land, 0.87 *mou*; low-grade paddy land, 0.65 *mou*; high-grade dry land, 0.81 *mou*; medium-grade dry land, 0.64 *mou*; low-grade dry land, 0.54 *mou*.
Unidentified locality (1581): 0.8 *mou*, paddy land; 0.4 *mou*, dry land. Unidentified locality, Ming dynasty: 1.2 *mou*, paddy land; 1.9 *mou*, dry land. Unidentified locality, 1654: 1.06 *mou*, paddy land; 0.57 *mou*, dry land.
Hsi-hsien (ca. 1654): 0.88 *mou*, paddy land; 0.14 *mou*, dry land.
Hsiu-ning (1654): first-grade paddy land, 1.07 *mou*; second-grade paddy land, 0.87 *mou*; third-grade paddy land, 0.77 *mou*; fourth-grade paddy land, 0.90 *mou*; first-grade dry land, 0.81 *mou*; second-grade dry land,

TABLE 6.6
Number of Plots Leased by Landlord Households

Number of plots leased	Number of landlord households	Number of plots leased	Number of landlord households
1-20	19	101-200	8
21-40	18	201-300	2
41-60	11	301-400	2
61-80	6	401-500	1
81-100	6	501-1000	3

SOURCE: Documents held in Nanking University.

0.92 *mou*; third-grade dry land, 0.89 *mou*; fourth-grade dry land, 0.69 *mou*.

Ch'i-men (1662-1722): paddy land, 1.58 *mou*; plain dry land, 0.74 *mou*; high dry land, 0.45 *mou*.

Because the plots were usually small, even a small landholder could own a number of plots.

It may be argued that official records of land and household registrations in the Ming and Ch'ing times are biased downward because the data were collected by local governments for taxation purposes, and there was thus a strong incentive for people to underreport their landholdings. Let us therefore turn to private rent collection records kept by some families in the period, which are more likely to be free of such distortion. These private ledgers contain records of the rents collected from each plot of leased land but do not indicate the size of the plot. Consequently, it was possible to compute only the number of plots leased by each landlord. Keeping in mind the small average size of plots, we can visualize the land distribution pattern in the region.

Most major landlords who leased more than 100 *mou* were not private households. They were either bursaries collecting rents on behalf of small landowners or communal charity organizations operating relatively large estates. As for genuine landlord households, most had less than 60 plots of land for leasing (Table 6.6); they cultivated most of their land themselves but rented the land beyond their tilling capacity.

Equally revealing are the land purchase records of landowning households. As a common practice, Chinese families transcribed original land deeds or purchase agreements of other fixed assets into a single volume, often keeping such records for several hundred years. I computed the

TABLE 6.7
TABLE 6.7
Total Land Accumulations of Various Families, 1568-1914

Name	Year	Amount of land accumulated (*mou*)	Name	Year	Amount of land accumulated (*mou*)
Hu	1568	152.8	Chin	1727	92.0
Wang	1583	167.2	Chu	1742	14.4
Hsieh	1616	71.3	Pan	1745	28.8
Wang	1643	33.3	Wang	1752	140.7
Wang	1645	80.5	Wang	1772	99.0
Hsu	1654	169.8	Huang	1776	191.5
Hsiang	1655	86.3	Yeh	1794	39.6
Wu	1656	41.8	Wu	1819	33.5
Wu	1662	221.6	Hu	1824	115.0
Sun	1675	22.5	Hung	1839	313.4
Chen	1678	33.5	Wang	1844	32.0
Fang	1692	645.7	Wang	1849	37.6
Huang	1705	68.0	Hu	1867	32.8
Yu	1725	40.9	Wang	1912	34.6
Wu	1726	37.9	Wang	1914	46.2

SOURCE: Documents held in Nanking University.

total landholdings of various families to discover how fast, on the average, holdings were accumulated.

Table 6.7 presents the data on land accumulated by thirty families up to the dates indicated. The largest landowners had 645 *mou*. Six families, or about 20 percent of the total, purchased between 100 and 200 *mou*; another six families fell in the range of 50 to 100 *mou*. Half the sample—fifteen families—acquired less than 50 *mou*.

Most important for our purposes is the dynamic dimension of the data: how fast, on the average, land was acquired. Table 6.8 includes families whose records have been used to compile Table 6.7 as well as families whose land purchase records sometimes failed to tell the sizes of the plots they bought. For the latter group I computed the average number of plots purchased per year.

Of the 39 families, 21 were able to buy less than 1 *mou* or one plot each year on the average; another twelve families had managed to acquire 1 to 3 *mou* or plots each year. The Hung family (1826-39), an exception, acquired 22 *mou* per year. The records of the Hung family cover only fourteen years; it is unlikely that they could have continued at that pace indefinitely. Usually, land transactions were concentrated in the first years after a family shifted the capital they had accumulated in commerce or government services to the rural sector; thereafter the tempo gradually

TABLE 6.8

Average Size of Land Acquisition per Year for Various Families, 1332-1912

Name	Period	Average size per year	Name	Period	Average size per year
Cheng	1332-1593	0.31 plots	Wang	1640-1914	0.17 *mou*
Hsieh	1339-1616	0.25 *mou*	Wu	1641-1656	2.78 *mou*
Li	1374-1661	0.55 plots	Chen	1649-1678	1.10 *mou*
Wu	1403-1758	0.32 plots	Chang	1652-1744	2.25 plots
Hu	1437-1568	1.15 *mou*	Sun	1653-1675	1.00 *mou*
Pan	1473-1745	0.10 *mou*	Yu	1657-1725	0.58 *mou*
Wang	1480-1607	0.34 plots	Wang	1690-1844	0.21 *mou*
Wang	1491-1643	0.22 *mou*	Wang	1690-1848	0.24 *mou*
Cheng	1491-1681	0.45 plots	Yeh	1964-1794	0.39 *mou*
Wang	1537-1583	3.60 *mou*	Wu	1706-1726	1.90 *mou*
Wang	1562-1583	5.00 plots	Wang	1717-1752	3.90 *mou*
Wang	1572-1645	1.09 *mou*	Wu	1736-1819	0.35 *mou*
Hsu	1590-1654	2.65 *mou*	Huang	1741-1776	5.30 *mou*
Hsiang	1608-1655	1.80 *mou*	Cheng	1742-1902	0.24 plots
Huang	1612-1705	0.47 plots	Hu	1755-1824	1.64 *mou*
Huang	1622-1647	0.65 plots	Wang	1760-1772	1.21 *mou*
Chu	1623-1742	0.12 *mou*	Hung	1826-1839	22.38 *mou*
Hsieh	1627-1655	2.90 plots	Hu	1829-1867	0.84 *mou*
Wu	1633-1662	7.40 *mou*	Wang	1886-1912	1.30 *mou*
Chin	1636-1727	1.00 *mou*			

SOURCE: Documents held in Nanking University.

slowed. The longer the period covered by the land purchase records, the lower was the average rate of acquisition.

The three types of empirical data from independent sources (official land and household registers, private rent collection records, and private land purchase records) consistently point to the same phenomenon—the dispersion of land ownership among small landholders. It may well be true that there were not too many major landlords throughout the Ming-Ch'ing period except for the large amounts of manor land given to members of the royal families by the Ming emperors. These few ultrawealthy families left disproportionately large historical footprints, which later scholars cited repeatedly as evidence for an extremely high degree of land concentration.

As far as the new data can suggest, increased population pressure seems to be a more crucial factor in the Ming and Ch'ing than in the Sung, when commercialization played the most important role in improving land distribution. The man-farmland ratio was so high in the region that each rural household could operate only on a tiny piece of land. Taking the larger sample in Table 6.3 as illustration, if we identify household families owning 10 or more *mou* of land as landlords, there were 104 such households with a total amount of 2,121 *mou*, or 20.4 *mou* each. Let us further assume that, when absentee landlords and cultivator landlords are taken together, each landlord retained an average of about 5 *mou* for self-cultivation; then there would be 1,600 *mou* of land available for leasing. If 400 of the 445 landless families were tenants, each one could rent roughly 4 *mou*. If the 147 families who owned less than 1 *mou* each, however, were actually partial tenants demanding some leased land, the total of 1,600 *mou* for leasing would have to be distributed among 547 households (pure tenants plus partial tenants), or about 2.9 *mou* per family.

Given such an unfavorable man-land ratio, the rate of return in agriculture must have been exceedingly low. The low rate of return means that it must have taken a long time for a family to expand its landholdings through agricultural accumulation.

Table 6.8 shows the slow rate of land acquisition. We may easily imagine how long it would have taken to accumulate a large estate—consisting of, say, 10,000 *mou*—at an average rate of a few *mou* per year. In this connection two interesting cases found among the private land purchase records are pertinent. One is the Wang family (1640-1914), which maintained the longest records of land acquisition—about 280 years. Starting as tenant farmers in the Ming dynasty, this family bought the right of "permanent tenancy" in 1640 on a small piece of land, which was equivalent to joint ownership. They were able to buy their first piece of land with full ownership only 68 years later (1707). The second is the Sun family (not included in the table), who converted their status from that of ordinary tenants into partial owners in 1733 by acquiring the right of "permanent tenancy" on a plot; 46 years later (1779), they purchased a plot with full ownership.

Another important factor that may be held responsible for the slow accumulation of wealth in the rural sector was the traditional tendency among many Chinese families to spend extravagantly on cemetery sites. The Wang family (1690-1848) spent 632 taels of silver in 159 years to buy 37 *mou* of farmland. But during the same time they expended 435 taels of silver on cemetery sites and graveyards. In fact, numerous land transaction records I saw indicate that the prices of cemetery plots were generally much higher than those of high-grade farmland.

123

The study by Ching and Lo seems to imply a higher rate of land accumulation in Shantung than elsewhere in China: The Pi family in Tzuch'uan bought 900 *mou* of land in 190 years (1720-1910), or 4.7 *mou* per year; the Meng family in Chang-ch'iu bought 1,050 *mou* in 200 years (1710-1910), or 5.2 *mou* per year; another Meng family in Chang-ch'iu bought 845 *mou* in 195 years (1718-1912), or 4.3 *mou* per year; the Li family in Chang-ch'iu bought 515 *mou* in 145 years (1761-1905), or 3.4 *mou* per year.[14] The average annual acquisition was larger probably because of the much lower man-land ratio in Shantung.

Occasionally, we find exceptional cases in which people could acquire land at a quicker pace under special circumstances. For instance, the surviving ledgers of a landlord family named Liu Li-ho-t'ang in Luanhsien, Hopei show that a total of 4,983 *mou* were purchased between 1880 and 1922, averaging 118 *mou* purchased per year.[15] Altogether, 422 transactions were involved, averaging 12 *mou* per transaction. A close examination of the data, however, reveals that virtually all the lands were purchased by this family from bankrupt "banner" families (Manchus) immediately after the Ch'ing government removed the ban on sales of so-called "banner fields" by the Manchus to any Han Chinese. In fact, the ban was lifted and reimposed between 1859 and 1907; the variation of acquisition rate coincided perfectly with changes in the law.

Another exceptional case is the land purchase records of Feng Kuei-fen cited in Muramatsu's study.[16] Feng bought large quantities of land, as shown (in *mou*), in Su-chou after the area was retaken by the government troops from the T'aip'ing rebels:

1866	48.21	1869	397.06
1867	428.20	1870	320.92
1868	393.98		

Transactions of such large quantities were possible in the immediate postwar years after numerous original owners had fled or had been killed in the war. Feng bought no land after 1870.

Quantitative data are relatively abundant for the Republic. Especially valuable are two comprehensive national surveys from the 1930's conducted respectively by the Land Commission of the Chinese government and John Buck of Nanking University, though the latter study was not much concerned with land distribution. In addition, numerous reports of small-scale rural surveys survive, including those done by the Research Department of the South Manchuria Railway Company.

In its summary report, the Land Commission presented land distribution data collected from a sample of 1,295,001 landowning households in 163 counties;[17] we learn further that an additional 303,166 households in the sample owned no land. A combination of the two sets of data yields a Gini coefficient of 0.66. Again, this indicator has concealed some important changes in land distribution. The proportion of landless households declined remarkably, from around 50 percent in the Sung to 18.9 percent in the Republic. The latter figure was generally confirmed by the findings of Buck's study, which revealed 17 percent landless households among 16,786 farm households taken from 154 counties.[18]

Perhaps more reliable and revealing than the national studies are the small-scale field surveys, because in most cases these data were personally collected by field investigators. The relevant data from a selection of such reports, along with the computed Gini coefficients, are presented in Table 6.9. Out of 47 samples, the Gini coefficients are more than 0.7 in five; between 0.6 and 0.7 in eleven; between 0.5 and 0.6 in thirteen; and below 0.5 in eighteen. Except for the six cases in which information is not given, 28 samples show a proportion of landless households below 20 percent; thirteen cases fall between 20 percent and 37 percent.

In examining some land distribution data compiled by earlier scholars for Hopei during 1880-1937, Ramon Myers concludes that land distribution in that province either remained relatively constant or became more equal, but most certainly did not become more unequal.[19] Based on the statistics gathered by Sidney Gamble for a village in the province between 1910 and 1931, Myers is able to construct a Lorenz curve clearly showing the improved distribution over time.

A more important question is whether there were major landlords possessing, say, more than 1,000 *mou* each. The largest landholding discovered by the sample in Table 6.9 had only 942 *mou*. This finding is confirmed, in a general way, by two other surveys conducted by the Research Department of the South Manchuria Railway Company. In one survey covering 453 villages in north China, the investigators attempted to identify the size of the largest estate in each village. Only two families in the 453 villages were found to have owned more than 1,000 *mou* of land. A detailed breakdown is presented in Table 6.10. The other survey of the same organization identified the largest property in each county in Hopei Province. It is clear from Table 6.11 that the leading landlords in many counties owned less than 1,000 *mou* of land. The biggest landowners of all owned 7,500 *mou*.

TABLE 6.9
Land Distribution Revealed by Local Surveys, 1930-1942

Code number and area	Date	Number of households surveyed	Gini coefficient	Percent of landless households	Largest landholding (*mou*)
1 Chia-ting, Shanghai	1941	50	.59	24%	34
2 Nan-tung, Kiangsu	1941	94	.52	18	49
3 Sung-chiang, Kiangsu	1941	65	.40	3	21
4 Ch'ang-shu, Kiangsu	1941	56	.40	32	8
5 Wu-hsi, Kiangsu	1941	80	.32	21	8
6 Su-chou, Kiangsu	1932	105,717	.79	26	—
7 Wu-hsi, Kiangsu	1932	119,120	.54	3	—
8 Ch'ang-shu, Kiangsu	1934	214	.42	0	—
9 Hsien-ning, Hupei	1937	678	.58	11	300
10 Chiang-pei, Szechwan	1938	150	.36	—	550
11 T'ai-an, Shantung	1939	80	.46	5	23
12 Hui-min, Shantung	1931	82	.48	0	53
13 Lin-ching, Shantung	1942	89	.41	1	86
14 Chi-hsing, Hopei	1936	128	.67	34	120
15 20 villages, Hopei	1936	2,174	.69	31	942
16 4 counties, Hopei	1937	479	.69	24	320
17 Kuang-chung, Hopei	1936	92	.30	0	—
18 Chao-ch'ang, Hopei	1936	—	.69	0	—
19 Nan-kung, Hopei	1936	200	.46	7	230
20 An-tsi, Hopei	—	100	.75	—	—
21 1st dist., Ting-hsien, Hopei	1931	—	.49	16	—
22 2d dist., Ting-hsien, Hopei	1931	—	.53	9	—
23 3d dist., Ting-hsien, Hopei	1931	—	.39	5	—
24 4th dist., Ting-hsien, Hopei	1931	—	.52	5	—
25 5th dist., Ting-hsien, Hopei	1931	—	.47	9	—
26 6th dist., Ting county, Hopei	1931	—	.45	7	—
27 7th dist., Ting county, Hopei	1931	—	.86	29	—
28 8th dist., Ting county, Hopei	1931	—	.48	8	—
29 Pao-ting, Hopei	1930	—	.54	5	—
30 Kao-chun, Ting county, Hopei	1934	—	.65	—	—
31 Nan-chun, Ting county, Hopei	1934	—	.58	—	—
32 Ming-chen, Ting county, Hopei	1934	—	.62	—	—
33 Li-chen, Ting county, Hopei	1934	—	.54	—	—
34 Niu-chun, Ting county, Hopei	1934	—	.72	36	—
35 Tsun-hua, Hopei	1933	1,018	.66	16	—
36 T'ang county, Hopei	1933	1,935	.61	16	—
37 Han-tan, Hopei	1933	580	.65	22	—
38 12 villages, Hopei	1936	—	.58	11	—
39 Yang-kao, Shansi	1934	11,125	.61	0	—
40 P'ing-shun, Shansi	1934	17,789	.57	16	—
41 33 villages, Chekiang	1933	1,418	.70	0	—
42 28 villages, Kiangsu	1933	952	.67	0	—
43 14 counties, Anhwei	1935	109,661	.56	37	—
44 Yunnan	1933	642	.49	30	—
45 13 villages, Shensi	1933	765	.34	0	—
46 Kwangsi	1933	983	.40	28	—
47 15 villages, Honan	1933	1,248	.57	3	—

SOURCE: See Chao and Chen 1982, pp. 234-38.

NOTE: "—" means unknown.

TABLE 6.10

Largest Landholdings in 453 North China Villages, 1935

Largest landholding (mou)	Number of villages	Largest landholding (mou)	Number of villages
Below 50	7	350-399	22
50-99	81	400-499	16
100-149	126	500-999	14
150-199	83	1,000-1,500	1
200-249	42	Over 1,500	1
250-299	29	TOTAL	453
300-349	31		

SOURCE: South Manchuria Railway, p. 53.

TABLE 6.11

Largest Landholdings in Various Counties of Hopei, 1935

County	Largest landholding (mou)	County	Largest landholding (mou)
Ta-ch'eng	1,200	Wu-ch'iang	200
Wen-an	1,500	Hsien-hsien	1,600
Hsin-chen	800	Wan-p'ing	2,000
Pa-hsien	1,000	Liang-hsiang	3,500
Hsin-ch'eng	900	Fang-shan	1,300
Hsiung-hsien	5,000	Cho-hsien	1,000
Yung-ch'eng	400	Lai-sui	1,000
An-hsin	7,500	I-hsien	1,300
Jen-ch'iu	200	Ting-hsing	1,000
Ho-chien	1,700	Hsu-sui	500
Shu-ning	400	Ch'ing-wan	200
Rao-yang	300	Man-ch'eng	425
An-p'ing	250	Wan-hsien	300
Shen-hsien	400	Lai-yuan	400

SOURCE: South Manchuria Railway, pp. 42, 63.

Obviously, over a period of a thousand years or so, large landlords in China were virtually extinguished by natural forces, that is, without any explicit land equalization policy on the part of successive governments. The few still remaining were too small in number to constitute an influential social class. Those who were called landlords in the early twentieth century for political reasons were actually owners of small- and medium-sized properties. According to the Land Commission report, the average property size of those persons classified as landlords was 34 *mou*.[20] On the average, each landlord cultivated 7 *mou* by himself and leased out 27 *mou* to tenants. A survey conducted by the Rural Reconstruction Commission in the early 1930's found that the average landlord in Kiangsu province owned a total of 57 *mou*, out of which 11 *mou* were for self-operation and 46 *mou* for leasing.[21] Even William Hinton, who witnessed and praised land reform in a Chinese village in the early 1950's, admitted that the Chinese landlords he saw owned about 3 acres each.[22]

Commercialization and Land Prices

As mentioned earlier in this chapter, there are two prevailing views among historians concerning the effect of commercialization on rural land markets in traditional China. Many argue that the rapid expansion of commercial activities in the Ming-Ch'ing led to further concentration of land because wealthy merchants invested in land with the enormous amounts of capital they had accumulated in trade. Scholars like Mark Elvin hold, on the other hand, that the growth of commerce curtailed enthusiasm for investment in land and diverted some capital from the rural land markets to the urban sector. I postulate here that economic development in general and commercialization in particular tended to equalize land distribution through their dual effect of enhancing rather than reducing the demand for land. The preceding section has demonstrated the dispersion of land ownership. The task that remains is to ascertain whether the demand for land rose or fell in the past few centuries. The fluctuation in demand for land may be tested against the movement of land prices during the period, as variation in market demand would ultimately be reflected in price changes. South Anhui region for which the new land data were discovered, provides a good testing ground because it was well known for its merchants, who did business all over the country during the Ming-Ch'ing period.

From these land purchase records and deeds I have compiled several thousand land prices spanning a period from 1342 to the twentieth century. I took two steps to minimize the effect of quality variation on land prices. First, I excluded prices of hilly land and dry land, which show a wider range of variation, presumably reflecting quality differences. I used only the prices of paddies for computation because paddies are relatively homogeneous in quality; the total number of prices considered was 1,519. Second, I chose a decade as the time unit within which to average paddy prices; I hoped that average prices would minimize the effects of quality variation and other short-run factors during the decade. My selected price data cover 430 years, from 1480 to 1910, or 43 decades. Moreover, prices of paddy land in traditional China were usually expressed in two forms: taels of silver per unit of area (*mou*) and taels of silver per unit of rental income (25 catties of rice). These two price forms permitted me to construct two separate time series of price indexes and check them against each other. All price data and the resulting index numbers are presented in Table 6.12. When plotted on a semi-log paper, the two curves based on the two time series of price indexes almost coincide, an outcome that strengthens confidence in the reliability of the price data.

Both price indexes show a high degree of price stability in 1510-1750 and a rising trend after 1750. Except for the period of the Manchu invasion and the T'aip'ing Rebellion, land prices in the region did not fall, a phenomenon consistent with the hypothesis that little agrarian capital flowed out of the sector.

Theoretically, a rise in price is a result of either increased demand, or reduced supply, or a combination of both. Since farmland acreage in this region did not decrease during the period, the steady rise in land prices must have been generated solely by demand changes. The rising market demand did not merely represent a stronger desire to buy land, it was the realized demand embodied with an increased flow of capital that actually entered the land market. The question, then, is where the additional flow of capital came from.

Perkins believes that the new capital came from other sectors; that is, most of the new landowners attained their initial wealth from some sources other than farming and then came to the countryside to buy land.[23] To support his conclusion, Perkins has cited some surveys done in the 1930's, which showed the initial occupations of large landowners. The fact that the rate of return in agriculture was then still relatively low—2.5 percent according to Buck and 5 percent according to Perkins, as compared to 10 to 20 percent in commerce[24]—suggests that the agricultural fundamentalist mentality of "earning wealth through superficial occupations but preserving it through the fundamental occupation" still prevailed. When Tawney says that the yield of the soil was too low to make it an attractive investment for the capitalist, he must have been referring to the modern Chinese entrepreneurs he observed in the Chinese treaty ports.

There might have been some extra demand for land generated within the agricultural sector. Improved land distribution gave rise to a larger proportion of efficient and enthusiastic peasant-farmers who were also thrifty and eager to acquire land.

Other developments during this period may also be interpreted as

TABLE 6.12
Prices of Paddy Land, 1480–1910

	Price per *mou*			Price per 25 catties rent		
Decades	Number of prices	Average price (taels)	Index	Number of prices	Average price (taels)	Index
1481-1490	n.a.	n.a.	n.a.	1	1.00	95.2
1491-1500	n.a.	n.a.	n.a.	3	1.20	114.2
1501-1510	17	11.83	122.9	n.a.	n.a.	n.a.
1511-1520	30	10.07	104.6	n.a.	n.a.	n.a.
1521-1530	11	10.70	111.2	2	1.12	106.6
1531-1540	7	9.21	95.7	n.a.	n.a.	n.a.
1541-1550	17	9.62	100.0	10	1.05	100.0
1551-1560	37	9.18	95.4	33	1.04	99.0
1561-1570	64	9.28	96.4	50	0.96	91.4
1571-1580	90	9.07	94.2	80	0.98	93.3
1581-1590	11	8.57	89.0	7	0.83	79.0
1591-1600	4	8.38	87.1	n.a.	n.a.	n.a.
1601-1610	12	9.93	103.2	4	1.12	106.6
1611-1620	10	9.02	93.7	6	0.79	75.2
1621-1630	24	8.69	90.3	19	1.01	96.1
1631-1640	11	8.69	90.3	44	0.88	83.8
1641-1650	57	10.00	103.9	87	1.02	97.1
1651-1660	23	8.82	91.6	33	1.02	97.1
1661-1670	5	7.37	76.6	6	0.83	79.0
1671-1680	37	5.60	58.2	27	0.62	59.0
1681-1690	29	5.63	58.5	17	0.66	62.8
1691-1700	20	6.80	70.6	17	0.78	74.2
1701-1710	19	7.10	73.8	16	0.81	77.1
1711-1720	25	8.01	83.2	9	0.89	84.7
1721-1730	33	8.04	83.5	23	0.95	90.4
1731-1740	28	7.90	82.1	30	0.98	93.3
1741-1750	18	8.68	90.2	17	1.16	110.4
1751-1760	20	12.66	131.6	16	1.57	149.5
1761-1770	24	17.26	179.4	23	1.96	186.6
1771-1780	16	17.30	179.8	17	1.89	180.0
1781-1790	15	17.46	181.4	12	1.80	171.4
1791-1800	8	16.35	169.9	3	1.78	169.5
1801-1810	16	17.72	184.1	11	1.87	178.0
1811-1820	12	19.69	204.6	17	2.12	201.9
1821-1830	11	21.16	219.9	14	2.42	230.4
1831-1840	6	22.54	234.3	5	2.52	240.0
1841-1850	2	16.10	167.3	2	1.95	185.7
1851-1860	11	12.34	128.2	7	1.32	125.7
1861-1870	13	4.93	51.2	16	0.65	61.9
1871-1880	6	10.63	110.4	6	1.33	126.6
1881-1890	5	11.95	124.2	1	1.19	113.3
1891-1900	12	14.73	153.1	n.a.	n.a.	n.a.
1901-1910	12	19.48	202.4	n.a.	n.a.	n.a.

SOURCE: Documents held in Nanking University.
NOTE: n.a. = not available.

having improved the relative position of agricultural production, though its rate of return was still below that in other sectors. If true, this could enhance both the external demand and the internal demand for land. In other words, the effect mentioned earlier would have been reinforced by the new factors.

One writer has connected the rising demand for farmland to tax reform in the late Ming.[25] He argues that the so-called single whip tax scheme introduced in the second half of the sixteenth century—in which most corvée labor services were combined into one, commuted to cash, and assessed as a small surcharge on acreage—had lightened the burden of landowners. The tax system was accepted by the Ch'ing rulers and was further improved. This would raise the demand for land relative to its supply as rich families from the cities became eager to buy land, whereas poor people in the countryside were unwilling to alienate land.

The rising demand for farmland may be partially attributed to the spread of such cash crops as cotton and tobacco and the burgeoning of manufacturing activities using cash crops as raw material. These crops would inevitably boost the rate of return on land. Another contributing factor was probably population growth. Without substantial imports, the population expansion would naturally bid up the prices of foods, which would in turn augment the rate of return on land investment. The indexes of land prices generally dovetailed variations in the man-land ratio. During the turmoil years of 1660-90 as well as the period of the T'aip'ing Rebellion (1850-64), which had an especially severe effect on this region, land prices of the region declined sharply. The ascendent movement of land prices after 1760 also coincides quite well with the similar trend of rice prices in Anhwei during the same period.[26] Yeh Meng-chu, a seventeenth-century writer, also describes the rush to buy land caused by the sudden rise in the price of rice, as he personally observed in Kiangnan.[27]

Whether to buy land and how to manage the land once it is bought are two distinctly separate decisions. We have just examined the important factors influencing the land market and the distribution of land ownership in traditional China. The next two chapters will examine farm operating systems and their changes over time.

7
Managerial Landlordism

Historical Development of Managerial Landlordism

After the third century B.C., Chinese agricultural institutions showed a greater similarity to the agrarian system found in the United States before 1860 than to the systems of medieval Europe. When making economic decisions, cultivators faced a minimum of cumbersome institutional restrictions, leaving them free to develop individual modes of agricultural organization within the constraints of existing technology. Consequently, various types of farms existed simultaneously until a general equilibrium was reached. Over time, however, agricultural organizations would change in response to new conditions of resource endowment that altered their relative advantages.

For the better part of two thousand years, China remained basically an economy comprised of free peasants working independently on their own small pieces of land. The typical peasant household was what Li Ke called "a family of five persons farming about 100 *mou* of land." Their general plight was described in greater detail by Tsao Tso, a famous scholar of the early Western Han:

> These days a family of five has at least two persons who are liable for labor service and conscription, while they farm no more than 100 *mou* of land, the yield from which does not exceed 100 *shih*. With their plowing in the spring and hoeing in the summer, harvesting in the autumn and storing in the winter, with felling firewood, repairing government offices and rendering service, they are unable to escape the windblown dust of spring, the heat of summer, the heavy rains of autumn or the chill of winter. In none of the four seasons do they have a day of rest. . . . In spite of all this painful toil, they still have to endure such natural disasters as flood and drought and also the cruelty of an impatient government that imposes taxes at inconvenient times, and gives orders in the morning and rescinds them in the evening. When the time comes that the levy must be met, those who own something sell it off at half price; and those who own nothing borrow

132

at doubled rates of interest. It is for this reason that some dispose of their lands and houses, and sell their children and grandchildren to redeem their debts.[1]

There were also numerous landlords at any given point in time who owned more land than they could cultivate by themselves, or who possessed large amounts of land they did not wish to farm. These men were free to choose between renting land to tenants and independently managing large latifundia. In the latter case, they had a further choice among alternative means of obtaining labor: buying slaves with large sums of initial capital; keeping retainers on the basis of long-term contracts; or hiring farm workers on a pay-as-you-use basis. This chapter will investigate the nature of managerial landlordism and the operation of latifundia in premodern China.

Unfortunately, the historical record suffers from lack of clarity in this area, for two reasons: different systems of labor acquisition overlapped, and relevant terms were often used loosely. For example, the term "enslavement" was often used by early Chinese historians to dramatize the unpleasant relations between landlords and their subordinates regardless of whether the latter were actually slaves. Equally often, the terms *k'e*, *p'u*, and *t'ung* were used indiscriminately by writers to denote people who depended, in various ways, on rich families for their livelihood. Thus, the numerous passages in official Han histories that state that wealthy and powerful families had enslaved hundreds or thousands of poor households to cultivate their lands might be describing virtually any set of relations ranging from tenantry to the employment of true slaves. Official Han histories also mentioned large plantations producing fruits, jute, bamboo, and vegetables without indicating the type of labor used.

On the other hand, the terms *yung* and *ku* had a standardized usage and an unequivocal meaning: both mean "to employ" (as a verb) or "hired hands" (as a noun). The term *yung* appears frequently in the historical record and from as early as the Warring States period, implying that hiring workers on a wage basis was already a common practice at that time.[2] According to these records, wage-earning workers were employed in house construction, tomb building, salt making, restaurant work, transportation, construction of irrigation facilities, gardening, and farming. There were labor markets, called *yung shih*, in which a large number of workers were available for employment. Agricultural production in the state of Ch'i, for example, depended on hired farm hands to the extent that the Ch'i government had to ban the hiring of workers by the salt-making industry during the spring season, when labor was badly needed for plowing the fields.[3]

The relationship between the employer and his hired farmhands was succinctly described by Han Fei, a famous legal philosopher of the Warring States period:

> In employing workers for cultivation, the master provides good food and pays good wages, not because he likes the workers but because only then the workers will plow deeply and prepare the land properly. When working for the master, the worker plows quickly and prepares the land properly, not because he likes his master but because only then he can get good food and good wages.[4]

Such transactions were apparently carried out on a voluntary basis and involved cash payments.

Workers were free people, although their social status was low. Prince Fa Chang of the Ch'i worked for wages as a gardener when in exile after his country had been conquered by Yen.[5] Another well-known story about wage-earning workers involves Chen She, who was employed as a hired farmhand before he became the leader of a rebellion against the tyranny of the Ch'in emperor: "One day, he halted his farming work and told his fellow workers indignantly, 'Let us not forget each other after we become rich and famous.' His fellow workers replied, laughing, 'As hired farm hands, how can we become rich and famous?'"[6] Similar cases have been cited in official Han histories in which people had first served as wage earners before becoming prominent.[7] Occasionally wage rates were quoted.[8]

Slavery was legal in China until the twentieth century. During the Han, people were required to report the number and value of their slaves along with other types of property, in their household registration. A comparison of the monetary values of slaves recorded on tablets from Chü Yen (20,000 cash for an adult slave and 15,000 cash for a juvenile slave) and the contemporary wage rate for hiring workers in the same locality (424 cash per month or 5,088 cash per year)[9] easily demonstrates that buying slaves and hiring workers were two alternative ways of acquiring labor and that the two costs had to be maintained in balance. At the 20 percent interest rate prevailing during the Han, the interest cost for .

keeping an adult slave was 4,000 cash (= 20,000 × 20%). The master had to pay a double poll tax for his slave, which amounted to 240 cash (= 2 × 120). The master probably had to spend 500 cash on the slave's clothing, an amount barely enough to buy 40 *chih* of white coarse linen cloth in that locality. These items would add up to 4,740 cash, a sum very close to the annual cost (5,088) of hiring a worker.

Slaves in Chinese history came from a number of sources. Prisoners of war and criminals might first be made public slaves serving in certain government offices but were later sold to private households. By far the most important source of slaves in peaceful times, however, was those private citizens who sold themselves, and often their offspring as well, for economic reasons. In this case the slaves would have to sign papers pledging that the transactions were voluntary. Therefore, the supply of slaves was also affected by the economic advantage of selling one's labor as a worker versus selling oneself as a slave. This is one of the reasons why slavery in China was such a persistent institution.

A third type of latifundia used mercenary retainers as labor. As far as can be discerned from documented data, this system began in the Eastern Han, when the government was too ineffective to protect its subjects from both external invasions and internal bandit attacks, thereby compelling many powerful houses to hire soldiers for purposes of self-defense. Such private armies, known as *pu-ch'ü*, consisted of the clansmen of the leaders, unrelated natives, and fugitives from other places. They erected fortifications surrounding a certain amount of farmland on which cultivating activities could continue. The leaders of these fortified camps maintained strict military discipline over their retainers, although the command was established on the basis of personal influence and mercenary relations rather than government authorization. When no battles needed to be fought, the private mercenary armies would be diverted to farming. After the restoration of a more durable peace, these retainers essentially became professional farmers working for their masters under long-term contracts. Because of their origin, they still continued to be subject to military discipline. In a sense, it was a system that fell somewhere between slavery and employment of free workers.

Apparently, prolonged civil turmoil after the second century A.D. increased the supply of slaves and retainers relative to free workers. The total number of private slaves swelled to dramatic proportions, almost exhausting the sources of military manpower available to the Chin government. Thus, Emperor Wu of the Chin issued edicts forbidding private households to recruit retainers and forcing them to release slaves.[10] Subsequently, the governments of the Southern Dynasties even conscripted private slaves directly into the state armies.

Public policy towards the retainer system was transformed after the Chinese government evacuated to the south when faced with a massive invasion by the northern tribes. Recruitment of subordinates by wealthy families was then considered as a desirable mechanism to absorb the migrating population. Thus, those units that began as expedient private organizations at the local level were fully legalized by the Eastern Chin government in A.D. 321. In the capital of the Liu Sung, generals and captains were all said to have recruited private retainers.[11] Many entered service either to avoid conscription or because they were attracted by the generous pay; some merely enrolled their name with the recruiting families but did not actually enter service.[12]

In the Northern Dynasties, however, the equitable field system provided strong incentives for acquiring slaves, because each master would receive land allotments on the basis of both the size of his family household and the number of slaves he owned. Furthermore, the taxes levied on slaves were substantially lower than the taxes set for commoners. On the other hand, since each able-bodied commoner was entitled to a certain portion of public land for use during his lifetime, very few were compelled to offer their services on the labor market, especially as retainers. More important, since retainers were not entitled to receive land, there was no demand for them. During the latter part of the sixth century, the government of the Northern Chou made serious attempts to check the slavery system but felt it necessary to maintain the retainer system in the newly occupied territory in the south, where the equitable field system had never been implemented.[13]

This policy was followed by the Sui and T'ang after the unification of the country, and consequently the status of retainers was still stipulated in the T'ang code. Nevertheless, enforcing the equitable field system on a nationwide basis rendered the retainer system utterly useless as an institution. There are no surviving records, to my knowledge, that can demonstrate the employment of retainers during the T'ang period. For the Sung dynasty, similarly, the term "retainer" can be found only in the legal code. However, two new categories of persons—*p'u* (servants) and *ti-k'e* (field helpers)—with a status somewhat comparable to that of retainers, came into being during the Sung. It is probable that the restoration of private land ownership once again created a need for retainers, but people had forgotten the old term *pu-ch'u* after such a long interruption and instead coined a few new terms.

It is necessary here to take a slight detour to reexamine the notion of parallel historical development that is frequently assumed to exist between Europe and China. Despite the fact that the pattern of European history has never been duplicated in any other part of the world, such a Chinese-European parallel is still often taken for granted. This false analogy has generated improper translation and interpretation of important Chinese economic institutions that in turn have reinforced or even perpetuated the parallelism. The terms "slavery" and "feudal" in the Chinese context have little in common with these systems in Europe. Yet many students of Chinese economic history insist on tailoring Chinese historical material to fit the European framework. Identifying the *chuang yüan* of the T'ang and Sung as "manorialism" is a good example of this practice.

A careful examination of the historical data on *chuang yüan* reveals that this was a new term that arose in the latter stages of the equitable field system to distinguish purely privately owned land from lands allotted by the government to individual households. The meaning of the term was even more obvious in records from the Sung, in which *chuang yüan* was nothing more than a synonym for "private landed property."[14]

Three "unique features" have been frequently cited to support the contention that *chuang yüan* represented a special land institution: (1) the term was never used by writers before the T'ang, (2) *chuang yüan* of the T'ang and Sung appeared to be very large in size, and (3) each *chuang yüan* was a self-sufficient economic unit engaging in multiple lines of production. Unfortunately, none of these reasons withstand close scrutiny. That the term had never been used before the T'ang merely proves that it was a new term, not necessarily a new land institution. Before the equitable field system was implemented, private ownership of land was too commonplace to require any special descriptive term. As discussed in Chapter 6, the relatively large size of *chuang yüan* may be briefly explained as follows: under the equitable field system, only privileged and powerful persons were able to acquire private estates and hence these would naturally be large in size. If the estate were sufficiently large, there were likely to be numerous production activities underway within its

137

confines, a situation found as early as the Han and as late as the twentieth century.[15] The T'ang and Sung were by no means unique in this respect.

Nor did *chuang yüan* represent a new way of operating farms. Available data show that, like private estates in all other time periods, *chuang yüan* of the T'ang and Sung drew labor from a variety of sources. Although the decree issued by the T'ang Emperor in A.D. 752 implied that the newly established *chuang yüan* depended on tenants for their labor supply, the *T'ai P'ing Kuang Chi* (Miscellaneous Notes about a Peaceful Period), a collection of short stories written in the T'ang, mentions that slaves and wage earners were used on *chuang yüan* as well.[16] In one case, it states, the owner of a tea garden in Szechuan hired hundreds of workers every year to pick tea leaves.[17]

The dependence of latifundia on diverse sources of labor continued in the Sung dynasty. Sung slaves, however, seem to have acquired some unusual attributes. In some cases, the so-called slaves had to pay rent to their masters;[18] in others, they cultivated independently, with considerable decision-making powers.[19] It is likely that either the term "slave" was used more loosely or that there was a liberalizing trend during the Sung. Quantitatively, there seem to have been fewer slaves in the Sung than in previous dynasties. For farming labor, landlords largely depended upon the *k'e hu* or nonresident households, which accounted for nearly half the population throughout most of the dynasty. Nonresident households— which, unlike slaves, were separately registered in local government offices—consisted of tenants, wage earners, *t'ien-p'u* (farm servants) and *ti-k'e* (field helpers). Workers were hired by relatively short-term contracts with fixed wage rates and were mostly paid in cash.[20] They were free to quit and to move from place to place. Farm servants and field helpers, however, were of a lower social status because of their long-term, usually lifetime, service contracts. In a sense, their position was comparable to that of retainers before the T'ang.

The Ming and Ch'ing dynasties may be identified as the time frame within which traditional managerial landlordism underwent drastic change. First, the Ming government announced, upon assuming control, a prohibition against the maintenance of slaves by private citizens who held no official titles or offices.[21] To bypass the new law, many families converted their slaves into "hereditary servants" (*shih p'u*), "adopted sons," or "adopted son-in-laws," while allowing them to do the same work as before. Others promoted their slaves to a status somewhere between that of bona fide slaves and free tenants, called *tien-p'u* (tenant-servants). After receiving a piece of land for farming, a tenant-servant paid rent to his master but at a rate somewhat lower than would have been charged to normal tenants. In addition, a tenant-servant was obliged to perform various chores for the master without pay. This category of people was bound to hereditary service partly because they had been converted from slave status, and partly because most of them had buried their grandparents or parents on the masters' land, which was more than just a renting transaction. Tenant-servants still had an independent family life, individual property, and some privileges that could not previously have been enjoyed by slaves.

A more important factor producing institutional change in the Ming-Ch'ing was growing population pressure. As the mathematical model in Chapter 1 showed, the existence of surplus population in China's rural sector rendered latifundia operated by managerial landlords employing diverse types of labor less profitable than renting land to tenants. To some extent, the conversion of slaves into tenant-servants was also a reflection of this force at work. In other words, the tenant-servant represented a transitional institution between managerial and tenurial landlordism.

This process of transition also took the form of converting farm workers into tenants. Passages from Sung literature concerning free farm workers are numerous; the same is true for the early Ming. The brothers T'an Hsiao and T'an Chao are a frequently cited case:

> T'an Hsiao was born in the east side of the city. He and his brother were both endowed with entrepreneurial talent. Much of the land along the lakeshores in the countryside was swampy and barren. The village people had left it alone and became fishermen. There were tens of thousands *mou* of such land, which Hsiao and Chao obtained at a very low price. They then hired more than a hundred village people, fed them, asked them to dig pools out of the lowest-lying portions, then converted the rest into farmland surrounded by high dikes.[22]

Another famous novel from the Ming told the following story: "Lu Yen had vast lands and about one hundred hired workers, not counting his family members. In mid-December of each year, he prepaid all workers' annual wages for the coming year. On that payday, all workers gathered together and entered the house."[23] Perhaps a more useful piece of information concerns the estimated proportion of farm workers for hire in Ch'ang-shu, Kiangsu: "Those who served permanently as hired hands to

139

do hard farmwork numbered about 20 to 25 per *li*."[24] which suggests a ratio of at least 10 percent in the total rural labor force.

In a recent study, Li Wen-chih states that the gazetteers of the following counties and prefectures in the Kiangnan area mentioned the widespread use of farm workers during the Ming (publication dates in parentheses):[25]

Wu-chiang	(1488-1505)	Ch'ang-su	(1522-1566)
Sung-chiang	(1506-1521)	Chiang-yin	(1522-1566)
Hua-t'ing	(1506-1521)	Yang-chou	(1573-1619)
Hu-chou	(1522-1566)	Chia-hsing	(1573-1619)

To use workers in place of slaves could cut the expenses of farm operation. Tenancy and the hiring of farm workers appears to have been the two most common procedures for landlords in those areas. Each locality had a regular marketplace in which landlords could acquire workers in any number.[26] Some local residents might have been able to find employment opportunities in other places.

The common practice of hiring farm workers reached a turning point by the latter part of the Ming dynasty. The reason underlying this institutional shift is clear from Shen's *Nung Shu* (Agricultural Handbook), which provided a detailed cost analysis for hiring workers during the early seventeenth century.[27] On an annual basis, each worker would cost the following (in taels of silver):

Yearly wage	3
Food	6.5
Travel subsidy	1
Depreciation of implements	0.3
Fuel and other expenses	1.2
TOTAL	12.0

After deducting land rent, the yield per worker (in taels) would be:

Cultivating 4 *mou* of dry land	4
Cultivating 8 *mou* of paddy land	10
TOTAL	14

Shen concluded that if the labor cost of the master himself, which would be worth at least 9.5 taels, were included, there would be no profit at all. He stated further: "People in the neighboring village on the west side have all rented out their land, so that the landowners not only receive the same amounts of income as we do, but also are free of the type of toil we

TABLE 7.1
Cost Analysis for a Ch'ing Farm, 1854-1859
(copper cash)

Year	Total revenues	Total expenditures	Profits or losses
1854	87,227	118,095	−30,868
1855	126,871	153,155	−26,284
1856	108,751	167,893	−59,142
1857	162,419	126,523	34,896
1858	195,407	189,019	6,388
1859	237,551	218,360	19,191

SOURCE: Li Wen-shih 1957, 1:675.

are suffering. Unfortunately, in our village none of us has yet rented out the land to tenants."[28]

Similar cost analyses can be found in Ch'ing records. For instance, a managerial landlord in Hsiu-ning, Anhwei, left the operation records of his farm for six years (1854-59). By eliminating irrelevant items of expenditure, one may rearrange and sum up the accounts as shown in Table 7.1. During these six years, there were net losses in three years and profits in the other three years; the combined losses exceeded the combined profits. More important, if the cost of the owner's labor, which was not included in the above accounts, is added, all six years would have shown net losses. In a study published in 1927, Tao Shü made a cost calculation for a managerial landlord in the late Ch'ing using the same format as Shen's.[29] The total gross income earned per worker was 61,000 cash whereas the total cost per worker was 60,600 cash, leaving 400 cash as the residual income for the owner. Again, as in Chen's case, the residual income of 400 cash was certainly insufficient to compensate for the labor of the owner himself.

Similar comparisons were conducted in 1888 by a British consul and several missionaries in five localities. Their findings have been carefully checked and a few data gaps have been closed with materials from other sources by Li Wen-chih, whose results are shown in Table 7.2. The last case shown in this table is an exception, with an earning from land renting lower than that from hiring workers. As Li explains, the wage cost in this case was underreported in the original study.

The most important data collected for this purpose are the farm household statistics from nineteenth-century Shantung compiled by Ching Su and Lo Lun.[30] The manner in which the researchers have treated this valuable set of data, however, leaves something to be desired.

141

TABLE 7.2

Comparative Earnings of Landlords, Five Localities, 1888

Locality	Unit of currency	Net earnings from hiring workers	Net earnings from renting out land	Difference
Southern Kiangsu	copper cash	11,261	15,122	3,861
Hang-chou, Chekiang	tael	3.98	11.10	7.12
Swatow, Kwangtung	tael	19.23	30.00	10.77
Kuang-chi, Hupei	copper cash	6,438	13,200	6,762
Lai-chou, Shantung	tael	16.29	13.60	−2.69

SOURCE: Li Wen-chih et al., p. 216.

Except for data from a few ultrawealthy landlord families, which were taken from actual account ledgers, the statistics used in the study were provided from memory by numerous senior villagers in 1957. While no sample of the original questionnaires used by the investigators is available for inspection, recollections of events that took place 60 years in the past can hardly be perfectly accurate. Unless carefully double-checked by the investigators and corrected by follow-up questions, statistics compiled from such sources are easily marred by internal inconsistencies. Let us cite two examples: First, according to the study, Lung-ho, a village in Po-hsing county, had 130 tenant households but no tenurial landlord renting out land to those tenants.[31] (The situation is possible but highly unlikely.) Second, in Kuan-chia, a village in Pin county, 95 percent of the residents were hired farmworkers and 5 percent were small owner-cultivators. (One wonders who actually owned the land in this village. Again, it is possible but improbable that all the land belonged to outside owners.)

There are also a few cases of questionable classification. Let us take two examples. First, the authors have included 22 villages in north Shan-tung in the category of villages in which managerial landlordism had replaced tenurial landlordism. Yet the detailed data do not show a single landlord of any type in 18 out of the 22 villages listed by the authors. Second, according to the study, Wu Hsi-hsien of T'ai-an owned 1,000 *mou* of land, of which 970 *mou* were leased to tenants. Li Hsü-t'ien of Chi-hsia owned 3,000 *mou*, of which 2,920 *mou* was leased to tenants. Yet both landlords are classified by the authors as managerial landlords.

Attempting to demonstrate that managerial landlordism was a more advanced form of operation than tenurial landlordism, the authors have repeatedly shown higher unit yields from lands operated by the managerial landlords than from ordinary farms. But the superiority of latifundia cannot be established solely on the basis of yield; one must include cost data in the comparison. The authors have almost defeated their original purpose by indicating that higher yields came as a result of using better-quality land, more fertilizer, better implements, and more labor per area.[32] The fact that all these inputs had higher opportunity costs renders the superiority of managerial landlordism completely uncertain.

Logically, to determine which system is the more recent institution of displacement, we must use data collected from different time periods and make comparisons. Static data collected from a given point of time, as presented by Ching and Lo, are inconclusive. Even if we accept the proportion of managerial landlords in Shantung, it is still negligible. With no temporal comparison, this small percentage taken by itself could mean either that managerial landlordism was brand new or that it was merely the remnant of a decaying institution.

In fact, the authors did collect some dynamic data, but they failed to see the implications. In studying the Yen Shu T'ang household of the Meng family, identified as tenurial landlords, the authors learned that the family were previously managerial landlords and that many of their present tenants were their former hired farm workers.[33] The authors, however, made no effort to trace the process of evolution suggested by such information.

Nevertheless, this study has contributed a great deal to our knowledge about the development of land institutions in China. Among the 131 managerial landlords identified by the authors, the average landholding was 1,780 *mou*, of which 360 *mou* were cultivated by hired workers. For 80 percent of the managerial landlords, less than 500 *mou* of land was devoted to self-operation. This fact suggests that the cutoff size of latifundia in Shantung during this period was around 500 *mou*. Given the nature of intensive farming, the enforcement cost of supervising hired hands per unit of output tends to increase as the size of the farm is enlarged. Therefore, a critical point must exist beyond which operation with hired hands is definitely uneconomical as compared to tenurial operations. This critical size tends to decrease as the rent level of tenantry rises. It was probably through this process that the latifundia of premodern China gradually shrank and finally disappeared.

Aside from the work by Ching and Lo, many researchers cite another set of data as convincing evidence that managerial landlordism was a

143

new and rising land institution during the Ch'ing. It has been discovered that, among cases of capital crimes reported by local magistrates and provincial governors to the central ministry of justice, the number of cases involving farm workers sharply increased from the Ch'ien-lung reign (1736-95) to the Chia-ch'ing reign (1796-1820); such increases are believed to have reflected the spread of managerial landlordism during this time period. While there is no doubt about the reliability of the statistics, the interpretation is, again, highly questionable.

Li Wen-chih took a sample of such cases and within this sample counted the number in different reigns as follows:[34]

Yung-cheng (1724-1735)	12
Ch'ien-lung (1736-1795)	259
Chia-ch'ing (1796-1820)	437

A more thorough screening of the archives by Liu Yung-ch'eng uncovered a total of 6,100 such cases in the 60 years of the Ch'ien-lung reign. These were broken down by decade as follows:[35]

1736-1745	45	1766-1775	1,855
1746-1755	643	1776-1785	1,055
1756-1765	1,235	1786-1795	1,267

These numbers signify anything but a natural development of a labor institution because in a natural labor market the system of employment could never change so abruptly. It is utterly inconceivable that very few farm workers existed before 1736 and then suddenly increased more than fourteenfold (from 45 to 643) in a short period of ten years.

In actuality, the statistics reflect an important change in the justice system that took place during the early part of the Ch'ien-lung reign. To understand their true significance, one must understand the nature of the archives from which these legal cases have been drawn and the point of law at stake.

Under Ch'ing law, criminal cases were classified into three categories, each with different trial and execution procedures.[36] First, minor cases were tried, sentenced, and executed locally in county courts. Second, more serious cases up to the sentence of banishment were tried and sentenced in local courts, but the sentences became final only after review by the prefectural or provincial governments. If necessary, the prefectural or provincial courts might retry the cases. Third, all cases of capital crimes involving death penalties were further divided into two types. If both local and provincial courts considered the case a serious crime and returned a sentence of "first-degree death penalty without delay" (*li-chüeh*), the case was to be reported to the justice ministry in Peking and the execution would take place as soon as the ministry sanctioned the verdict. For a second-degree death penalty (hanging or beheading after a period of retrial), the governor or an equivalent official would hand over the case, along with all documents and records, to the ministry of justice. The ministry would then organize a review board, known as the *san-fa-ssu* (board of three judges), to reexamine the case, a procedure called *ch'iu-shen* (autumn retrial). The verdict became final if the review board upheld it and the emperor signed his name; the criminal would be executed "after autumn," meaning any time after the beginning of autumn. There was a department in the justice ministry, known as the department of autumn trials, which processed all such cases. The archives from which the preceding labor statistics were drawn were the records of autumn retrials and accompanying documents.[37]

The point of law involved in these case records was whether a landowner who had killed a farm laborer he hired or a farm laborer who had killed his employer should receive the death sentence and if so, whether he was entitled to an autumn retrial. These factors determined whether retrial cases involving farm workers were present in the justice ministry's archives, but the absence of such cases does not mean there were no farm workers at this time. The whole issue began in 1588 when the Ming emperor Wan-li added the following new law to the criminal code: "Henceforth, in the families of officials and commoners, all hired workers who have signed written contracts, [and] have agreed on the number of years of employment, shall be treated as *ku-kung-jen* [hired hands]. Only those who have been hired for a short period of months or days, and have not received any great amount of wages, shall be treated as commoners."[38] A new category of persons was thereby created—*ku-kung-jen*, or hired hands—whose status in the criminal code lay between that of bondservants and commoners. Under the new law, when a landowner killed his hired hand, for whatever reason, he was not considered to have committed a capital crime; hence, he would receive a penalty of three years' hard labor instead of a death sentence. Consequently, such a case was not sent to the ministry for autumn retrial. On the other hand, when a hired hand killed his employer, he was subject to the first-degree death penalty, which had to be executed without autumn retrial by the ministry of justice. Thus, there were likewise no retrial documents for these cases.

The problem was: What would qualify a farm laborer as a *ku-kung-*

145

jen to be so discriminated against? Because of the ambiguous wording of the 1588 law, the word "and" was not explicitly expressed. In interpreting the law, either an "and" or an "or" might be inserted in the place of the missing word. The standard interpretation during the Ming was an "or": that is to say, as long as a farm laborer had agreed to work for his employer for one year or longer, he would be considered a *ku-kung-jen* and a written contract was no longer required.[39] Thus, all long-term farm laborers automatically had this legal status conferred on them whether or not there were written contracts between them and their employers. Until 1728, this standard interpretation of the law was generally accepted by Ch'ing officials. Because all long-term farm laborers were classified as *ku-kung-jen*, their cases were never sent to the justice ministry for retrial. That is why no cases involving hired hands have been found in the archives of the ministry before the Yung-cheng reign, although such a class of workers existed long before this time.

In 1727, the fifth year of the Yung-cheng reign, the emperor issued a mandate that abolished the servile status of certain categories of bondservants in the Kiangnan area and converted them to commoners.[40] This action immediately led to the question of whether hired hands, who supposedly held a higher legal status than bondservants, should be discriminated against by the law. Consequently, some local officials began to interpret the 1588 law as requiring the two conditions concurrently, that is, the interpretation using an "and." Thus, a long-term farm laborer would be treated as a *ku-kung-jen* only if he had signed a written contract in which he accepted this discriminatory designation. The diversity in interpretation was clearly demonstrated by the well-discussed case of Shih Mao-er, which took place in Hsin-ch'eng, Chihli, in 1735.[41] Shih Mao-er, a long-term farm laborer with no written contract, was killed by his employer. The provincial court treated Shih Mao-er as a *ku-kung-jen* by virtue of the long duration of his employment. When the case was finally referred to the ministry of justice, the ministry changed the verdict on the ground that there was no written contract, thus making Shih Mao-er legally a commoner.

Disputed cases of this sort reached the ministry every year thereafter in increasingly larger numbers. The issue was finally clarified by the Ch'ing government's new ruling in 1759, which unambiguously defined *ku-kung-jen* as persons who were hired as long-term farm laborers under written contracts.[42] This is why the foregoing statistics reveal a sharp in-

TABLE 7.3
Ratio of Farm Worker Households to
Total Rural Households, 1936

Province	Ratio (%)	Province	Ratio (%)
Kiangsu	0.60%	Shansi	7.39%
Chekiang	2.03	Shensi	0.57
Anhwei	0.58	Chahar	0
Kiangsi	0.42	Suiyuan	2.17
Hunan	0.84	Fukien	0.21
Hupei	0.56	Kwangtung	0.61
Hopei	4.41	Kwangsi	2.00
Shantung	2.26	National	
Honan	2.54	average	1.57

SOURCE: Land Commission, p. 35.

crease up to the decade 1756-65 and stabilize thereafter. Under the un-equivocal definition, all cases of capital crimes involving noncontractual long-term farm laborers were subject to death penalties and would have to be routinely retried by the ministry of justice. What the statistics faith-fully reflect, therefore, is a change not in labor institution or farm opera-tions, but in the law—and its gradual application. It is unfortunate that these records have been so long misunderstood by so many scholars.

It is equally unfortunate that many scholars have ignored the abun-dant data collected in the 1920's and 1930's that clearly show the transi-tion from self-operation to tenantry in Chinese agriculture. A good ex-ample is the compilation of findings from several dozens of local surveys explaining why and how managerial landlords gradually switched to land-renting.[43] Yet these data seem to have attracted little attention.

Quantitative data of this nature for the modern period are equally abundant. The most comprehensive set is that compiled by the Land Commission in the 1930's. According to these statistics, presented in Table 7.3, the ratio of farm worker households to total rural households was generally below 1 percent in the southern provinces. Even in the northern provinces, where the ratio was generally higher, the maximum was only 7.39 percent (Shansi). The national average was 1.57 percent.

There are also a number of small-scale rural surveys dating from this period that covered selected localities. These sample studies usually produced more reliable results than national surveys because the inves-tigators conducted on-the-spot household interviews. Their findings, as presented in Table 7.4, were generally consistent with the Land Commis-

TABLE 7.4
Ratio of Farm Worker Households to Total Rural Households
in Various Localities, 1933-1941

Place	Date	Ratio (%)
Yunnan	1933	5.6%
Ting county, Hopei	1933	1.1
5 counties, Kwangsi	1933	5.5
3 counties, Honan	1933	2.5
P'an-yü, Kwangtung	1933	8.9
Yang-kao, Shansi	1934	14.9
Ting county, Hopei	1933	1.2
Wang-tu, Hopei	1933	1.2
P'ing-shan, Hopei	1933	4.3
I county, Hopei	1933	6.2
P'ing-hu, Chekiang	1936	3.3
Ch'ing-yuan, Hopei	1935	3.0
9 counties, Shantung	1934	7.9
T'ai-an, Shantung	1939	0.9
Hsien-nien, Hupei	1937	1.6
16 counties, Hopei	1936	10.0
Feng-jun, Hopei	1939	11.3
Hueh-lu, Hopei	1939	12.4
Hui-min, Shantung	1939	0
Chang-te, Honan	1940	0
Nan-t'ung, Kiangsu	1941	1.5
Sung-chang, Kiangsu	1940	0
Ch'ang-shu, Kiangsu	1939	0
Wu-hsi, Kiangsu	1941	0.8

SOURCE: Chao and Chen 1982, p. 309.

TABLE 7.5
Allocation of Land by Landlords, 1933
(percent of total land owned by landlords)

Place	Rented to tenants	Self-operation	Other use
Yen-ch'eng, Kiangsu	99.3%	0.2%	0.5%
Chi-tung, Kiangsu	98.4	1.0	0.6
Ch'ang-su, Kiangsu	97.9	1.7	0.4
Yu-lung, Chekiang	68.6	20.5	10.9
Yung-chia, Chekiang	90.8	5.4	3.8
Wei-nan, Shensi	68.6	2.2	29.2
Sui-te, Shensi	92.7	4.1	3.2
Chen-p'ing, Honan	95.9	2.1	2.0
Hui county, Honan	96.5	1.3	2.2
Hsu-ch'ang, Honan	85.8	1.9	2.3

SOURCE: Li Wen-chih 1957, 3:810.

sion report. The percentage of farm worker households is slightly higher in a few cases, but the statistics show the same regional pattern—higher in the north than in the south.

The relative lack of importance of managerial landlordism in early twentieth-century China may also be seen from the land allocation of landlords as a whole. The statistics obtained from sample surveys, shown in Table 7.5, clearly show that, except for the case of Lung-you, Chekiang, only a tiny proportion of the total land owned by landlords was self-operated, and that most of their land was leased to tenants. No indications can be found to support the claim that managerial landlordism was a new and rising land institution in modern China.

The Status of Slaves, Retainers, and Wage Earners

Slaves and Retainers

Slavery in traditional China differed markedly from the European institution. Slavery in Europe was supplanted by feudalism; in China no such precise developmental stages ever appeared. The institution of slavery was present throughout Chinese history, but slaves never formed a caste comparable to that found in Europe. Moreover, Chinese slaves differed significantly from their European counterparts in crucial class characteristics.

The first point of difference was that Chinese slaves could upgrade their status, an option that made slavery a less rigid class system in China than in Europe. Apart from prisoners of war and certain categories of criminals, who were enslaved by the government as a punitive measure, Chinese law traditionally permitted commoners to sell themselves and their immediate family members into slavery. Even in early times, Chinese officialdom considered this type of slave transaction a purely economic activity and thus granted interested parties the freedom to carry out such transactions as long as they were conducted on a voluntary basis. Beginning in the Han period, a person who intended to sell himself as a slave was required to sign a contract or sale agreement declaring that the sale was willingly made; otherwise, the transaction would be regarded as illegal. Thus, the Han government allowed those who had been kidnapped and sold as slaves to private households to appeal to local magistrates, as a result of which they would very probably be granted their

149

original status. Other dynasties even promulgated so-called *lüeh jen fa* (antikidnapping laws), imposing heavy penalties on those parties who had abducted free persons by force for the purpose of enslavement. Of course, few laws could be fully enforced; stories of kidnapping and selling slaves by force or enslaving people by forging sale contracts abound in Chinese historical literature.

Slaves often regained the status of commoners when the government indemnified or released them. This happened to public as well as private slaves. For instance, an edict issued by the founding emperor of the Han in the summer of the fifth year of his reign declared: "All who have sold themselves as slaves because of starvation shall be restored to the status of commoners."[44] More often, slaves accumulated enough funds and redeemed themselves, or masters freed their slaves without asking for any redemption payment. The right of self-redemption, however, was not always an automatic option in slave contracts. For instance, the Manchu government of the Ch'ing designated two categories of slave contracts.[45] The so-called "red" contracts carried no redemption option; under such contracts slaves had to be listed in the slave registers of the local governments and their status, theoretically, became permanent. The other category, "white" contracts, consisted of those slaves who had reserved the self-redemption option and no official registration was necessary.

In fact, the slave contract could stipulate any special clause as long as it was agreed upon by the two parties. In a well-known case, a slave refused to fetch wine on the grounds that the contract he signed had specified that his only work assignment was to be a security guard for the master's house.[46] This was, of course, an extreme case; the standard slave contract would grant the master full command over his slave.

Unlike European feudal society, except for royal family members the power, titles, and offices of Chinese nobles and magnates were seldom hereditary. Slaves as a whole constituted an inferior caste deprived of certain personal freedoms and political privileges. For an individual slave, however, the presupposed hereditary service might not actually turn out to be such because the master family might not maintain its wealth and power for many generations. These conditions provided slaves with a certain degree of leeway and prevented rigid stratification of the slave class. In fact, considerable fluidity existed among the different social classes. To cite some well-known but extreme cases, a slave girl named Wei Tzu-fu became the queen of Emperor Wu of the Western Han; her brother, Wei Ch'ing, married a royal princess and was made a general of the highest rank; Li Shan, a slave of the Eastern Han, was ultimately appointed the governor of a province.

Even Chinese law provided slaves with better protection than the European feudal system did. Under the laws of various dynasties, a master had limited power to punish his slaves. Killing slaves for any reason was prohibited. Slaves who had committed major crimes were to be tried and punished under state law, though sentences were more severe than those imposed on commoners committing identical crimes.

Because employing slaves and acquiring labor through other means all involved contractual rights and obligations, it was difficult to distinguish this inferior class from other labor suppliers. Traditional Chinese statutes used the duration of the contractual obligation as the criterion: the longer the contractual period, the more inferior the status of the worker. Thus, directly above slaves on the ascending scale as stipulated by the statutes would be retainers who had sold their service for a long but definite period of time. As explained earlier, the retainer system began in the latter part of the Eastern Han in the form of local militia organizations. Retainers were recruited from the populace and received compensation for the services they rendered.

The status of retainers under traditional Chinese legal codes rested somewhere between that of slaves and free commoners. Instead of being registered in the local government offices as independent taxpayers, they were registered, as were slaves, as subordinates of their masters. But retainers enjoyed a higher social status than slaves. When the Northern Chou ruler ordered rich families in newly occupied territories to liberate their slaves in A.D. 575, he allowed slaves to choose between registering in the local government as common taxpayers and staying with their former masters as retainers.[47] Although there were no records stating that retainers could be resold by their masters, T'ang law stipulated that a retainer could be transferred from one master to another as long as the latter repaid the former the full cost of food and clothing spent on the retainer.[48] Under the Sung antikidnapping law, abduction for the purpose of enslavement was punishable by death, but the kidnapper would only be sentenced with banishment if he had coerced the kidnapped person into becoming a retainer. T'ang law also specified that retainers were entitled to own property.

Shortly after the retainer system disappeared completely during the

Sung dynasty, it was replaced by a variety of labor-supplying procedures. These differed from each other primarily in the duration of employment contracts. We may arrange all types of employment, from slavery to short-term wage earning, as follows: *nu* (slave), hereditary servitude, permanent or until redemption, no wage; *shih-p'u* (hereditary servant), hereditary servitude, wage payment; *tien-ku* (mortgage hiring), servitude until repayment of loan; *ti-k'e* (field helper), very long-term employment; *ch'ang-kung* (long-term worker), employment of usually over one year; and *tuan-kung* (short-term worker), employment usually less than one year.

Obviously, these categories form a continuum rather than clear-cut classes. Yet Sung law insisted on maintaining the tradition of identifying a humble class (the *chien min*) in order to differentiate them legally from the so-called ordinary people or commoners (*liang min*). The way to do this was to draw an arbitrary line of demarcation, again on the basis of duration. In the law promulgated in 1019, a five-year employment span was made the dividing line.[49]

In addition to legal discrimination on the basis of social class, or what was called *liang chien* (differentiation between the good and the humble), a new element of inequity was added to the legal system during the Southern Sung. Some individuals received punishments harsher than the established sentences for a given offense. The rationale for this disparity was not based on class status, but was related to the person's standing in the family system, such as son versus father, wife versus husband, and younger brother versus elder brother. In each pair, the former was the inferior (junior) and the latter the superior (senior). In Confucian thought, the notion that the inferior should respect the superior provided justification for legal discrimination against the inferior, or what was called *tsun pei* (the differentiation between the superior and the inferior). Therefore, a heavier penalty than the established sentence was to be imposed on the son for killing his father, but not vice versa.

Since the two types of legal discrimination were so similar in form, their combination in the same set of codes has caused enormous confusion among early Chinese writers as well as modern researchers. Yet the two types of legal discrimination were not without significant differences. First, the impacts of the two types of unequal treatment were not comparable because class status was more static than personal standing in the family. A son would become a father after he grew up and got married; at this time his family status automatically changed from inferior to superior, and he began to enjoy new privileges accordingly. Second, legal discrimination based on personal status was applicable on a much more limited range than that based on class. When a slave killed a commoner, he was subject to a stricter punishment regardless of whether or not the victim was his master, whereas a person who killed not his own father but the father of some unrelated person would be sentenced normally. In other words, a son was inferior only to his own father and elder brothers, not to all other people. Third, legal discrimination based on inferior position in the family did not restrict basic freedoms. Thus, a son or younger brother could travel freely, for instance.

The Sung dynasty witnessed some conflicting changes in legal institutions. During the early part of the period, the government made significant efforts to minimize legal discrimination among social classes, and the distinction between "commoners" and the "humble" was least pronounced. This desirable trend was tarnished, unfortunately, by the application of the new element of legal discrimination based on personal standing to the area of employment. The theoretical justification was obviously based on Chinese clan and family ethics, which emphasized the distinct but related positions of family members. The relevancy of including the master-servant relationship within this ethical framework is not clear, except in the case where servants were disguised as "adopted sons."

This change in Chinese legal thought probably derived from the decisive influence enjoyed by neo-Confucian scholars during the Southern Sung, who reiterated the importance of Confucian familial ethics. Chu Hsi, spokesman for the neo-Confucian school, once protested in his memorial to the emperor:

> According to what I have seen in recent years, when a wife kills her husband, a son kills his father, or a *ti-k'e* kills his master, the court imposes only the ordinary punishments on the killer. . . . Whenever there is a lawsuit, in my opinion, the court should first determine the relative positions of the persons involved in the family and their superior-inferior order, and then listen to their reasoning. When the inferior has offended the superior, even if the offender had good reasons to do so, he should be judged guilty. If the offender did not have good reasons, he should be sentenced more severely by one degree than ordinary persons committing the same crime.[50]

During the Ming and Ch'ing, the law still singled out the *chien min* or so-called humble people for harsher treatment. Interestingly, however, what was then included in this category were certain "specialty" groups, such as beggars, prostitutes, and low-class musicians. Moreover, these groups of people actually were at liberty to move, to own property, and even to build their own ancestral worship temples, a privilege previously reserved only for elite families.[51] On the other hand, slaves and all types of workers hired under long-term contracts were lumped together under the same general terms in the Ming legal code, and their relation to their master was seen in terms of the familial analogy. The question that then arose was how long a term of employment under contract should be to qualify a labor employer as a "master" and putative "father."

The demarcation line was drawn in Emperor Wan-li's 1588 law cited earlier. Now that the two different types of legal discrimination were embodied in the same set of codes, the dividing line was moved from five years to one year. Confusion and misinterpretation were inevitable. Most writers during the Ming tended to use the status terms even more loosely, often indiscriminately categorizing workers, tenants, servants, and genuine slaves as slaves. As a result, many modern students of Chinese economic history hold the opinion that there was a sudden expansion of slavery in China during the Ming dynasty. When legal discrimination based on class distinction and legal discrimination based on family relationships are presented simultaneously, many scholars interpret the latter as class discrimination as well. But this is obviously a misleading interpretation when the meaning of social classes has become ambiguous. How can we label those employed for fewer than 365 days as one social class, and those employed for more than 365 days as another? Moreover, as we have seen, the inferior-superior relationship applied only to members of a given family. By extension, a worker hired for a long-term duration was legally inferior to his own employer, but not at all inferior in relation to the heads of other households.

Another phenomenon of the mid-Ming, "commendation" (*t'ou hsien* or *t'ou k'ao*) has been taken by many writers as a sign of expanding slavery. Numerous commoners begged official households to accept them as slaves even without payment. Still others who owned small parcels of land would sign over their property to official households besides surrendering themselves voluntarily as slaves. The most frequently quoted material for this practice is a statement by the scholar Ku Yen-wu in the early eleventh century: "There is a common practice nowadays among elite families in the Kiangnan area. As soon as one has been appointed to an official position, commoners would rush to his door, a practice known as *t'ou k'ao.* Sometimes the number of persons can reach several thousands."[52] The same was true in Honan: "In Kuang-shan county, as soon as someone passed the provincial examination [for the civil service], people, in tens and hundreds, would come to commend their land and ask to be taken as slaves."[53]

The standard interpretation today is that commoners only resorted to this action to avoid heavy tax burdens, and the result of such actions was inevitably the further spread of slavery in the country. This interpretation is highly questionable from an economic viewpoint, however, for Ray Huang has convincingly demonstrated that the level of land tax in the Ming dynasty was fairly low.[54]

In economic terms, the phenomenon of widespread commendation after the mid-Ming has the following significant implications: First, the tremendous increase in population during the Ming depressed the marginal product of labor in the rural areas far below subsistence level, so that even the prospect of slavery appeared attractive to many people. Thus, there was a sharp increase in the supply of slaves.

Second, however, the demand for slaves was almost inelastic, partly because of the government regulation allowing only official households to keep slaves and partly because of the lack of profit in using more slaves when their marginal product had dropped below subsistence level, a situation amply described in Chapter 1. What has escaped the notice of Ku Yen-wu, a keen observer who is nonetheless untrained in economics is the crucial clue that the commenders would rush primarily to those newly appointed to offices and to those who had just passed the provincial examination; both types of officials would soon be qualified to own slaves. In other words, the number of slaves had already reached the saturation point in existing official households, so that hopeful commenders could only appeal to those families that had just acquired the privilege of owning slaves. This is an unmistakable sign of an inelastic demand in the slave market.

Third, given the state of supply and demand as such, it is hardly surprising that prices in the slave market would drop to near-zero. This circumstance easily explains why people would beg to be taken as slaves without asking for payment. It naturally follows that the excess supply of

155

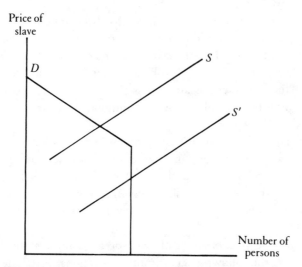

Fig. 7.1. The value of slaves in the Ming dynasty.

slaves would further aggravate the miserable plight of existing slaves, a crucial factor responsible for the frequent slave uprisings towards the end of the Ming dynasty.

This analysis can be conveniently demonstrated by the graph in Figure 7.1. Government restrictions had more or less prevented the demand schedule in the slave market from shifting to the right. Households that could legally own slaves would determine the number of slaves they wished to own by comparing the price of slaves with their marginal product. By the time the marginal product of additional slaves dropped below subsistence level, official households would stop buying more slaves; the demand schedule then became vertical. On the other hand, the supply schedule was being constantly pushed to the right by population increase until the equilibrium price of slaves in the free market became depressed to near-zero.

In short, properly interpreted, no data prove conclusively that the relative importance of slavery increased after the Southern Sung, even though the absolute number of slaves possibly increased. In fact, it was common practice among wealthy Ming households in the Kiangnan region to convert hereditary servants into tenant-servants by leasing some land to them. As Chapter 8 will show in greater detail, tenant-servants had their own families, owned property, and enjoyed the privilege of sending their sons to local schools. This category of workers may be regarded as a transitional institution in providing agricultural labor.

Wage Earners

The status of agricultural workers before the Sung, in contrast, is clear-cut and has never posed problems of interpretation. Judging from the Han materials that mention the circumstances under which workers were employed, no long-term or hereditary servitude was required. During the Sui and T'ang, workers were hired legally by farm households under the equitable field system. Surviving documents from this period show that employers and workers signed employment contracts that usually specified the following: (1) the person to be hired was a *fan-jen* (ordinary person); (2) there was an agreed-upon length of employment, usually one year; (3) the agreed-upon wage rate, usually a certain amount of grain per month, was stated; (4) the type and nature of the work were specified; and (5) the amount of penalty payment in case of contract violation was stated.[55] This contract form was almost standardized, and in no case can we find indications that workers were reduced to an inferior position.

Nor can we find from the materials of the Northern Sung any sign that workers were not free persons enjoying both full freedom of movement and the right to resign from a particular workplace. The status of the so-called *ti-k'e*, however, was different. They were wage-earning farm hands hired by contracts with terms of employment so long as to qualify them as slavelike subordinates. A *ti-k'e* wishing to terminate his contract prematurely was compelled to pay a sum comparable to redemption money.

As explained earlier, it was during the Ming that workers hired for a period of one year or longer were accorded an inferior status relative to their employers. This was not a sign of enslavement, strictly speaking, because no additional economic exploitation was incurred as a result of this new inferior legal standing. As soon as the work contract terminated or the worker resigned, his inferior status relative to his employer would be automatically removed.

Ironically, the Manchus, who as a people were rather dependent on the use of slaves, took several effective measures after they came to power to improve the status of workers and tenant-servants. As noted earlier,

157

a number of imperial decrees issued after 1727 abrogated legal discrimination against some categories of people on the basis of the inferior-superior relationship. Except for those whose inferior status was clearly substantiated by sale agreements, all suppliers of labor were equals with their employers and landlords.

Slavery was officially banned by the Manchu government in 1909 as part of its modernization program. A continual increase in population had ultimately rendered the use of labor from other sources more economical than slaves, whose cost of supervision was high. Therefore, the abolition of slavery in China was a relatively peaceful and smooth process.

In conclusion, three observations may be made. First, the Chinese rulers and their laws considered all types of labor transactions as market activities and emphasized the voluntary principle and the freedom of making contracts between consenting parties. Even in a slave sale agreement, the slave might ask to reserve the right of self-redemption or to specify the type of services to be rendered. The Ch'ing government's 1759 ruling, which defined *ku-kung-jen* as long-term farm workers under written contracts, merely reiterated the old tradition of freedom to make contracts. In effect, the government legalized discrimination as long as the worker had signed a written contract in which he accepted this discriminatory master-servant relationship and his inferior status.

Second, farm workers always had the freedom to accept or reject long-term employment as well as the full right to quit. Based on this general foundation, the inferior status accorded to farm workers, for whatever reason, should be regarded as part of the terms of employment, just like the wage rate. For a person could reject an opportunity of long-term employment if he considered the wage rate too low; by the same token he could reject an employment opportunity if he felt the status specified in the contract too inferior to be acceptable.

Third, for terms of employment in general, we observe a deteriorating trend in Chinese history. The status of farm workers during the Han was not at all inferior, as evidenced by the fact that several famous Han scholars served as farm workers or even brought classic works of literature along with them while hoeing in field. Likewise, no sign of inferior status can be detected in workers during the T'ang. Their status began to deteriorate after the Sung, a trend that was accompanied, as Chapter 9 will show, by a decline in the real wage rate. As part of the terms of employment, both trends reflected the oversupply of labor. In an economy with a scarcity of labor, people could obtain sufficient labor either by enslaving others forcibly or by enticing the voluntary supply with good wages. To enforce legislation like the 1588 law under such conditions would be impractical because it would raise the wage rate substantially in the labor market. The deterioration in both wage rates and the legal status of workers during the Ming-Ch'ing period was clearly a result of the oversupply of labor.

8

Tenurial Landlordism

The Historical Development of Tenancy

Private land ownership and tenancy have been intimately connected over the past two thousand years of Chinese history. One of the earliest records of tenancy is the famous statement of the Confucian scholar Tung Chung-shu during the Western Han: "When people cultivate the land of the powerful families, 50 percent of the yield is taxed away [by the landlords]."[1] Apart from indicating the level of rent at that time, this passage suggests two interesting attitudes toward rent collection. First, the notion of paying rent to a landlord on the basis of land productivity had not yet been distinguished from the notion of paying taxes to the state under the old system of public ownership; rent was in effect seen as a private tax. Second, Han scholars, still nostalgic about the ancient well field system, were reluctant to endorse the right of landowners to collect payments from tenants on the basis of land ownership. This attitude was sharply opposed to that of the Confucian scholars in later dynasties who accepted the private ownership system as the natural order of things.

Another important Han statement about finances was Wang Mang's proposal that private land ownership be abolished: "The powerful families suppress the common people by dividing land [*fen t'ien*] among them, and then steal the land taxes that should go to the state. Although the official rate of land tax is merely one-thirtieth, the powerful families actually tax the common people at a rate of 50 percent for the use of land."[2]

Fen-t'ien was the term used in Han times to denote the sharecropping system. Since Wang Mang did not consider private ownership of land an acceptable institution, he equated the collection of rents by landlords from their sharecroppers with "stealing" the land revenues (*chia*) that should have gone to the state. The confusion between a land tax and a land rent is again apparent here. This passage confirms not only the prevailing rent of 50 percent for land rents but the confusion between taxes and rents.

These two documents indicate that tenancy was a common practice in Han China. Many prominent figures, such as Cheng Hsuan and Yang Chen, are said to have rented land for cultivation at one time or another in their lives.[3] Tenants were also recorded in individual household registers at the local government level.

A number of significant changes in the tenancy system took place under the Western Chin in the late third century. On one hand, the government transformed the right to have tenants into a privilege extended only to those holding offices or honorary titles. Tenant farmers were thus reclassified as subordinates of those landlord-officials and were no longer entered in separate household registers. On the other hand, the government restricted the number of tenants who could lawfully be retained by landlord-officials: a first-rank official was entitled to up to 50 tenant households, an eighth-rank official to one.[4] It is not clear whether or not these measures represented the ruler's efforts to curb the total number of tenants countrywide.

The aggregate number of tenants, however, was definitely reduced when the equitable field system came into force. The universal land allotment instituted by the government rendered tenancy unnecessary except in two special cases. First, the so-called office land (*chih-t'ien*) might be leased to tillers with the rental income serving as the officeholder's salary.[5] Second, fragmented plots separated by long distances could be leased by mutual exchange to minimize inconvenience. The T'ang archives unearthed from Turfan show that such tenancy arrangements were legal and openly registered (and perhaps required by law) in the government files.[6]

As the equitable field system degenerated, both private land ownership and regular tenancy gradually revived. Historical records reveal that some *chuang yuan* used their tenants as a labor pool. During the Sung, all landless people were registered as nonresident households, in contrast to resident households, which owned at least some land. According to government regulations, registration forms requested the following information:[7]

For upper-class resident households:

> Name (head of household)
> Classification
> Have you been conscripted into public service?
> Number of household members

161

For lower-class resident households:

> Name
> Occupation
> From whom do you rent land?
> Number of household members

For nonresident households:

> Name
> Where did you live before moving to this village?
> How many years have you been in this village?
> From whom do you rent land?
> Number of household members

Many lower-class resident households were actually partial tenants or owner-tenants, typically owning a small quantity of land while simultaneously leasing additional land from a landlord. A nonresident household was one that had migrated and owned no land. Nonresident households in fact consisted of tenant farmers together with a few other categories of landless people. According to an account by Ou-yang Hsiu, a landlord with about 10,000 *mou* of land usually supported several dozen non-resident households, which fell into the following categories: (1) hired hands who contributed their labor but used the landlord's oxen; (2) share-croppers who used their own oxen to work on the landlord's land; (3) the so-called *she-t'ien-fu* (hired hand for slash-and-burn agriculture) who came once every two or three years on a fallowing schedule to use the slash-and-burn method to cultivate mountain fields.[8] The third category of farmers was perhaps not common except in Hupeh, Szechwan, and Kweichow, the areas that Ou-yang Hsiu described.

Migrant landless households ranged from one-third to one-half of all households during the Northern Sung. As noted in Chapter 6, this percentage shifted downward because of wider distribution of land ownership. If we combine landless, nonresident households and partial tenants, who belonged to the lower class or fifth grade of resident households but owned tracts of land inadequate for subsistence, the ratio must exceed 50 percent for most of the Sung period. Precisely what proportion of these people were tenants is not known, but nonquantitative data suggest that the incidence of tenants was greater where population density was high, as it was in the south.

A low population density provided stronger incentives for landlords to keep slaves, since the cost of using tenant-cultivators in such regions was high because of heavy competition for scarce labor. As one writer remarked in 1087 about the high mobility of tenants. "Rich people invite migrants to be their tenants. Before harvest each year, they make loans and lend other things to the migrants. If they once fail to show generosity and care, the tenants are certain to go somewhere else the following year."[9] A more detailed account was given for a district in Anhwei: In the region of An-feng, resident households are handicapped by the lack of migrants. Some migrants have arrived this year. There is keen competition among resident households to get hold of the migrants by lending them seeds, houses, oxen, and implements, which add up to several hundreds or thousands of cash. As a rule, no interest is charged in such cases.[10]

In some places, the competition between landlords for tenants was so intense that tenants would leave for other farms offering better terms even before they finished reaping the harvest and completed a year's contract. In some remote areas in Szechwan and Kweichow, where population density was exceedingly low and government control was weak, local magnates, instead of enticing tenants, retained them by force. Both situations created difficulties for the Sung government, which had simultaneously put forth an antidesertion law to prevent tenants from leaving farms before harvest and a law prohibiting the retention of tenants by force.

Because of continued population expansion, the Ming dynasty witnessed a dramatic change in the nature of agricultural institution. This change took two forms. First, a decline in the marginal product of slaves relative to the high cost of using them, together with the government restrictions against slaveowning by ordinary households, caused a decrease in relative importance, if not the absolute numbers of slaves as a source of agricultural labor. As an interim step, many households converted their slaves and hereditary servants into *tien p'u* (tenant-servants). The second form of institutional transformation was the increased use of farm workers, which was followed, toward the late Ming, by a further shift to tenancy. By these means managerial landlordism gradually gave way to tenurial landlordism, a change lucidly and convincingly documented by Shen's *Agricultural Handbook*, cited in Chapter 7. The same trend continued through the Ch'ing.

163

TABLE 8.1
Proportion of Tenanted Land by Province in the 1930's

Province	Buck	Land Commission	Province	Buck	Land Commission
Hopei	9.8%	12.9%	Chekiang	31.0%	51.3%
Shantung	9.8	12.6	Fukien	55.7	39.3
Honan	19.7	27.3	Kwangtung	59.6	77.0
Shansi	15.8		Kwangsi	26.0	21.2
Shensi	17.4	16.6	Yunnan	27.6	
Kansu	9.1		Kweichow	25.8	
Kiangsu	33.3	42.3	Suiyuan	5.0	8.8
Anhwei	51.0	52.4	Ningsia	0.2	
Kiangsi	51.4	45.1	Tsinghai	9.5	
Hupeh	31.2	27.9	National		
Hunan	36.9	47.8	average	28.7%	30.7%
Szechwan	52.4				

SOURCES: Land Commission, p. 37; Buck, statistical volume, various tables.

Some quantitative data on tenurial landlordism in the Kiangnan area during the Ming and Ch'ing dynasties are available from four fish-scale land registers I have examined. These furnish, for each plot of farmland registered, information about whether a plot was cultivated by the owner himself or leased out to a tenant. If the plot was leased to a tenant, the name of the tenant was sometimes recorded on the register as well. From these registers, all for unknown locations, I have calculated the percentages of owner-cultivated land as follows: (1) 34.4 percent (1581); (2) 53.4 percent (sometime between 1645 and 1655); (3) 24.7 percent (1676); (4) 37.5 percent (year unknown). Obviously tenant farming was common in the sixteenth and seventeenth centuries. It is unclear, however, what percentage of tenants were free tenants and what percentage tenant-servants.

More data on land tenure were collected in the 1920's and 1930's by the Chinese government, private scholars, research organizations, and the Japanese-operated South Manchuria Railway Company. In 1937, John Buck of Nanking University estimated that 28.6 percent of the total farmland in the country was leased to tenants.[11] A slightly higher proportion (30.7 percent) of land leased to tenants was given by the Land Commission.[12] The provincial data from these two sources, shown in Table 8.1, are less close than the aggregate ratios, but both show the same basic regional pattern.

TABLE 8.2

Proportion of Tenant Households by Province in the 1930's

Province	National Bureau	Land Commission	Directorate of Statistics
Chahar	31%	8.3%	27%
Suiyuan	31	17.2	20
Ningsia	20		
Tsinghai	22		
Kansu	18		
Shensi	18	10.5	29
Shansi	16	1.9	13
Hopei	10	5.4	13
Shantung	10	4.6	9
Kiangsu	30	21.7	32
Anhwei	42	35.3	55
Honan	20	7.2	22
Hupeh	41	14.9	51
Szechwan	51		57
Yunnan	36		28
Kweichow	45		35
Hunan	50	19.4	34
Kiangsi	14	14.2	39
Chekiang	47	26.2	42
Fukien	44	14.5	69
Kwangtung	46	51.9	46
Kwangsi	38	9.3	31
National average	30%	15.7%	26%

SOURCES: National Agricultural Research Bureau, 5, no. 12 (Dec. 1937): 330; Land Commission, p. 35; Directorate of Statistics, p. 8.

Tenant households and partial-tenant households as a percentage of total rural households were computed by Buck as follows:

Category	Tenants	Partial tenants
National average	17%	29%
Wheat region	6%	18%
Rice region	25%	37%

Provincial statistics on tenant households were presented by the National Agricultural Research Bureau, the Land Commission, and the Directorate of Statistics, respectively, and are displayed in Table 8.2. The somewhat larger discrepancies stem from the different definitions for tenants used in those surveys. More reliable data are presented in the sample studies conducted by the South Manchuria Railway. Those findings, shown in Table 8.3, are more usable because unified definitions have been

165

TABLE 8.3
Proportion of Tenant Households in Various North China Areas According to Sample South Manchuria Railway Company Surveys, 1933-1940

Area	Year	Percent of tenant households
North China	1938	5.0%
Ting-hsien, Hopei	1933	4.6
Wang-tu, Hopei	1933	1.9
P'ing-shan, Hopei	1933	0
I-hsien, Hopei	1933	1.2
Lin-ch'ing, Shantung	1942	6.5
Ch'ang-shu, Kiangsu	1939	55.0
Nan-t'ung, Kiangsu	1941	43.0
Three counties, Honan	1936	25.0
Three counties, Hupeh	1936	46.0
Five counties, Anhwei	1936	65.0
Three counties, Kiangsi	1936	47.0
T'ai-an, Shantung	1939	5.5
Chi-hsien, Hopei	1935	7.8
Sixteen counties, Hopei	1936	20.6
Feng-jen, Hopei	1939	29.6
Huo-lu, Hopei	1939	11.2
Hui-min, Shantung	1939	5.8
Chang-te, Honan	1940	43.0

SOURCE: See Chao and Chen 1982, p. 354.

adopted throughout. It should be noted that all these studies classified permanent tenants as tenants. As will be discussed later, persons tilling lands on permanent tenure contracts, a system very popular in Kiangsu, Chekiang, and Anhwei, actually possessed partial property rights on the lands they were tilling; they were thus, strictly speaking, joint owners.

The quantitative data from the 1920's and 1930's are generally consistent with previous observations that managerial landlordism gave way to tenurial landlordism during the Ming Ch'ing and that the relative share of owner-cultivators in the rural sector increased during the same period of time. Both trends I believe to be a response to the same force—the rise in population.

Types of Tenancy and Levels of Rent

Historical documents of the Han, including those cited in the preceding section, suggest that the dominant, perhaps even exclusive, form of tenancy in the private sector during that time was the sharecropping system, or what Han writers called *fen-t'ien* (dividing or sharing land). Public tenants in state colonies paid fixed rents, probably for administrative convenience,[13] yet even such colonies had converted to sharecropping by the end of the Eastern Han.[14]

One notable feature of sharecropping contracts in traditional China was the remarkable stability of the distribution of shares, which remained almost unchanged for more than 2,000 years. According to the analysis in Chapter 1, the classic partial equilibrium theory of share tenancy asserts that the income share of sharecroppers ($1 - s$) is a price at which landlords hire sharecroppers. The latter are price takers who would supply their labor up to the point where

$$(1 - s) \frac{\partial F_3}{\partial L_3} = w$$

It follows that as the man-land ratio in the economy rises, the share for landlords (s) tends to rise, whereas the share for sharecroppers ($1 - s$) tends to decline. This effect is analogous to the case of price fluctuations in response to demand variations in product markets.

In contrast, general equilibrium theory contends that the landlord and the sharecropper are partners who negotiate an equilibrium compromise in which each party earns an income equal to the amount obtainable from alternative tenurial arrangements. This compromise may be attained through negotiating the distribution of shares—that is, s and $1 - s$, or relative contribution—that is, H_3/L_3, or both. Theoretically, it is possible for them to peg the distribution shares and merely negotiate their relative contributions of resources. This is precisely what happened in the long history of China. For more than twenty centuries, the usual distribution of shares under sharecropping was fixed at 50-50. The behavior of Chinese landlords and tenants thus clearly conformed with the postulates of general equilibrium theory; such a remarkable stability of share distribution over such a long span of time, and despite the continuously rising man-land ratio, is utterly inconceivable on the basis of partial equilibrium analysis.

The 50-50 distribution of shares not only seems to have been neutral but was also simple to effect. The tenant usually divided the land he farmed into two halves just before harvesting or else divided the grain harvested from the land into two equal piles; landlord and tenant would then toss a coin to determine who was to take which half. The chances

167

for the two parties were equal even if the two portions had not been equally divided.

The income of the landlord per unit of land increased under this arrangement—rather than remaining constant, as some scholars believe—because the amount of labor inputs per unit of land increased with the rising man-land ratio. It was, however, far easier to extract this higher income by increasing the number of tenants per unit of land than by keeping the number of tenants constant and gradually raising the landlord's share of the harvest. The 50-50 distribution was the basic formula used when the landlord supplied nothing but the land, as implied by all references to share tenancy before the T'ang.[15] Extra rent was required if oxen, farm implements, or seeds were provided by the landlord. State colonies in the third century, for example, stipulated: "The government and the public tenant will divide the crop equally if the latter provide oxen. . . . But, if oxen were supplied by the government, six-tenths go to the government and four-tenths to the tenant."[16]

Tenancy during the period of the equitable field system was somewhat complex. Of the tenancy contracts from the T'ang unearthed in Turfan and Tunhuang, all public and most private leases called for a fixed rent. The rental rates of contracts involving public land were considerably lower than those of private leases because the government had set a ceiling on the rent for common land. Yet even in this remote area at least one private contract was for share tenancy, calling for the fall harvest of wheat to be divided equally between landlord and tenant.[17] Elsewhere, however, all available T'ang data indicate a 50-50 distribution.[18] We may safely assume that, before this period, the basic form of land tenancy—with the exception of the Turfan-Tunhuang area—was sharecropping.

Between the tenth and twelfth centuries, share tenancy was restored as the exclusive form of tenancy contract.[19] The standard formula of division was again 50-50, with an additional 10 percent going to the landlord if he supplied oxen. There were only a few occasions during the early Southern Sung when the authorities of state colonies announced rent reductions of 10 to 20 percent because the land had been devastated by warfare or natural disaster.[20] More favorable shares were also given to tenants farming newly reclaimed lands.

Surviving records show that the fixed-rent system for public land was introduced in a given district after the adoption of the rice-wheat double-cropping system. Rent collection was greatly simplified by charging a fixed quantity of rice as payment for both crops. This formula was quickly imitated by the offices that managed income landholdings of the local public school systems (*hsueh-t'ien*) in various localities.[21] But the fixed-rent arrangement remained nonexistent among private landlords throughout the Southern Sung.

By the Yuan dynasty both forms of tenancy existed in the private sector. Although the Yuan literature continues to cite cases of sharecropping with a 50-50 income division,[22] a guidebook for peasants commonly used in that period contains a simple contract for fixed-rent tenancy.[23] The change from share tenancy to fixed rent accelerated in the Ming; most sample contracts contained in agricultural guidebooks published in that period were in the fixed-rent form. In a few cases there was an additional clause: "In any year of drought or flood, the landlord will be asked [by the tenant] to inspect the field and share with the tenant on an equal basis whatever can be reaped."[24] This arrangement was intended as an escape clause for tenants with fixed-rent contracts in the case of severe crop failure.

In the southern provinces the transition from share tenancy to fixed-rent tenancy went through an interim form, the so-called normal rent system (*cheng tsu*). The normal rent was calculated as half the highest historically recorded crop. Since the quantity was specified on the rental contract, it has the appearance of a fixed rent. After the harvest each year, however, the landlord was expected to lower the rent to accord with the actual yield. The reduction from the normal rent, called concession (*jang tsu*), theoretically would equal one-half the difference between actual and maximum yields. Thus, the rent actually charged was half the actual harvest, and the system was in effect a share tenancy.

Ming rental contracts collected by Fu I-ling from a few counties in Fukien indicate that the normal rent system was the dominant form. Contracts were printed in standardized format rather than individually handwritten.[25] The same transitional arrangement also prevailed in the Kiangnan area, as evidenced by the rental records of some Soochow bursaries collected by Muramatsu Yuji.[26] As a matter of interest, investigators found the normal rent system still in force in Sungchiang, Kiangsu as late as 1940.

During the Ming and Ch'ing, there were fewer instances of share contracts. Some stipulated the traditional 50-50 division,[27] whereas those in the double-cropping regions charged a rent of 60 percent of the early

TABLE 8.4
Distribution of Various Types of Tenurial Contracts in Kiangnan, 1522-1926

Name of landlord	Time period	Number of tenants	Type of contract (percent of total)		
			Share-cropping	Normal rent	Fixed rent
Wu	1522-1566	55		100%	
Cheng	1568-1790	207		72	28%
Chen	ca. 1600	63	3%	94	3
Ying	1600-1710	71		74	26
Unknown	1684-1696	96	2	76	22
Unknown	ca. 1690	556		100	
Unknown	ca. 1700	158		100	
Unknown	ca. 1700	93	56	34	10
Unknown	ca. 1700	36	13	55	32
Kuei	1723-1735	73	29	47	24
Unknown	1775-1780	151	2	62	36
Chang	ca. 1780	57	2	45	53
Li	1783-1800	59	12	35	53
Unknown	1783-1802	35	29	69	2
Unknown	1788-1801	17		6	94
47 families (paddy)	1790-1795	568	14	83	3
47 families (dry land)	1790-1795	365	1	88	11
Chung	1791	25	20	80	
Liao	1798-1828	19		89	11
Chi	1807-1814	51	25	75	
Chien	ca. 1820	50			100
Hsiang	1820-1830	50			100
Ting	1836	17	12	88	
Li	1851-1887	24	4		96
Yuan	1852	27	18		82
Unknown	1856-1869	35	9	68	23
Cheng	1856-1869	19	31	53	16
Wang	1857-1873	50	12		88
Chien	1861	17			100
Chung	1863-1888	63	5	63	32
Hsing	1864-1874	7		43	57
Hsu	1864-1880	35	34		66
So	1864-1880	57	23	77	
Sun	1866	62		100	
Sun	1866-1885	19		100	
Ching	1866-1903	11		73	27
Huang	1867	36			100
Yung	1868	33	18	27	55
Chuan	1868-1892	65	12	6	82
So	1869-1909	28	7	71	22
Tuan	1870-1890	149	2	92	6
Wu	1874	235	3		97
Yi	1879-1903	40			100
Piao	1881	166	8		92
Lou	1884-1889	50	4		96
Tuan	ca. 1890	83			100
Hsia	1894-1912	46	4		96
Wang	1894-1913	20		70	30
Huang	1894-1926	60			100
Cheng	1900	13			100
Chun	1900-1924	18	17		83

SOURCE: Documents held in Nanking University.

crop plus 40 percent out of the second crop.[28] In some cases of share tenancy, landlords personally supervised critical agricultural operations of tenants to ensure that tenants were exerting themselves.[29] But more often landlords or their agents would visit the farms only to observe the harvest. Thus the practice gave rise to a new term for sharecropping: supervised income division (*chien-fen-chih*).

The archives of the Ch'ing Ministry of Justice provide evidence of the decreased proportion of share tenancy contracts. Of the 888 lawsuits involving rent disputes during the reign of Ch'ien Lung (1736-95), 784 cases—about 88 percent of the total—involved fixed rent contracts. Of 102 lawsuits from the Chia Ch'ing reign (1796-1820) only 34 involved share tenants.[30]

An interesting new development is revealed in rent records from the Kiangnan region during the Ming-Ch'ing era: the simultaneous existence of a variety of contractual arrangements between a landlord and his tenants. Though it might seem a landlord would ordinarily prefer a uniform contract for all tenants, it appears that tenants had different preferences and were sometimes indulged in them. In several cases the landlords changed the type of tenant contract and remarked on the rent-collection books: "After consultation with the tenant, and with his consent, his tenancy contract has been changed from form x to form y."[31] Table 8.4 lists the three categories of tenant contracts and calculates the percentages of distribution for selected landlords. It is clear that very few landlords adopted one type of contract exclusively throughout the period recorded.

It is significant that landlords, at least in this region, switched their tenurial arrangements in the direction postulated by the general equilibrium theory as given in Chapter 1. Rent collection data in Table 8.4 are listed in chronological order, which allows us to see that the proportion of sharecropping decreased whereas the percentage of fixed-rent contracts gained over time.

Only in a few cases was the switch in the reverse direction—that is, from a fixed-rent contract to a sharecropping contract. Such cases occurred in only two special situations. At times share tenancy served as a temporary escape for poor tenants. The productivity of land often deteriorated drastically after two or three consecutive years of severe famine. Some landlords were then willing to share the suddenly increased risk with the tenants by temporarily suspending the fixed-rent contract and reverting to a share contract. I have found several such cases in two rent collection books, but the fixed-rent contracts were reinstated a few years later.

Another special circumstance under which a fixed-rent contract would be changed into a share contract was when the land was taken over by a new tenant, usually the son of the previous tenant. I believe that this change was most probably initiated by the new tenant who, being inexperienced and less knowledgeable, was more likely to be risk averse.

Even under the normal rent system there were occasions when the share arrangement was temporarily reinstated in years of extremely poor harvests. Ordinarily, under a normal rent contract the landlord had the right to evaluate the degree to which the actual harvest had fallen short of the bumper crop level, thereby determining the amount of concession to be allowed. This method, however, gave the landlord too much discretionary power and probably placed the tenant in an inequitable position during years of bad harvest; in such a situation a better and fairer solution would be an equal division of the actual harvest.

For five rent collection books that covered relatively long periods of twenty to fifty years, the average of actual rent payments as percentages of the stipulated normal rents were 72, 69, 73, 67, and 71 percent, for an overall average of 70 percent. The shortfall (i.e., 30 percent) may be regarded either as the average degree of concessions or as the difference between the average yield and the maximum yield of farmland in this region.

These historical data suggest that transaction cost was the primary factor responsible for the shift of the tenurial system from sharecropping to fixed-rent tenancy. As may be recalled, transaction cost here is broadly defined to include costs of administration and supervision. State colonies during the Han probably adopted the fixed-rent system because it required minimum supervision of fieldwork. This feature may also explain why fixed-rent contracts became prevalent during the same period as the equitable farm system; the leased lands of each landlord were so scattered that they rendered on-the-spot supervision impractical. As soon as the various parcels had been integrated into large tracts by the *chuang yüan*, however, fixed-rent contracts disappeared.

Costs of administration and supervision for share tenancy would be somewhat higher for absentee landlords, who in many ways resembled managers of public lands, but the cost was not high enough under the

172

single-crop system to compel absentee landlords before the Ming to give up share tenancy, as did the state colonies of the Southern Sung. The introduction of the double-cropping system and the further fragmentation of land in the Ming and Ch'ing raised enforcement costs to a level high enough to generate a gradual movement toward fixed-rent tenancy. The intensification of farming and the fragmentation of land ownership, however, were both the result of mounting population pressure. In the final analysis, therefore, it was population pressure, not the growth of absentee landlordism, that changed patterns of farm operation in premodern China.

Avoidance of risk might be responsible for some changes in the tenurial system in the short run, as evidenced by the "escape clause" in the fixed-rent contracts previously cited. Still, this factor could not influence the long-term trend of farm operation. In the long time frame of the Ming and Ch'ing, during which share tenancy gradually was transformed into fixed-rent tenancy, China's agriculture showed no discernible change in the risk factor. Moreover, many rent collection books kept by landlords during this time contain records of both share contracts and normal-rent contracts for leasing plots.

I have taken those books with relatively long records and computed the coefficients of variation for the actual rent payments under each type of tenancy contract. Let V be the coefficient of rent variation; it is defined as

$$V = \frac{\sigma}{M} \times 100$$

where M is the mean rent payment for each plot in N years covered by the rent records, and σ is the standard deviation. The results are presented in Table 8.5.

For each plot of tenanted land, the coefficient of rent variation V may be taken as a meaningful proxy for the degree of risk in production. The averaged coefficient of rent variation for the seven plots under share tenancy is 21.2, whereas that for the 31 plots under normal-rent tenancy is 17. The difference between the two figures is insufficient to demonstrate any significant difference in risk between the two categories of rent. In other words, share contracts were employed on the seven plots not necessarily because they involved greater risk in production.

Five rent collection books recorded a number of cases in which normal-rent contracts were converted into fixed-rent contracts during the record-

TABLE 8.5
Coefficients of Rent Variation for 38 Plots, Locations Unknown

Code number of plot	N	M	σ	V
Share contracts				
1	17	23.5	5.2	21.8
2	21	30.2	7.6	25.2
3	21	44.8	9.4	20.9
4	21	285.0	29.6	10.4
5	19	61.0	20.8	34.1
6	21	82.0	14.4	17.6
7	15	32.0	5.9	18.4
Normal rent contracts				
8	20	86.0	10.0	11.6
9	21	268.0	25.6	9.6
10	21	121.0	36.7	30.3
11	21	111.0	19.1	17.2
12	19	136.0	21.6	15.9
13	21	185.0	17.8	9.6
14	21	79.0	19.6	24.8
15	20	165.0	19.0	11.5
16	19	131.0	21.1	16.1
17	20	265.6	36.5	13.8
18	20	98.0	22.7	23.2
19	20	184.0	16.4	8.9
20	20	201.0	12.1	6.0
21	20	118.0	5.3	4.5
22	20	83.0	13.9	16.7
23	19	151.0	26.8	17.7
24	20	191.0	31.8	16.6
25	22	68.0	6.6	9.7
26	20	234.0	62.9	26.9
27	20	30.0	7.2	24.0
28	19	70.0	23.5	33.6
29	20	267.0	25.3	9.5
30	20	60.0	10.0	16.7
31	20	96.0	11.0	11.4
32	20	185.0	50.7	27.4
33	20	197.0	36.7	18.6
34	20	183.0	32.3	17.7
35	20	162.0	43.6	9.4
36	18	33.0	12.2	37.0
37	15	34.0	9.4	27.6
38	15	39.0	1.6	4.1

SOURCE: See Chao and Chen 1982, pp. 378-80.

ing period. We can easily compute the ratio of the new fixed-rent to the previous normal-rent level. Altogether there are 68 such cases in the five books; the average proportion is 67 percent.[32] This percentage is not significantly different from the average proportion (70 percent) of actual rent payments under normal-rent contracts to normal rents, as computed earlier. In other words, there is no statistical evidence that landlords raised the rents at the time of conversion to cover any increase in risk.

A similar comparison has been made for the cases in which share contracts had been converted into fixed-rent contracts during the recording period.[33] Six such cases exist; their rent comparisons are as follows:

Case	Avg. rent under share contract (catties)	Fixed rent (catties)	Case	Avg. rent under share contract (catties)	Fixed rent (catties)
1	55	60	4	157	160
2	85	90	5	125	120
3	240	252	6	171	180

Except for one plot, the fixed rent was slightly higher than the average share rent; evidently, the fixed rent was determined on the basis of the average of previous share rents. Fixed rents were slightly higher because even under the new contracts landlords still had to make some allowances to tenants during extremely difficult years.

The transformation of the tenurial system took place in other regions of the country as well and continued until the 1940's. This phenomenon is well documented in numerous twentieth-century survey reports. For instance, a survey conducted by the South Manchuria Railway Research Department in 1940 revealed the common practice throughout north China of converting share contracts into fixed-rent contracts.[34] In his collection of agricultural data from the years 1910-30, Li Wen-chih has also compiled numerous cases of this type along with the conversion agreements signed by the landlords and tenants involved.[35]

Table 8.6 presents the relative regional distribution of different tenurial contracts. Here the fixed cash rent and the fixed grain rent are combined without any differentiation. Based on Land Commission data, the proportion of share contracts in total tenancy exceeded 40 percent only in Chahar, Shansi, Shantung, and Honan; it was below 20 percent in all other provinces. In the southern provinces such as Chekiang, Kiangsi, and Kuangtung, where two crops were grown every year, the proportion was as low as 3 percent. The national average was 15 percent. The National Agricultural Research Bureau survey gave a higher national average, 28 percent, but it revealed a similar pattern of regional variation. Provinces with an incidence of share tenancy below 20 percent were important centers of double cropping. On the other hand, provinces with an incidence over 33 percent are north of the Yangtze river (except for

TABLE 8.6
Proportion of Share Tenancy Among All Tenants by Province in the 1930's

Province	Land Commission	National Bureau	Province	Land Commission	National Bureau
Chahar	52.0%	29.7%	Hupei	4.0%	21.8%
Suiyuan		45.7	Szechwan		15.8
Ningsia		35.4	Yunnan		24.9
Chinghai		35.6	Kweichow		50.5
Kansu		34.5	Hunan	18.4	18.4
Shensi	5.8	25.9	Kiangsi	1.9	12.8
Shansi	42.8	26.7	Chekiang	2.4	7.1
Hopei	16.7	26.1	Fukien	8.5	25.3
Shantung	40.2	39.1	Kwangtung	0	17.7
Kiangsu	11.9	19.5	Kwangsi	14.5	28.5
Anhwei	18.3	33.4	National		
Honan	71.6	44.0	average	14.9%	28.1%

SOURCES: National Agricultural Research Bureau, 3, no. 4 (Apr. 1935): 90; Land Commission, p. 42.

TABLE 8.7
Average Rental Rate of Share Contracts
by Province in the 1930's

Province	Average rent (percent)	Province	Average rent (percent)
Kiangsu	43.6%	Shensi	46.9%
Chekiang	48.1	Kansu	41.0
Anhwei	44.0	Tsinghai	60.0
Hupei	42.5	Kwangtung	44.7
Hunan	49.1	Kwangsi	43.8
Hopei	47.5	Yunnan	45.1
Shantung	53.8	Chahar	35.0
Shansi	51.4	Suiyuan	37.5
Honan	49.9		

SOURCE: Directorate of Statistics, p. 47.

Kweichow), where the colder climate prohibited extensive double crop-ping. Using Buck's data compiled in the early 1930's, I have computed the rank correlation between the multiple-cropping indices and the percent-ages of share tenancy in the eight agricultural regions.[36] The result is $P = -.80$, suggesting a close relation between the two variables.

The Directorate of Statistics of the Chinese government published a set of data on the average rental rate under share contracts in various provinces. The fact that most of the averages, as shown in Table 8.7, were not far off the 50 percent mark suggests that the dominant practice was still a 50-50 division. Indeed, this tradition had persisted for more than 2,000 years, a stability that is utterly inconsistent with the classic partial equilibrium theory of land rent.

Conditions of Tenancy

Social Status

The social and legal status of tenants in premodern China fluctuated considerably. At no time, however, were Chinese tenants debased to the status of the serf, as the term is construed in Europe. Traditionally, Chinese tenants were basically free men, though their freedom was at times restricted.

Han tenants were not classified as the subordinates of any private household; hence, they had their own household registration independent of that of their landlord. Nor were they bound to the soil, public or private. In fact, the high mobility of the rural population presented successive Han governments with the worrisome problem of coping with huge and politically sensitive migrations among regions. The historical data state unequivocally that written contracts existed between public tenants and offices managing public lands for rent.[37] Although no documented evidence of private tenurial contracts exists, the situation could not have been worse for private tenants. As mentioned earlier, many eminent scholars or high-ranking officials of the Han worked as tenants at some point in their lives, a situation that apparently was not frowned upon by society.

Han tenants and landlords were entwined in a purely economic relationship. This association began to change toward the end of the Han, when the population decline created a serious shortage of manpower and the demand for tenants increased substantially. Commenting on Chin state colonies in the third century, Fu Hsuan said:

> The operation of state colonies during the early Wei did not emphasize the quantity of land cultivated, but stressed the quality of cultivation. Consequently plain land yielded more than 10 *tou* of grain per *mou* whereas paddy land yielded several dozen *tou*. . . . But now it is the quantity of land cultivated that is emphasized. The tenant-soldiers are greedier and pay less attention to the quality of work, resulting in a meager yield of no more than a few *tou* of grain per *mou*. In the most serious cases, the harvest is not enough to compensate for the seeds consumed.[38]

177

This interesting phenomenon was described in Chapter 1. If the tenant under a share contract had strong bargaining powers that enabled him to lease any quantity of land, he tended to thin out his labor to the largest possible area of land until the marginal product of land dropped to zero.

This stronger bargaining power of tenants could not last, however, because in a general equilibrium model landlords had the option of acquiring labor in more economical ways. What they failed to obtain by using carrots they could try to obtain by applying sticks. Thus, after the third century, farming with retainers and slaves spread further at the expense of tenancy. Even those tenants that remained suffered more restrictions because a new law stipulated that tenants should be registered as subordinates of their landlords instead of as independent households. On the other hand, the same law restricted the numbers of tenants that each official's family could employ. In actuality, social mobility was reduced to a minimum during the Chin after elite families became virtually hereditary.

Tenancy relations in the early T'ang represent another extreme case. Tenancy contracts from the Turfan area suggest that leasers and lessees interacted as equals. This circumstance probably derived from the fact that many leasers were recipients of public lands rather than major landlords so that in reality the two sides were equal socially as well as legally. Furthermore, the fragmentation and scattering of land created a higher degree of dependence of leasers on lessees. Unfortunately, this equality quickly disappeared after the equitable field system collapsed in the late T'ang, when the monopolistic power of large private landowners again reduced tenants to an inferior position economically, if not legally.

In the early years of the Northern Sung, interestingly, the government first adopted a policy to promote the welfare of tenants and farm workers, then sharply reversed its policy orientation. To be sure, one important feature of the system throughout the Sung was to grant tenants and other landless people the right to register as independent households, *k'e hu*, rather than as subordinates of landlords or employers. As Hu Hung put it, "Both the *chu hu* and the *k'e hu* are *ch'i min* [equal citizens] in the country."[39] The detailed provisions in the law regarding the status of *k'e hu*, however, were revised later in the period.

During the early years of the Northern Sung, tenants enjoyed a high degree of mobility and a favorable bargaining position because of keen competition for farm labor among landowners. The government also made a strenuous attempt to provide better legal protection for less privileged people. The second emperor, T'ai Tsung, announced in 989: "According to the old system, slaves and servants who committed crimes were branded on the face by the masters themselves. Yet slaves and servants were originally ordinary people. They should be punished [by the government], and private branding by masters is to be strictly prohibited."[40] The same order was reiterated by T'ai Tsung's successor, Chen Tsung, in 1003.

The high mobility of Sung tenants generated considerable instability in landlord-tenant relations. This instability in turn triggered three reactions on the part of landlords: some attempted to retain tenants by coercive means, others were inclined to negotiate longer-term contracts with their tenants. A crucial issue was the best method of preventing the so-called "untimely departure" of tenants before harvest. Early regulations tried to forestall this occurrence by restricting the movement of tenants unless they could present letters of consent from their landlords. This provision was soon distorted by some landlords who compelled tenants to stay by refusing to furnish letters of consent even after harvest was over. Thus the original law was revised in 1027 to protect tenants' freedom of movement after the harvest.

> According to the old regulations for the prefectures of Chiang-nan, Huai-nan, Liang-che, Fu-chien, Chin-hu and Kuang-nan, agricultural tenants of private parties may not move away at an untimely moment. They are only allowed to live elsewhere if their masters send them and furnish them with permits. Many are maltreated by their masters and are prevented from moving. Henceforth, tenants shall no longer need a permit from their masters to move, but they must give notice of their intention only after they have gathered in the harvest from every field. Thus each side has his own freedom. That is, tenants may not move away at an untimely moment according to their personal whims. If their masters obstruct them, they may appeal to the magistrates.[41]

Competition for tenants was more complicated in the sparsely populated mountainous region of Kuei-chou, where there were numerous state-owned farms. The owners of private latifundia, mostly powerful tribesmen, were so desperately in need of farm labor that they resorted to "pirating" tenants from the state farms. As a countermeasure special regulations, known as the antirunaway law, were announced in 1052 to govern the movement of public tenants in that particular region. A Sung historical account recorded: "An order was issued in 1052 demanding that those who had run away from the state farms in Kuei-chou province and other provinces be forced to return to their previous farms and not be permitted to live elsewhere."[42] After an additional length of time, this law, specially devised for state farms in a special region, was broadened and revised so that it could apply to all tenants who had defected from private landlords. Thus, the Sung Ministry of Finance ruled in 1184:

> If, in the future, any household issues a complaint that its tenants have been pilfered, this should be dealt with in accordance with the special law [of 1052]. Henceforth, in dealing with tenants who have run away and gone to live elsewhere: (1) those who have done so within the past three years shall be compelled to return, with all their relatives, to their former masters. Notices will be posted throughout the prefecture that if runaway families return to their lands within two months, they shall not be recklessly seized because of their failure to fulfil their obligations; and (2) those who did so more than three years ago, and are living peaceably and do not wish to return, shall be allowed to do as they please. If, in the future, any families are made to move, then the authorities shall pursue them and bring them back regardless of any question of a three-year limit. If violence has been used to effect the forcible removal of a tenant, this shall be judged in accordance with the laws on kidnapping.[43]

Conceivably, in those areas where the population was unusually meager, landlords tended to distort this antirunaway law to their own advantage. The government was caught between its desire to stabilize landlord-tenant relations and its pledge to protect the basic rights of tenants. This was exactly the dilemma faced by the governor of Kuei-chou, Fan Sun, who finally announced a further revision to the antirunaway law in 1205:

> In the remote border areas of Shih-chou and Chien-chou, etc., which form part of this province, there are countless mountains and valleys, the land is vast, and inhabitants are scarce. Large proprietors need men for cultivation. Rich and powerful families compete for fieldhands. They either entice landless people [nonresident households] or force them to move. I would request a few revisions to the 1052 antirunaway law governing the tenants. The landless persons themselves may be recruited to serve, but this obligation shall not be extended to any of their families, or to their womenfolk. When [a peasant] has mortgaged or sold his fields and house, he shall be free in due order to leave the property and may not be made to act as a tenant paying rent. Nor may he be made to serve as a fieldhand, even if he

does not pay rent. All those who have borrowed either money or goods may only be required to return these as specified in their contracts. It is forbidden to coerce them into becoming fieldhands. When a tenant dies and his widow wishes to marry again, she should be allowed to do as she pleases; and the daughters of tenants ought to be freely betrothed and married. In this way, the people of the deep hills and barren valleys may live contented.[44]

Obviously the Sung government made serious efforts to protect the rights of tenants from the coercion of local magnates.

The high mobility of tenants had a positive as well as a negative side. Government legislation, which vacillated between the two conflicting goals of protecting the rights of tenants and maintaining a stable supply of labor inputs for all landowners, could hardly accomplish both. But it did compel landlords to devise an alternate approach in achieving stable relations with their tenants, namely, instead of using force to retain tenants, they began to negotiate long-term tenancy contracts with tenants. Thus, the practice of granting long-term contracts emerged for the first time and gradually spread; aspects of the arrangement ultimately evolved into the well-known permanent tenancy system found in Ming and Ch'ing China.

The high degree of mobility and freedom enjoyed by tenants in the early Sung triggered yet another reaction—the attempt by landlords to justify control over tenants and other types of farm labor supplies on ethical grounds. The landlord-tenant relationship was interpreted as a type of family kinship that was to be subject to the same set of familial ethics strongly advocated by the neo-Confucians of the Sung. This school emphasized the unconditional obedience of tenants to their masters and even called for a somewhat unbalanced handling of the two categories of people in the legal system. A typical argument of this type was provided by Hu Hung in a letter he wrote to General Liu Chi in the mid-twelfth century:

There is a chain of obedience stretching from masters down to tenants; and it is by means of this [chain] that the state is supplied. It cannot be dispensed with for a single day. Since this is so, how can tenants be allowed to do as they please? This would result in their masters being unable to control them! Tenants depend on their masters for their livelihood, and so they have to provide them with services and submit to their discipline. Officials should inflict vigorous punishment on tenants, and forbid them to

181

act in accordance with their own pleasures, in the event that a master issues a complaint on any of the following grounds: (1) that his tenants are behaving perversely and refuse to recognize the distinction between superior and inferior; (2) that they are practicing commerce and not working hard at farming and sericulture; (3) that they are drinking or gambling without restraint, and are unamenable to discipline; (4) that, being unmarried, they are seducing other men's wives; or (5) that, having many adult males in their families and more than enough food and clothing, they have been able to buy half an acre or an acre of farmland and a house, have set up a tax-paying household of their own, and wish to leave their master.[45]

The legal discrimination against tenants actually began in 1090, when the new law was passed, stating specifically: "If a tenant offends his master, he shall be punished one degree more severely than commoners. If a master offends his tenant and if the crime normally calls for flogging, he shall be pardoned; if the crime normally calls for a punishment of banishment or more severe sentences, his punishment shall be reduced by one degree."[46] Legal discrimination against tenants was further intensified during the reign of Shao Hsing of the Southern Sung (1131-62). The evolution of such discrimination was described by the historian Wang Chü-cheng:

> The case of killing a tenant by his master would be sentenced normally during the Chia You period [1056-63]. But it would be sentenced one degree lighter during the Yuan Feng period [1078-85]; instead of a death penalty the killer would be banished to the neighboring county. By the period of Shao Hsing [1131-62], the killer would be banished to a new location in the same city.[47]

The punishments for tenants, on the other hand, escalated accordingly. When the new discriminatory law was not faithfully enforced by some local magistrates, Chu Hsi, the greatest Confucian scholar of that period, submitted a serious protest to the emperor, insisting that the penalty should be determined not only on the basis of the crime committed but also according to the standing of the offender in his family.

Judging from available data, however, legal discrimination against tenants, unlike servants and wage earners, was not strictly enforced in the Southern Sung or in ensuing dynasties. Ming tenants suffered none of the penal inferiority imposed by the Sung code. The inferior status of tenants applied only in the area of personal relations. Thus, in 1372 the Ming government decreed that, whereas age and genealogical order were to determine seating at festivals and banquets, the seating of a tenant must be below that of his master regardless of their respective ages.[48] This ruling can hardly be interpreted as a sign of enslavement of tenants, for even in today's China the seating order at banquets is determined by official rank and employer-employee relations.

To my knowledge, none of the surviving tenant contracts from the Ming-Ch'ing period imply that the tenant was other than a free man. Some contracts clearly stated that the tenant had the right to terminate the contract and move to any place he chose. The fact that the actual turnover rate of tenants was low in the Ming was attributable partly to the widespread permanent tenure system and partly to the rigid classification of household registration, later abolished in the Ch'ing.

Ming and Ch'ing laws imposed heavy penalties on those landlords who flogged tenants or abused tenants' dependents. Forcing a woman from a tenant household to marry as a concubine, for example, was punishable by hanging.[49] Of course, there were always some whose behavior deviated from the law; Chinese history has no shortage of stories graphically relating how tenants and their dependents were abused by landlords.

The fact that the status of tenant-servants was distinguished from that of tenants has constituted an important source of misunderstanding regarding the status of ordinary tenants. Either converted from household servants by their masters or having commended themselves to their masters, tenant-servants possessed a status between that of free tenants and that of servants. The treatment they actually received varied considerably from area to area or from case to case, depending on local customs, the native population, and the power and wealth of their masters.[50] Generally, those who had become tenant-servants through commendation and especially when they had surrendered their own property, enjoyed better terms. They might have received, from their masters, land, farm implements, housing, and often a female slave or servant as wife; in return they paid reduced rent and performed various chores. Only in a few exceptional cases were tenant-servants literally bound to their master's land. For some, servitude was hereditary, but the large majority could leave and work elsewhere. Some were only nominally tenant-servants of a powerful family and actually maintained a high degree of independence in terms of property ownership and occupational freedom. Others owned fairly large tracts of land, lived in large houses,[51] and bequeathed their property to their offspring. Many tenant-servants had their obligations specified in contracts. Legally, any dispute between master and tenant-servant had to be adjudicated by the local magistrate; the master had no authority to punish his tenant-servants privately. Furthermore, as time passed, this category of people came to resemble free tenants more closely than servants or slaves.

Duration of Tenure

It is unclear whether written tenure contracts were in use among private households during Han times. Among the tenure contracts from the T'ang dynasty—to date, the earliest samples available—one carried a stipulated duration of 22 years and another of three years; the rest did not mention any specific duration. Most tenancy contracts before the twelfth century, written or otherwise, did not specify duration, which became a source of frequent dispute between tenants and landlords. Some landlords interpreted the unspecified, indefinite contracts as embodying long-term arrangements and demanded that their tenants do likewise, yet the annoying problem of the "untimely departure" of tenants who left the land before harvest remained.

Because Sung legislation was ineffective in stabilizing tenancy, in the twelfth century the stipulation of long and specific terms of tenure began to seem like a promising solution. There were many cases involving school lands in which contractual relations were so durable that the managing offices of these public lands even engraved the names of tenants on large stone tablets.[52] The Southern Sung, in fact, may be identified as the beginning of the permanent tenancy system in China.

Nevertheless, the long-term tenancy arrangement was, and still is, subject to controversy. Theoretically, a long-term contract could provide stability and assurance to both sides, but it could as easily become one-sided protection simply because the landlord could terminate a long-term tenancy contract at any time by selling his land to others and buying a new plot as a replacement. The only solution to this problem would be to write down the name of the tenant on the land purchase document and compel the new owner to honor the tenant's right to till the land as a necessary condition of the transaction. But this arrangement, sometimes called *sui t'ien tien hu* (tenants attached to the land), was construed as enslavement of tenants.[53] Consequently, a new decree was issued in 1153: "Henceforth, when private households mortgage or sell their lands, no names of tenants may be included in the contracts. The new owner of the land, on the other hand, may not abrogate the tenants' right to till the land involved. Whoever violates this law may be sued."[54] The beneficiaries of this new law were tenants under long-term contracts at the time of its passage. The permanent right to till the land eventually became a valuable asset to tenants because they could transfer the right at high prices.

Different regions of China witnessed great variation in duration of tenancy during the Ming-Ch'ing. According to Fu I-ling's report, residents of Yung-an, Fukien used standard printed ten-year tenancy contracts that were renewable.[55] Rent collection documents from Anhwei and Chekiang I have examined do not specify the terms of tenancy, but the turnover rate of tenants was low. This region was one in which the permanent tenancy system was highly popular, and so some of the tenants recorded in these rent collection books could well have been permanent tenants. In one case, during a year marking a change of tenants, the following remark was noted down: "The new tenant is the son of the previous tenant."

Cases in which tenants' names were written on the land purchase documents have also been found. Such provisions seem to have had the effect of protecting the tenants. A deed signed by a certain Wang family as the buyer in the seventh month of 1541 included the following clause: "The land is tilled by Wang Chi and Hsiang Yuan [as tenants], both parties [the seller and the buyer] agree. The rent is 147 catties per annum, both parties agree." Apparently, this clause was meant to provide assurance and security to the two tenants.

More frequently, names of tenants appeared on the deeds for transactions of mountainous lands that produced timber. Since trees took many years to grow, tenancy contracts for timber lands always involved long time periods. Tenants in Anhwei dwelling on such lands, known as *huo tien*, either paid a stipulated amount of rent every five or six years or promised to share with the master their timber production according to an agreed formula. A complication arose when the owner of a tract of timber land wished to sell the land for some reason. It would then be virtually impossible to synchronize the transaction time with the "harvest" time of all timber products. The labor performed by the current tenant in planting and nurturing trees was equivalent to an investment and hence deserved compensation. This problem could be resolved either by a lump sum payment to the tenant at the time of transfer of owner-

185

ship, or by recording the name of the tenant on the deed, signifying that the new owner was to assume the original tenant contract complete with all its terms. Unfortunately, deeds of this kind have been mistaken by some modern scholars as documents to substantiate their contention that Ming tenants were serfs bound to the land.

Moreover, even the permanent tenancy system has been sometimes interpreted by a few Chinese scholars as no more than the feudal bondage of tenants using the rationale that such arrangements tended to restrict the tenants' freedom of movement. Rather than regarding it as bondage, however, tenants in such an arrangement considered it a valuable "right" equivalent to partial ownership of the land. Such a right could be sold, mortgaged, and bequeathed. Among the more than 100 agreements I have seen involving the sale of permanent tenancy rights, the earliest was signed in 1640. The format of this type of sale agreement was almost identical to the sale document used for land transfers in that period.

The permanent tenancy system was one of the salient features of premodern Chinese agriculture. Though its origin may be traced to the Southern Sung, it spread under a variety of names to the Kiangnan areas and Fukien during the Ming-Ch'ing. Strictly speaking, under such an arrangement the tenant was entitled to use the land permanently or indefinitely unless he had defaulted on rent payments over a prolonged period. Because ownership and use rights were permanently separate for the same piece of land, ownership was fragmented. Therefore, peasants usually considered this system to be joint ownership between the landlord who possessed the *t'ien ti* (bottom of the land) and the tenant who possessed the *t'ien mien* (surface of the land). It followed naturally that either party could sell his part of the full ownership separately. In the strictly legal sense, such transactions were transfers of ownership and use rights respectively, and at times use rights might command a higher price than ownership per se on the market.

The permanent tenancy system in China evolved from a variety of sources for a number of distinct reasons. First, the earliest source, as noted in the preceding section, was a strong desire on the part of both landlords and tenants to stabilize their relationship by establishing long-term contracts. Many landowners during the Sung wrote the names of their tenants on the sale documents when selling their lands. Initially this practice was highly controversial because it assured tenants the right to work on the lands on one hand and restricted their freedom to move

186

away on the other. As the rural populace's demand to lease land increased over time, however, the merits of this system prevailed and its defects were either forgotten or ignored. The permanent right to cultivate the land became a valuable asset to tenants.

Second, the practice of mortgaging land or selling land with the right reserved to buy it back was another important source of the permanent tenancy system. Under such arrangements, the seller usually continued to cultivate the land he had sold and paid rent to the new owner, hoping that some day he might be able to repurchase the land.[56] Unless the seller waived his right to repurchase or redeem the land, the buyer's ownership remained incomplete in the eyes of the law. The right to repurchase was often extended for several generations, and eventually it evolved into a permanent right to use the land without any repurchase agreement.

Third, and deviating somewhat from the preceding case of mortgaging land, an owner could sell his land under a clear sale agreement except that the buyer allowed the seller to remain indefinitely as a tenant.[57] This arrangement was especially common among the tenants of school land. Some managing offices of school land during the Southern Sung even engraved the names of their tenants on stone tablets, attesting to the permanent nature of the tenancy relations.[58] It is unclear, however, whether this system was introduced because it would enable schools to buy land at lower-than-market prices or because stable, long-term tenancy simplified land management.

Fourth, some permanent tenants in the Kiangnan area may be traced to the land commendation popular during the mid-Ming. Some commenders surrendered their lands to powerful families and received in return the promise that they could cultivate the land indefinitely as tenants. From a legal perspective, this practice may be seen as a case of double ownership; the commender only nominally transferred the title of his land to the powerful family, while actually preserving control over it.

Fifth, in some mountainous or coastal areas, tenants might have helped owners develop hilly or sandy land for cultivation, resulting in augmented land productivity. In return, tenants received compensation in the form of a permanent right to cultivate the land.[59] It may be argued that this arrangement constituted a legitimate case of joint ownership because the tenant had invested his labor in the land. At the very least, joint ownership and permanent tenancy rights are difficult to distinguish in this case.

187

Sixth, in Suiyuan and Chahar, where population density was low, and in the Kiangnan region after the T'aip'ing Rebellion, when there was a temporary shortage of tenants, landlords were able to use the permanent tenancy right as a preferential condition in recruiting tenants.

Seventh, the deposit paid by the tenant on first leasing land from the landlord might in turn serve as the price for purchasing the right to use the land. To put it another way, the landlord refused to return the deposit to the tenant but allowed him to till the land indefinitely. Whenever the tenant wanted to leave, he might find a successor who was willing to pay him an amount comparable to the deposit. The whole transaction would be similar to the case in which the tenant sold his use rights on the open market.

Eighth, after the permanent tenancy system was well established in rural Chinese society, landowners could easily sever use rights from ownership of the land on a permanent basis and sell the former separately. Purchase agreements of this kind were frequently made during the early twentieth century.[60]

In short, regardless of its diverse origins, the eventual spread of the permanent tenancy system in China had a great deal to do with population growth, or more specifically the extremely unfavorable man-land ratio. First, because of the strong sense of land scarcity the land market turned into a seller's market; whenever a poor peasant had to sell his land under extreme hardship, he still made efforts to preserve his rights to repurchase or use the land. For buyers this arrangement was one effective way to lure potential sellers into alienating their ownership.

Moreover, as discussed earlier, the transformation of share tenancy to fixed-rent tenancy in China was, directly and indirectly, a consequence of population pressure. The spread of permanent tenancy in turn depended on the development of fixed-rent tenancy, because only then could use rights be separated from land ownership. With the rent already specified as an absolute quantity, the landowner was indifferent to the identity of the tenant and his cultivating techniques as long as the rent was paid regularly. In contrast, income accruing to the landlord in the case of share contracts depended on the operational efficiency of the tenant, making it desirable for the landlord to supervise field operations in some way. Thus, the right to use the land could not be made completely independent of ownership.

188

TABLE 8.8

Proportional Distribution of Various Types of Tenancy Contracts by Province, 1936

Province	Permanent	Definite duration	Duration unspecified
Kiangsu	40.9%	9.2%	49.9%
Chekiang	30.6	10.1	59.3
Anhwei	44.2	12.9	42.9
Kiangsi	2.3	0.3	97.4
Hunan	1.0	0.4	98.6
Hupei	13.4	4.6	82.0
Hopei	3.9	23.5	72.6
Shantung	4.5	5.6	89.9
Honan	2.6	7.8	89.6
Shansi	4.2	41.7	54.1
Shensi	0.5	2.8	96.7
Chahar	78.7	4.1	17.2
Suiyuan	94.0	3.9	2.1
Fukien	5.2	8.7	86.1
Kwangtung	1.7	17.7	80.4
Kwangsi	11.7	11.4	76.9
National average	21.1%	8.1%	70.8%

SOURCE: Land Commission, p. 45.

It is no surprise, therefore, that both the permanent tenancy system and the fixed-rent system became popular in areas in which population density was relatively high. These were also areas in which the tenancy rate itself was high relative to the rate of managerial landlordism. Two points must be noted here, however. First, because permanent tenancy was equivalent to joint ownership and tenants under this arrangement were equivalent to partial tenants, the tenancy rate in areas in which the permanent tenancy system prevailed was somewhat overstated. Second, the tenancy rate should not be taken as distribution of ownership per se, for leasing out land was only one of the various alternatives landowners could call upon in managing their lands.

Table 8.8 shows that the permanent tenancy system accounted for 21 percent of the total number of tenancy contracts during the 1930's. Its incidence was higher in Kiangsu, Chekiang, and Anhwei as well as in the two northern provinces, Chahar and Suiyuan, where landlords employed the permanent tenancy system to entice tenants. The proportion of contracts of specified duration was only 8.1 percent for the country as a

TABLE 8.9

Distribution of Specified Duration in Tenancy Contracts, 1936

Number of years	Percent	Number of years	Percent	Number of years	Percent
1	35.9%	8	2.1%	14	0.1%
2	1.6	9	0.3	15	0.2
3	35.2	10	3.9	16	0.1
4	3.1	11	0.1	18	0.6
5	11.8	12	0.3	20	0.4
6	3.8	13	0.2	over 20	0.1
7	0.6				

SOURCE: Land Commission, p. 46.

whole. About 70 percent of the tenancy contracts, written or oral, did not specify contractual duration. Table 8.9 shows the distribution of contracts by duration when duration was stipulated. Obviously, one-year, three-year, and five-year contracts were most preferred. About 87 percent of the contracts that had specified contractual durations were of five years or less.

Tenant Risk

Share tenancy is tantamount to a partnership whereby the tenant and the landlord share the risk of operation (equally, under the Chinese formula), whereas fixed-rent tenancy makes the tenant the residual claimant of the income, thereby assuming full risk for the operation. The huge increase in the Chinese population after the Sung dynasty compelled landlords to switch from share tenancy to fixed-rent tenancy and in the process forced tenants to bear the whole burden of risk.

One indication of the increased risk borne by tenants was the rising frequency of tenant revolts and rent resistance and defaults in areas where fixed-rent tenancy prevailed. In the 175 Ming-Ch'ing rent collection books I examined, in no case under the fixed-rent contract was the landlord able to collect the full rent payments from all tenants every year. There were two situations in which rent payments were defaulted or fell short of the agreed amount: some tenants who suffered unusual hardships due to bad crops might obtain permission from their landlords to pay reduced rents, cases known as *jang tsu* (special allowance or concession); the other situation included only straightforward cases of rent delinquency in which the tenants defaulted rents in part or in full.

TABLE 8.10

Rent Delinquencies of Tenants of Six Landlords in Kiangnan, 1906-1929

Landlord and year	Percent of tenants who defaulted in the current year	Percent of tenants who defaulted in all previous recorded years
Fei Kung Shou T'ang		
1906	19.4%	7.3%
1907	20.1	1.8
1908	38.2	1.8
1909	30.5	0.6
Ku Lo Shou T'ang		
1906	34.7	13.7
1907	20.0	3.2
1908	24.2	3.2
1909	40.0	2.9
Fu Hung Hsing Hao		
1907	47.2	10.3
1908	46.2	8.3
1909	50.6	8.9
1910	47.6	8.2
Ho Hao		
1909	42.7	2.8
1910	48.6	3.4
1911	38.2	0
1912	40.7	2.8
I Feng		
1909	37.5	0
1910	87.5	0
1911	0	0
Chün Hao		
1922	31.2	0
1927	27.7	0
1928	29.9	0
1929	47.8	0

SOURCE: Yuji, p. 196.

In an exemplary rent collection book covering records of six years for a total of 120 tenants, the numbers of rent delinquencies were:

1775	31 tenants	1778	30 tenants
1776	31 tenants	1779	44 tenants
1777	43 tenants	1780	25 tenants

In other words, more than one-quarter of the tenants defaulted.

More interesting, some landlords appeared to have no effective control over rent delinquencies. One outstanding case involved the rent collection records of Wu Ch'i-hsien in Ming-chou covering the years 1895-1921, in which the number of tenants varied from 81 to 90.[61] Among them, 80 tenants, or more than 90 percent, defaulted in part or in full during some years. The landlord was apparently totally powerless in dealing with his delinquent tenants; all he could do was to set up a separate book to record the names of delinquent tenants every year. In this book, entitled "The List of Delinquent Tenants," he remarked occasionally "This fellow never paid a penny, I hate him." Based on the records, a simple computation yields the following statistics: 4 tenants defaulted in more than 40 years, 12 in 11-40 years, 13 in 10 years, 4 in 9 years, 8 in 8 years, 7 in 7 years, 11 in 6 years, 17 in 5 years, and 4 in 4 years.

In his study of Kiangnan bursaries, Muramatsu Yuji also mentions frequent rent defaults by tenants. These data are reproduced in Table 8.10. The bursaries, charged by absentee landlords to manage their tenanted lands, had close connections with local governments and could enforce contractual terms with the assistance of the tax authorities. Yet they were unable to collect rents in full. This fact suggests that rent delinquencies constituted a problem beyond the power of both private landlords and local governments to resolve. Conceivably, some landlords must have attempted to protect their interests by resorting to coercive and inhumane means, but in the long run the effectiveness even of violence was highly doubtful. In the final analysis, the worsening plight of tenants, and for that matter of small owner-cultivators as well, was created primarily by the increasingly unfavorable man-land ratio in China, a development for which landlords alone cannot be held responsible. Nor could the landlords themselves, or removal of them as an economic institution, alleviate the problem.

9

Changes in Productivity and Living Standards

Choice of Farm Implements and Cropping Systems

Economic institutions in traditional China were inherently conducive to the development and diffusion of agricultural technology. The abolition of the well field system made it possible from very early on to avoid the kind of waste associated with the open field system of medieval Europe. Furthermore, the lack of artificial restrictions on the peasant economy, which consisted of small, independent family farms,[1] and the centralized political system that mostly prevailed in the empire[2] contributed to the rapid diffusion of useful technologies. It is not surprising that China's early spurt in agricultural development gave the country an enormous lead over Europe, at least up to the twelfth century, when mounting population pressures compelled the Chinese to adjust their preferences in selecting technology and economic institutions in a different direction, which eventually turned out not to be viable for modernization.

A variety of factors affected productivity in traditional agriculture, including improvement of farm implements, water irrigation, introduction of higher-yield strains or crops, fertilization, and better field management. There were other developmental activities whose effects were less obvious and whose contribution is difficult to assess. A shift from single cropping to double cropping, for example, might reduce the yield substantially per unit of sown area unless it is accompanied by adequate fertilization to replenish soil fertility depleted under the double-cropping system. Moreover, to grow the same crop twice a year without long intervals might enhance survival and reproduction rates for the type of pests depending on this crop, making the problem of pest control more difficult. Reclamation usually involved removal of the natural vegetation on a piece of land before replacing it with the cultured crop, because any land not covered by natural vegetation was most probably also unsuitable for

193

cultivating crops. Thus excessive reclamation may upset the ecological balance in a given region and become harmful to long-term agricultural production.

This section presents a brief summary of the major historical technological changes in China's agriculture. I will attempt to describe the nature of those innovations without going into excessive technical detail. Although I agree with Cho-yun Hsu that many intensive farming techniques were introduced in the Han,[3] I tend to believe that intensive farming did not become necessary and widespread in China until the twelfth century. This, in fact, is a crucial ingredient of Boserup's theory: intensive farming techniques may become available long before the people in a country actually apply them widely.[4]

Generally speaking, agricultural production in China followed a pattern of extensive development before the Southern Sung but gradually changed thereafter. Taking cultivating implements as an example, we may observe that virtually all important innovations and inventions took place before the fourteenth century, at the latest, and all were labor saving in nature. These innovations were noticeably guided by two principles. First, new implements were made of increasingly better materials so that their operational efficiency could be enhanced. During the Warring States period, iron became widely used in manufacturing farm implements, as evidenced by the fact that iron farming tools from that period have been excavated in every one of the eight northern provinces that were occupied by the seven major states.[5] Attesting to the paramount importance of those items in agricultural production, the *Yen-t'ieh-lun* (Debate on the Monopoly of Salt and Iron) which contained the great debates among scholars in the early Western Han over the issue of government monopoly of iron and salt production, declared: "Iron tools are the life of farmers."[6] The second material revolution in farm implements took place in the T'ang, when steel was introduced, especially for the cutting edges of plows, hoes, sickles, and the like.[7] All these changes were meant to raise labor productivity so that each farmer could handle a larger acreage.

The other area of improvement in cultivating implements was structural refinement to cope with new farming conditions. Although people knew how to drive oxen to work in the field as early as the Warring States period, horses remained the main draft animals on farms before the time of Emperor Wu of the Western Han (140-87 B.C.). It was Chao

194

Kuo, a general under Emperor Wu, who urged peasants of the Western Han to replace horses with oxen, which were not only stronger but cost less to raise.[8] Plows and other animal-drawn implements were gradually modified to fit the new type of draft power. In his famous book *The Handbook of Plows*, Lui Kuei-meng described a typical plow used in the T'ang. It boasted a sophisticated construction of eleven parts and could be adjusted to vary the depth and width of the furrows it was to plow. Thus it could properly function in different types of soil or under different topographical conditions. During the Sung plows were further modified or redesigned to cope with the rising prevalence of farming in paddy fields, where plows tended to sink into the soft muddy bottom.

In sum, improvement and refinement of plows and other implements in China up to the Sung took a pattern similar to that in medieval Europe—toward the direction of extensive farming. Innovation of farm implements practically came to a halt after the Southern Sung, however. As Perkins points out, of the 77 farm implements illustrated in Wang Chen's *Nung Shu* (Treatise on Agriculture) published in 1313, all but one were listed in the treatises or handbooks on agricultural production published subsequently.[9] A more recent study has identified the dates of invention or innovation after 221 B.C. for 68 major farm implements in Chinese history,[10] distributed over time as follows:

Dynasty	No. of implements invented
Ch'in and Han (221 B.C.-A.D. 220)	13
Wei, Chin, Southern and Northern Dynasties (221-580)	10
Sui and T'ang (581-906)	3
Sung (961-1279)	35
Yuan (1280-1368)	3
Ming (1369-1644)	4

The invention rate declined sharply after 1300 and finally came to a complete halt after 1700. Among the four items invented in the Ming period, two were plows pulled by man, known as the "wooden ox," clearly labor intensive rather than labor sparing in nature.

We may also conclude that the plows illustrated by the T'ang writer, Lu Kuei-meng, were not surpassed in quality by plows in use during the early twentieth century in terms of function, quality, and engineering sophistication.[11] In fact, many plows of the 1930's appear inferior to their counterparts of earlier times. According to Lu Kuei-meng's illustration and description, a typical plow used in the T'ang had two parts made of iron—a plowshare and a moldboard. Yet one careful survey of implements used by farmers in twelve provinces during 1920-46 reports that most plows had only plowshares made of iron, some plows had no moldboards, and a few plows were made entirely of wood.[12]

Obviously, this change signifies not merely a decline in the rate of innovation but a drastic shift of technological preference on the part of Chinese peasants. Until the twelfth century, a primary concern was to save labor through invention and perfection of implements so that each farmer could handle a larger and larger amount of land. Development in this direction reached its climax in the Sung, during which time the number of significant inventions not only increased, but the new implements also embodied the best engineering skills and the most advanced mechanical ideas, such as wooden cogwheels.[13]

In contrast, the previously cited survey of farm implements during the early twentieth century implies that farmers were now more concerned with cost than with operation efficiency. They preferred implements built with poorer, hence cheaper, materials to more efficient, but more expensive, ones. A plausible explanation seems to be that the higher man-land ratio not only made the saving of labor unnecessary but also impoverished peasants to such an extent that they could no longer afford to invest in efficient but expensive implements.

Until the Sung, the invention of labor-saving implements enabled the average peasant to work on an increasingly larger area without substantially extending his number of working days in a year. As explained in Chapter 5, the per capita acreage of farmland rose slightly between 200 B.C. and the early part of the eighth century. Perhaps a more important avenue through which peasants expanded their farming acreage over this long period was the gradual elimination of fallow land.

In view of the frequent discussions of various fallowing arrangements dating from the period of the well field system, fallowing appears to have been a necessary and widely applied pattern of land use before 200 B.C.[14] Farmlands were classified into three categories: those to be tilled once every three years, those to be tilled every two years, and those tilled annually. For China as a whole, the average multiple-cropping index—that is, the ratio of sown area to cultivated area—was probably below 0.5. This index gradually rose to a level slightly above 0.5 until the fourth century. The *ch'an-t'ien fa* (law of land occupation) and *k'o-t'ien-fa* (law of land taxes) promulgated by the Chin government around 280 A.D. shed light on this issue, because land-use legislation could not have been formulated without reference to the current cultivating ability of peasants and prevailing practices. Taking a standard-sized family with two working adults, husband and wife, as a basis of computation, a holding of 100 (70 + 30) *mou* was permissible under the *ch'an-t'ien fa*, whereas taxable acreage under the *k'o-t'ien-fa* was 70 (50 + 20) *mou*. Logically, taxable acreage meant the sown area in a fiscal year, implying a multiple-cropping index of about 0.7 (70/100).

There are indications that the man-land ratio improved after the third century as prolonged warfare reduced China's population. The equitable field system adopted by the Toba Wei in A.D. 485 allotted 60 *mou* of cropland to a standard family with two working adults for annual cultivation. In addition, the law would double or triple the allotment for such a family if fallowing was necessary. Sixty Wie *mou* is equivalent to 67.68 *shih mou*, which is larger than the 70 *chin mou* of taxable acreage (= 52.78 *shih mou*). This increase partly reflected the improved operation efficiency of the average peasant and partly the more favorable man-land ratio. The Toba Wei was replaced by the Northern Chi in 550. The new government revised the equitable field system by abolishing the provision of additional land for fallowing and raising the regular allotment for a standard family from 60 *mou* to 120 *mou*. Although the revision was mainly intended to simplify the administration of land allotment, it implied that, on the average, half of the land in the territory of the Northern Chi was left idle for fallowing in each year. In other words, by that time the multiple-cropping index had probably decreased to 0.5.

As discussed in Chapter 2, the T'ang dynasty witnessed a rapid expansion of population. By 730, more than 80 percent of Chinese districts had been classified as "narrow areas" in which land allotments were reduced by as much as 50 percent from the stipulated quotas. Hsin-t'ang-shu states that around 810 the state colony in Ching-hsi (Honan) recruited 1,950 men to cultivate 1,900 *ch'ing* of land each year in an area totaling 3,800 *ch'ing*.[15] The implied index of 0.5, however, is believed to have been an exceptional case, for the state colony was established in a relatively sparsely populated region after the devastation of the An-Shih Rebellion. For the country as a whole, the average index must have been higher. The writings of Ou-yang Hsiu, Fan Ch'eng-ta, and other Sung scholars mentioned the common practice of slash-and-burn, locally known as

197

she-t'ien, in the mountainous areas of Hupei, Hunan, Kueichow, and Szechwan during that period.[16] An official report to the Sung emperor in 1070 stated that a sizeable portion of the 36 million *mou* of farmland in Su-chou, Kiangsu were left for fallowing each year.[17] The fact that Chen Fu, in his own *Nung Shu* (Treatise on Agriculture) published in 1149, emphatically criticized the fallowing system as unnecesssarily wasteful suggests that even then fallowing was still practiced in Kiangnan. A drastic change in this practice must have taken place shortly afterward.

Although by the early Sung the per capita acreage of cultivated land already fell slightly below the level of the first century, per capita sown acreage continued to expand for some time through the gradual elimination of fallowing land. As long as the multiple-cropping index remained less than unity, no more than one crop was grown in any piece of land and the number of working days in the growing season remained approximately unchanged. Thus, more efficient implements were needed as per capita sown acreage expanded.

The twelfth century marked a crucial turning point in Chinese agricultural history, after which rising population pressure compelled the populace to produce more food chiefly by means of three approaches. First, whenever and wherever possible, more than one crop was grown on a given piece of land, resulting in a multiple-cropping index above unity. Second, cultivation was extended by reclaiming lands that were either inferior in quality or entailing more initial investment for development. Third, total output was enhanced by intensified fertilization and introduction of higher-yield strains or crops.

Since double cropping was carried out by extending the number of working days in a year, there was little need to invent better labor-saving implements to cope with the expansion of sown areas. The same implements could be used for growing both crops. Moreover, as the population continued to increase, not only the per capita cultivated acreage but also the per capita sown acreage would decrease, so that even the older implements would become underutilized.

Although the possibility of "harvesting twice in a single year" was first discussed in the Han, there is no evidence that it was actually practiced then. The system of planting three crops in two years, alternating millet, wheat, and soybean, is known to have existed before the sixth century.[18] But as far as historical data can indicate, the double cropping of rice first appeared in a few coastal counties in Fukien during the early years of the Northern Sung. During the early Sung, attempts were made to plant wheat in the Kiangnan region along with the local rice crop, but the results were not successful. It was only after the Sung government evacuated to the south that the local populace in the Kiangnan region was compelled to reconsider this idea. In view of the unprecedented density of population and the relative scarcity of farmland in Kiangnan, Chen Fu recommended a year-round operation in that region.[19] To promote the new cropping system, the Southern Sung government promulgated an incentive policy under which tenants were exempted from rent payments for the wheat crop if it was planted after a rice crop.[20] During that period a large number of northerners, who were knowledgeable wheat growers, migrated to the south in the face of the Chin Tartar invasion. The combination of their expertise and the government's promotional measure resulted in the widespread practice of rice-wheat double cropping in the Kiangnan area. In contrast, the rice-rice double-cropping system extended rather slowly, only to the southern parts of Chekiang and Anhwei by the Ming.[21] There is a high probability that the multiple-cropping index for China as a whole reached a peak, approximately 1.40, by 1850, declining slightly thereafter because of the development of the vast single-crop region in Manchuria.

Based on the foregoing observations and other relevant information, the evolution of the multiple-cropping index in China may be provisionally reconstructed as follows:[22]

3rd century B.C.	below 0.5	12th century	1.00
1st century A.D.	0.60	17th century	1.30
3rd century	0.70	19th century	1.40
6th century	0.50	1940	1.30
8th century	0.80		

The selection of crops in China was closely related to the intensity of land use. Although Chinese classical writings often used the terms "five grains" and "hundred grains" to indicate variety, there was a high degree of concentration on a single crop (millet, or *shu*) until the Han; all grain crops other than millet were only secondary crops planted on limited acreages. The concentrated pattern was firmly established because the choice of peasants was relatively simple under the fallowing system—selecting a crop that could promise the highest and most stable yield. Millet, a crop that is suitable for most types of soils, flexible in planting time, drought resistant, and tolerant of wind, met the requirements best in virtually all parts of the country.

The importance of other crops as popular staples tended to rise only

199

after farmers gave up the fallowing system. To plant the same crop in a piece of land year after year would either deplete the land's fertility too quickly or provide a much higher survival rate for the pests that depended on this crop, thereby aggravating the problem of pest control. Thus, an optimal combination of crops for rotation, rather than a single optimal crop, had to be selected to maximize the yield. This is believed to be the main reason why wheat was chosen as the second important crop to accompany millet during and after the Han time.[23] The selection of crops, however, still remained highly concentrated until the revolution of rice cultivation during the Sung.

Based on the findings of recent excavations, the existence of cultivated rice in China may be dated as early as 5000 B.C.,[24] even earlier than the estimated origin of rice cultivation in India (4530 B.C.). It failed to spread in the country as a staple grain primarily because of the heavy requirement of labor input per unit of output. As the next section will show, the yield record of rice grown in the region occupied by the Kingdom of Wu during the period of Three Kingdoms (220-80) was about 176 catties per *shih mou*, which is 80 percent higher than the normal unit yield of millet during that period. An official document from the period 713-41, however, demonstrated that it would take 948 working days to grow rice on 100 *mou* of land, whereas it would take only 283 working days to grow millet over the same land area, a labor input differential of 3.35:1.[25] Even the high population density of the T'ang dynasty could not justify the adoption of rice cultivation over a large area.

During the early years of the Northern Sung, the coastal area of Fukien was perhaps the only region where rice was extensively planted, largely because farmers there imported Champa rice for local adoption. The history of rice cultivation in China reached a turning point in the early eleventh century when the Sung emperor Chen-tsung brought a large quantity of Champa rice via Fukien and made it available to the peasants in Kiangnan.[26] Compared to the Chinese indigenous strains, Champa rice was characterized by a higher yield, better ability to resist drought, and earlier maturity. The profound impact of the new strain on China's agricultural production is too well known among historians to require detailed exposition.[27] When planted on high or arid lands with poor soil, its drought-resisting power could assure a much higher yield than other crops. Its feature of early ripening, on one hand, made double cropping possible in Kiangnan and some other regions, where the growing season was only moderately long, and allowed rice on the other hand

200

to be planted as a single crop further north, where the short growing season had previously impeded rice cultivation. More important, the new strain of rice not only produced a higher yield but also demonstrated a great potential for further improvement in yield. In short, Champa rice ushered in a new era of agrarian history in China, during which time the country witnessed a continuous rise in the unit yield of rice crop. It met the altered preferences of Chinese farmers perfectly—promising a higher total output by absorbing more labor.

A few New World crops were subsequently introduced to China. Although the source and date of corn importation remain debatable, sweet potatoes and Irish potatoes are known to have been brought from the Philippines to China around 1570. Those crops were well accepted by the Chinese as a sort of poor man's staples—corn for its unusual adaptability to poor growing conditions and potatoes for their high yields per unit of land. Sorghum was introduced from Western Asia to Szechwan and Yunnan, probably during the Yuan period. The wider variety of good food crops enabled Chinese peasants to arrange diverse cropping patterns, such as various systems of double cropping, interplanting, and rotation most suitable to local growing conditions, so that total output could be increased everywhere. Based on 1952 statistics, the distribution of cultivated acreage among the major food crops in China was as follows:[28]

Rice	22.9%	Sorghum	7.6%
Wheat	20.0%	Millet	7.9%
Corn	10.1%	Potatoes	7.0%

Reclamation, Deforestation, and Their Ecological Consequences

In the long history of China, some activities of the expanding population did irremediable ecological harm to the environment. Such ecological alterations eventually led to a decline in land productivity. Thanks to our modern knowledge of ecology and the great contribution of several Chinese historical geographers who have recently made accessible enormous quantities of meteorological data, hydrological records for major rivers, and descriptions of forests from a large number of historical writings and local gazetteers, we are much better informed today than ever before about the serious constraints population pressure placed on ecological conditions and agricultural production.[29]

One type of desperate effort made by the inhabitants of north China

201

under mounting population pressure was to expand farmland by clearing trees. The line of cultivation along the northern frontiers, except for the region of Manchuria, had been stretched out almost to the limit as early as 100 B.C.; subsequent reclamation activities in north China hardly went beyond what Emperor Wu of the Western Han had accomplished. But after each major war, the populace would reoccupy and recultivate farmland that had been laid to waste during wartime. In times of peace, farmland on the northern plains was usually expanded, primarily at the expense of timber land, by deforestation and the removal of trees around farms.

A careful study by Shih Nien-hai presents a large quantity of historical materials that clearly indicates the existence of vast forests in north China, especially in the mid-reaches of the Yellow River, before Sung times.[30] The proportion of "mulberry land" to "unshaded land" stipulated in the equitable field system of the Northern Wei suggests that at least 30 percent of cultivated land was covered by trees. These large forested areas gradually shrank, according to Shih, and finally disappeared completely by Ming-Ch'ing times.

Large quantities of timber were also consumed as fuel. The local populace cut trees to provide firewood; they even dug out the roots for the same purpose after they had used up the trees.[31] Forests were also the necessary source of charcoal consumed by urban residents. This process of deforestation occurred with striking speed around national capitals and large urban centers, where huge amounts of charcoal and contruction timber were consumed annually. The neighboring forests of Ch'ang-an, Lo-yang, and Pei-ching were quickly wiped out shortly after these cities were designated as national capitals, and the local population soon had to procure charcoal from locations as much as several hundred *li* away.[32]

As a result of accelerated and destructive deforestation, land in north China lost its natural protection and became more vulnerable to floods and droughts. Farmland along the northern frontiers gradually converted into semidesert. Shortly after Pei-ching was made the national capital of the Yuan dynasty—it was then called Ta-tu—the surrounding area was noted as a region "studded with 99 lakes." In the next few hundred years all these lakes dried up and disappeared, though their names—such as Hai-tien in the west suburb of Peking—are still recognizable today.[33] Based on available data, a leading Chinese meteorologist has convincingly calculated that the annual mean temperature in north China today is about 2° C lower than it was two thousand years ago and the mean January temperature is about 3°-5° C lower.[34]

Deforestation caused by excessive reclamation activities led to aggravated soil erosion, which in turn caused siltation in rivers. The result was reduced land fertility after topsoil washed out on one hand and the silted rivers flooded more frequently on the other.

Ever since the Sung, Chinese historians and water control experts had been puzzled by the fact that the Yellow River was relatively stable and trouble-free between the fourth and seventh centuries A.D. According to a recent study, the Yellow River became tame during that period because north China was occupied by a few nomadic tribes who converted a large portion of the farmland previously cultivated by the Han people into pastoral land. The altered land use and the increased natural vegetation as ground cover are believed to be mainly responsible for the reduction of soil erosion and rates of siltation, hence the new behavior pattern of rivers.[35]

The rivers in north China became less stable after the Sung dynasty. According to historical records, the frequency of major floods along the Hai river was once every 31 years during the T'ang dynasty, once every 30 years during the Sung, and once every 5.3 years during the Ch'ing.[36] As for the Yellow River area, the changed frequency of natural disasters can be clearly seen from the following statistics.[37]

Century	Major floods	Major droughts	Century	Major floods	Major droughts
7th	9	4	14th	9	9
8	4	2	15	8	5
9	3	0	16	11	17
10	6	5	17	15	22
11	2	4	18	13	7
12	0	2	19	25	11
13	2	2			

The frequencies of major floods and droughts in the area both increased significantly after the thirteenth century.

Beginning in the fourth century, major efforts were made in China to develop new farmland in the south, and pockets of small plains in that region were quickly settled. Between the eighth and eleventh centuries, the main pattern of development in south China was opening up hillside fields for cultivation. A T'ang writer noted that mid-eighth-century cultivators "became so diligent as to bring their plows and harrows to high mountains and deep valleys."[38] The term *t'i t'ien* (terraced land) appeared frequently in the literature of the Northern Sung.[39]

A new pattern of land development began to loom sometime in the Southern Sung, when cultivators attempted to create polders by building dikes surrounding lakes or along riverbanks to contain water. Before 1100 or so, all lakes were owned, legally speaking, by the state and no private party was allowed to occupy them for any purpose. Some powerful families during the T'ang enclosed small lakes illegally as their private property, but they made use of the lakes for purposes other than that of creating land.[40] Pressed by the serious shortage of farmland, the Southern Sung government formally abolished the traditional prohibition and encouraged people to reclaim lowlands from the sea, lakes, or other bodies of water by constructing dikes, dams, and the like.[41] The most commonly used terms for those polders in that period were *wei-t'ien* (enclosed land) and *yu-t'ien* (diked land). In many counties in the Kiangnan, polders accounted for as much as 25 percent of the total farmland. This practice was equally widespread in Hunan and Hupei.

Following the lead of Chi Chao-ting, Dwight Perkins has compiled from local gazetteers the data for water control projects constructed throughout Chinese history.[42] It is clear from his table that the number of new water control projects constructed in each period, not counting major repair works, increased sharply after the eleventh century. Most of the projects built before that time were in north China, whereas major projects built thereafter were in the south, especially in Anhwei, Chekiang, and Kiangsu. It is important to note that the primary function of the northern projects was irrigation and flood prevention, whereas many projects in Kiangnan were polder dikes. By 1183, for example, a total of 73 km of dikes had been built along the shores of T'ai lake, used primarily for forming polders.[43] The twentieth century saw 990 dikes surrounding Tung-t'ing lake in Hunan with a total length of 6,400 km.[44]

In the process of creating polders in the south, many famous lakes disappeared forever. Chien lake in Shao-hsing, whose beauty was greatly appreciated by the T'ang poet Tu Fu, disappeared entirely by 1180.[45] More dramatic were the changes in total surface area of Tung-t'ing lake.[46] The maximum recorded surface area was 14,000 square km. Later recorded areas were as follows: 6,000 square km (1825), 5,400 square km

(1896), 4,350 square km (1949), 2,740 square km (1949). This sort of activity accelerated after 1949 because of even greater population pressure. For example, there were 1,066 lakes in Hupei in 1949 but the number was reduced to 326 by 1977, meaning that 740 lakes disappeared in a period of 28 years.[47] No one knows how many lakes had been filled up before 1949.

Although reclamation activities and the creation of polders had their positive contribution to food supply in China, they produced harmful ecological consequences. The shrinking surfaces of lakes in the south meant that they had lost part of their water-retention capacity and hence could no longer properly serve as natural reservoirs. The dikes surrounding lakes were also apt to prevent water from flowing into those lakes during periods of excessive rain, and thus the southern regions also became more vulnerable to flooding.

Some keen observers in these times realized the disastrous results and served warning to the government. On several occasions Chinese governments even seriously considered the possibility of converting polders back into lakes. But the temptation of gaining new land was too great to resist over a long period of time. Thus, as noted in a recent study, this pattern of reclamation proceeded in cycles.[48] Increasing population pressure intensified reclamation activities, which invited more natural disasters; awareness of environmental deterioration tended to slow down the process until the next wave of intensified reclamation began.

Similar warnings have been served by modern Chinese scholars who can present the argument more convincingly by showing relevant statistics. By reviewing the records of past natural disasters, recent studies point out the obvious changes in frequency of floods and droughts in the areas where polder creation was rampant. Only 14 major floods and droughts occurred in the T'ai lake area between 200 B.C. and A.D. 1100, but the number rose to 26 during the 360 years of the Ming and Ch'ing dynasties. In the Tung-t'ing lake region, there was one major natural calamity in every 83 years before the Ming dynasty, one every 20 years between the fourteenth and nineteenth centuries, and one every five years after the nineteenth century.[49]

For the T'ai lake region, detailed data of droughts and floods have been compiled from the relevant gazetteers and may be arranged by century as follows:[50]

Century	Floods	Droughts	Century	Floods	Droughts
10th	6	3	15th	48	19
11	16	8	16	57	38
12	31	24	17	56	50
13	29	10	18	48	39
14	47	17	19	48	28

In both cases the rising trend after the thirteenth century is clearly discernible.

A more comprehensive set of data of this sort, with nationwide coverage for the past 500 years, has been recently published by the Chinese government's Bureau of Meteorology. The bureau has canvassed an enormous number (2,200 volumes) of local gazetteers and annals since the fifteenth century for climatic records and related materials. It has divided the territory of China into 120 districts, or observation points, each covering an area of one or two prefectures, with climatic materials or records systematically classified into the following five grades: grade 1, very wet; grade 2, wet; grade 3, normal; grade 4, dry; and grade 5, very dry. Unfortunately, the editors of this volume fail to mention if recordkeeping was uninterrupted for all 120 observation points over 500 years. It is possible that the documents from which meteorological data have been taken might be missing for some localities in some years. Theoretically speaking, nationwide data are less reliable than regional data, which are based on an uninterrupted time series with a fixed coverage. Notwithstanding this possible shortcoming, the nationwide data show analogous results to the regional data.

For purposes of investigating possible changes in ecological conditions, I shall concentrate on grades 1 and 5—namely, what we call major floods and major droughts—which no local gazetteers could have ignored or failed to document. To compute the frequency of occurrence, I have combined the annual records into twenty-year intervals. The processed data are presented in Table 9.1.

These data can be tested statistically to determine if they manifest any significant trends. The following is the equation for major droughts, in which H and t denote the frequency in a twenty-year interval and the time factor (every twenty years), respectively.

$$H = 125 - 0.941t$$
$$(15.2) \quad (1.16)$$

TABLE 9.1

*Frequency of Major Floods and Major Droughts in China
by Twenty-Year Period, 1470-1909*

Period	Number of major floods	Number of major droughts
1470-1489	91	129
1490-1509	63	123
1510-1529	105	157
1530-1549	113	102
1550-1569	143	81
1570-1589	127	144
1590-1609	152	90
1610-1629	118	108
1630-1649	124	220
1650-1669	198	103
1670-1689	119	128
1690-1709	111	94
1710-1729	100	106
1730-1749	137	73
1750-1769	132	66
1770-1789	92	113
1790-1809	109	88
1810-1829	125	108
1830-1849	192	99
1850-1869	140	94
1870-1889	177	115
1890-1909	165	163

SOURCE: Bureau of Meteorology, pp. 321-32.

Judging from the standard error in parentheses, the constant term is highly significant. The negative sign of the t term seems reasonable, too, because, as time passed, construction of more and more irrigation projects was expected to serve the function of reducing the occurrence of major droughts. The fact that the coefficient of the t term is not significantly different from zero implies that the water projects did not serve this function as well as expected, hence the frequency of major droughts in the country was not significantly reduced over time.

More interesting is the equation for major floods, whose frequency in twenty-year intervals is represented by F:

$$F = 99.8 + 2.52t$$
$$(13.0) \quad (0.988)$$

This demonstrates a discernibly rising trend, for the coefficient of the t term is significantly different from zero at the 1 percent level. In other

207

words, in the past 500 years or so, the frequency of major floods in the whole country increased by 2.5 occurrences every twenty years, convincing statistical evidence of worsening ecological conditions.

Among the 120 observation points selected by the Chinese Bureau of Meteorology, twelve are located in Manchuria, which is not immediately relevant to this study. Even when the records for the twelve points are excluded, however, the foregoing statistical results remain basically unchanged, because the climatic conditions in Manchuria were fairly stable, relatively free of major floods and droughts. This circumstance actually reenforces the preceding conclusions.

Major floods recorded by different observation points in the same year were not necessarily independent of each other because flooding of a major river might affect a vast region covering several observation points. Thus the increase in frequency of major floods so measured may signify an expansion of the disaster area.

Measurement of Unit Yields

Dwight Perkins and his research associates have compiled from local gazetteers nearly 900 items of historical data on crop yields in China, far exceeding what other researchers have achieved in this regard.[51] One can hardly quarrel with Perkins on his careful examination of the problems and possible biases associated with the yield data and his analysis of the findings derived therefrom. My only reservation, however, is that he has assumed a more or less stable level of per capita grain output during the period under investigation, namely, from the Sung to 1968. On the contrary, we are told by Boserup that because the transition from a system of extensive farming to one of intensive farming is accompanied by a decline in output per unit of labor, a country would be reluctant to shift to the latter system until population density reached such a level that they would have to accept a decline of output per unit of labor.[52]

Therefore, that per capita grain output was maintained at a constant level over a long time period during which the population increased enormously is a hypothesis still to be verified. Verification begins with estimating grain yields. It is also highly desirable to extend the inquiry to pre-Sung times, with whatever meager data available, so that we can detect if contrasting patterns of development in unit yields existed before and after the transition. Furthermore, attempts should be made to measure the yields of millet and wheat, two staple foods in North China. Since the two crops have demonstrated lower potentials for yield increase than rice, the exclusion of them from the calculation of average yields may lead to overstatement.

To compare yield data from different time periods, they must first be converted into standard *shih mou* and *shih shih* according to the following ratios:[53]

Period	Shih mou/mou	Shih shih/shih
Early West Han (206-140 B.C.)	0.273	0.1937
Late West Han (141 B.C.-A.D. 8)	0.691	0.3425
East Han (9-220)	0.731	0.1981
T'ang (619-906)	0.810	0.5944
Sung (961-1279)	0.865	0.6641
Ming (1369-1644)	1.040	1.0737
Ch'ing (1645-1911)	1.040	1.0355

For intercrop comparisons, the capacity unit (*shih shih*) is then converted into catties (*shih chin*) according to the following ratios: millet, 135 catties; wheat, 140 catties; husked rice, 150 catties; unhusked rice, 130 catties.[54]

1. *Millet.* The earliest statement concerning unit yields of millet was given by Li Ke sometime in the period 403-397 B.C. and referred to the prevailing situation in the state of Wei. According to Li Ke, 1.5 *shih* of *shu* could be produced per *mou* of average-quality land in a normal year (*p'ing nien*). A recent archaeological discovery indicates that the state of Wei adopted a new land gauge during this period that was about twice the size of the official Chou *mou*.[55] Thus the implied average yield would be

$$\frac{0.1937 \times 1.5}{0.273 \times 2} \times 135 = 72 \text{ catties per } shih \ mou$$

The best land with adequate water supply, however, could produce as much as 186 catties per *shih mou*, suggesting a wide variance of crop yields in the early stages of Chinese agricultural history.[56]

As cited in Chapter 7, Tsao Tso, a famous stateman who died in 154 B.C., described the plight of the average peasant household during the early West Han. "These days a family of five has at least two persons who are liable for labor-services and conscription, while they farm no more than 100 *mou* of land, the yield from which does not exceed 100 *shih*."[57] Since the observation was made in the early Western Han, before Emperor Wu changed the Chou measuring systems into new gauges,[58] the unit yield is estimated to be

$$\frac{0.1937}{0.273} \times 135 = 96 \text{ catties per } shih\ mou$$

Three other pieces of data from the Western Han give unit yields as 117 catties, 157 catties, and 250 catties per *shih mou*, respectively.[59] These are probably references to lands with above-average grades.

Altogether nine items of data have been collected from T'ang documents reporting the following unit yields of millet: 5 items, 1 *shih*; 2 items, 0.8 *shih*; 1 item, 2 *shih*; 1 item, 6.4 *shih*.[60] Among them the most reliable is a production report, around the year 810, from a state colony in Honan, which had 1,950 men cultivating 380,000 *mou* on a two-year fallowing schedule. The actual yield was 1 *shih* per *mou*, which may be converted as

$$\frac{0.5944}{0.810} \times 135 = 99 \text{ catties per } shih\ mou$$

An official document from the Tartar Chin (1115-1234) recorded that in the region south of the Yellow River, upper-grade land produced 1.2 *shih*; middle-grade land, 1.0 *shih*; and lower-grade land, 0.8 *shih* of millet per *mou*.[61] The yield of the middle-grade land would be equivalent to

$$\frac{0.6641}{0.865} \times 135 = 104 \text{ catties per } shih\ mou$$

After the twelfth century, millet was gradually relegated to a kind of secondary grain, on which no yield data have been found. The latest statistic is the national average yield of millet in 1952, as officially released by the Chinese government: 156 catties per *shih mou*. The foregoing historical yield data may be arranged as follows: 400 B.C., 72 catties; 160 B.C., 96 catties; A.D. 810, 99 catties; 1130, 104 catties; 1952, 156 catties.

This set of yield estimates is surprisingly consistent with the analysis in preceding sections. The early spurt of millet yield, from 72 catties around 400 B.C. to 96 catties around 160 B.C., coincided with the first round of innovation in the manufacture of farm implements. Although millet does not demand good soil, its yield depends decisively on how thoroughly the field is prepared. Because the millet seed is relatively small, it cannot grow well if the field is full of large lumps. The in-

210

ventions of iron plowshares and iron-tooth harrows and the installation of moldboards on plows, which functioned to turn over the soil and break lumps, assured better preparation of fields during this period. Consequently, there was a rapid rise in the yield of millet.

In the next twelve centuries, however, millet yield virtually stagnated. Following the extensive pattern of agricultural development, farmers in this period were interested primarily in the expansion of per capita cropping area rather than the promotion of unit yields. The remarkable rise in yield materialized only after China had nearly exhausted the potential of expanding the cropping acreage and turned to intensive farming.

2. *Wheat.* Information on yields of wheat, then a secondary crop, was seldom documented before the Sung. The two early pieces of data on wheat yields collected by researchers are from the Northern Sung. One official document quoted the average wheat yield in the period as 1 *shih*, which may be converted to[62]

$$\frac{0.6641}{0.864} \times 140 = 108 \text{ catties per } shih\ mou$$

This is confirmed by an actual report of farm output from a temple (Kuang-hui Yuan).[63] Although there are no wheat data for the Han and T'ang, the yield must be somewhat below the level of millet. Because both millet and wheat could be grown on the same type of soil in most parts of north China, wheat could have been the leading crop if its yield were higher than that of millet. The estimated yield of wheat during the Northern Sung was slightly higher than millet, explaining why the former was gradually overtaking the latter as the leading crop in north China.

Unlike millet, however, and for reasons that are still unclear, wheat failed to improve substantially in yield after the Sung. Li Wen-chih has compiled a few pieces of data for wheat yields, in *shih* per *mou*, for 1820-1911:[64]

Ching-kou, Kiangsu	0.5-1.0	Chu-yung, Kiangsu	2.0
Chen-chiang, Kiangsu	1.4-1.5	Pao-t'ing, Hopei	2.91
Huai-an, Kiangsu	0.7-1.0	Yen-t'ai, Shantung	0.2-0.5

The figures are extremely low for some localities. The wheat yields measured by Buck in his sample study during the 1930's were 127 catties per *shih mou* in the wheat region and 142 catties in the rice region.[65] His figures are proven to be upward biased, and the adjusted national average is 120-22 catties per *shih mou*.[66] Even this level of yield could not be maintained in the period 1952–57, for which average wheat yields were officially given as 117 catties for the wheat region and 103 catties for the rice region.[67]

Whether wheat yields have remained at a low but stable level throughout the period since the Northern Sung remains a question. Fairly convincing evidence suggests that wheat yields rose after the Sung, peaked sometime before the nineteenth century, then began to decline. Yield data collected by some scholars for the summer harvest in nine provinces—Hopei, Honan, Shansi, Shensi, Anhwei, Kiangsi, Hunan, Hupei, and Fukien—formed the following yield indices, with average yields in 1821-30 as 100.[68]

1821-1830	100.0	1851-1860	88.7	1881-1890	82.8
1831-1840	94.1	1861-1870	82.4	1891-1900	81.0
1841-1850	93.9	1871-1880	81.0	1901-1910	81.0

The main weakness of the study is that yield figures used in the computation were originally provided by nonexperts as "averages" of some undefined large areas and in very approximate terms. To compare changes in yield, one should ideally collect yield data at different points of time from a fixed sample of farms or a narrowly defined small district with relatively homogeneous farmland.

A more conclusive study of yield changes is made possible by the recent publication of the extensive archives of *K'ung Fu* (The Mansion of Confucius). The archives include rent collection records and grain crop reports from K'ung Fu farms located in four counties in Shantung between 1653 and 1940. The fixed locations and stable sizes of these estates make them an ideal sample to study yield variations over time. The relevant data from K'ung Fu are presented at the end of this book as Appendix C.

The rental records for wheat and other grain crops from seven K'ung Fu estates under fixed-rent contracts show that the rent collections per *mou* declined by 20 percent to 43 percent on those estates between 1653 and 1788 but became stable at the lower levels thereafter. More revealing is the complete set of yield and rent data from Mei-hua Chuang, Wenshang county, where K'ung Fu leased out about 900 *mou* of land to tenants, mostly under the 50-50 sharecropping arrangement. The records are complete for twenty years in the period 1736-75. Against these statistics we are able to test the following equation for various crops:

$$X = a + bt + e$$

where X denotes the unit yield of the crop, t the time factor, and e a random variable representing the natural variation of yields, whose mean value is zero. The following are the resulting coefficients for the trend factor along with their standard errors in parentheses for four crops.

Crop	a	b
Wheat	3.6155 (0.3040)	−0.0440 (0.0126)
Kaoliang	4.5044 (0.5408)	−0.0425 (0.0224)
Brown and black beans	2.4296 (0.3772)	−0.0413 (0.0156)
Miscellaneous grain	5.3508 (0.6832)	−0.0912 (0.0283)

In the four equations, the negative trend coefficients are significant, three being significantly different from zero at 1 percent and one at 5 percent. The evidence of reduced crop yields in this area is too overwhelming to be ignored.

3. *Rice.* The earliest rice yield figure is based on a harvest report of a farm in Yung-hsing, Hunan, during the third century.[69] The amount stated may be converted to 176 catties of unhusked rice per *shih mou*. Although this yield was about 80 percent higher than the millet yield of the same time period, the high requirement of labor per unit of output prevented rice from becoming a popular crop.

The nearly 900 items of rice yield data collected by Perkins for later periods are easily usable. By employing his averaged rice yields for four major rice-producing provinces during the Sung and a set of weights constructed on the basis of cultivated acreages in these provinces during the same period, we may estimate a weighted mean of rice yields. Perkins's underlying data are:[70]

Province	Rice yields (catties per *shih mou*)	Weight
Chekiang	402	23.3%
Kiangsu	326	45.3%
Hupei	255	16.6%
Szechwan	178	14.8%

Thus, a weighted average of 310 catties is obtained for the Sung.

His data manifest a clearly discernible rising trend of rice yield in virtually every province for subsequent periods up to the nineteenth century. Even when all the necessary qualifications of data have been made, it is still reasonable to conclude, as Perkins argues, that rice yields per unit of land rose slowly but significantly over the past nine centuries.

Muramatsu Yuji has presented some data on rent payments by the tenants to a bursary in Su-chou during 1878-94 for leased lands located in six subdivisions in Ch'ang-chou and three subdivisions in Wu-chiang.[71] It is a happy coincidence that similar rent records exist for leased lands located in these subdivisions for much earlier dates (1204-1311). If the assumption that rents as a share of land yield remained stable during this period is accepted, the following indices of land productivity may be derived from these two sets of rent statistics:

Chang-chou	153.8%
Wu-chiang	131.9%
Unweighted average	142.8%

Again, there is strong evidence that the rice yield increased before the eighteenth century and either declined slightly or stagnated thereafter. According to the *Pu Nung Shu* (Supplement to the Treatise on Agriculture), an agricultural handbook published in the mid-seventeenth century for the Kiangnan region, the measured rice yields in three Chekiang counties (Wu-hsing, Tung-hsiang and Hai-yen) ranged from 518 to 681 catties per *shih mou*. Comparing with the average rice yield of 402 catties per *shih mou* cited earlier for Chekiang during the Sung, the implied growth varied from 28 percent to 69 percent. Yet rice yields reported for the same three counties were lower in 1928, between 300 catties and 400 catties.[72] Even the record yield on the best farmland with the most efficient labor in this district reached a mere 550 catties per *shih mou* before 1949, which is slightly above the low yield figure of 518 catties but still 24 percent short of the high yield of 681 catties given by *Pu Nung Shu* for the mid-seventeenth century.

4. *Composite grain yield.* Theoretically, a composite indicator of land productivity at a given point in time is the weighted average of unit yields of individual crops produced at that time. For the very early period of the Chinese agricultural history—say, 200 B.C.—even the weighting problem is simple, because grain production was dominated almost exclusively by a single crop—millet. It cannot be too far off, if the unit yield of millet, 96 catties per *shih mou*, is taken as the composite productivity indicator for that period.

For the twelfth century, the other benchmark period, there were three main crops—millet as the leading crop in the north, rice in the south, and wheat as a secondary crop in both north and south. The importance of rice in the Sung is demonstrated by the annual shipment of as much as 6 million *shih* of rice from Kiangnan to the north via the grand canal. The fact that Wang Chen still listed millet as the primary staple in the country in his *Nung shu* (Treatise on Agriculture) published in 1313, however, suggests that millet had not been surpassed by rice and wheat in popularity by then. Based on such nonquantitative information, we assign an arbitrary set of weights to the three crops for the purpose of computing a weighted average:

Crop	Unit yield	Weight
Millet	104	40%
Wheat	108	30%
Rice	310	30%

The average unit yield in the twelfth century is then estimated at 167 catties per *shih mou*. Because the unit yields of millet and wheat did not differ greatly, a redistribution of weights between them would not alter the result substantially. The weight for rice is a crucial factor, which, if reduced to 25 percent, would render a lower average yield of 157 catties per *shih mou*. This figure may be regarded as the lower limit.

No computation is necessary for modern times. The unit yield for composite grain was officially given as 176 catties per *shih mou* of sown area in 1952. If the multiple-cropping index for grain in 1952 is assumed to be 135,[73] the unit yield of grain per *mou* of cultivated area would then be 238 catties, or 42.5 percent higher than that in the twelfth century.

Even without similar estimates for the intervening periods, and notwithstanding the short-run fluctuations, the general trends of development can still be detected. The yield increase was faster after the transition of agricultural production. But this was realized primarily through the expansion of rice cultivation, and to a lesser degree through the planting of potatoes. As soon as the potentials of those approaches had been exhausted, improvement in yield came to a halt. This point probably arrived by the eighteenth century,[74] after which the average yield in China remained approximately the same, except for some short-run fluctuations, for about a hundred and fifty years.

Per Capita Grain Output and Living Standards

The previous sections have demonstrated that Chinese farmers were compelled by population pressure after the eleventh century to switch to intensive farming by providing more labor per unit of land each year and that yields increased as a consequence. But whether the rise in yields was sufficient to avoid a decline in per capita output remains a question. Perkins admits the high possibility of a decline in per capita grain output and a general deterioration in economic conditions in China after 1770.[75] I am able to strengthen his contention by showing that this deterioration probably came much earlier.

From Table 5.1 and the preceding three sections I have assembled the following data for estimating per capita grain output for two specific periods.

Measure	1st century	11th century
Per capita cultivated area (*shih mou*)	9.67	5.50
Percent fallow land	40%	0%
Percent grain land	90%	80%
Unit yield of grain (catties)	96	167
Per capita grain output (catties)	501	735

Obviously there was a rising trend of per capita grain output between the two benchmark dates. Because there existed an upper limit of human consumption of grain and both nonhuman consumption and exports of grain were negligible in Chinese history, a per capita grain output of 735 catties was probably the peak level, or at least very close to it.

There are more reliable data for computing per capita grain output for 1949-52:[76]

Year	Grain output (billion catties)	Population (000)	Per capita output (catties)
1949	216.2	536,370	403
1950	249.4	546,820	456
1951	270.1	557,480	484
1952	308.8	567,910	542

The average for the four years was 471 catties, or 64 percent of the Sung level, a discrepancy too large to be fully explained by errors of estimation. There was probably a long trend of decline, if short-run respites are ignored. This declining trend must have begun long before the eighteenth century, perhaps as early as the fifteenth century, because if such a sharp drop had taken place over a period of a hundred years or

216

less, it would inevitably have caused some drastic social responses. But when the deterioration came only gradually and accumulated over five hundred years or so, the change might not be shocking, or even noticeable, during any short time interval. Although the populace might be fully aware of their present sorry plight, they might not be equally aware that they were poorer than before.

This contention may be supported by a tentative estimate of per capita output for the intervening years. Per capita cultivated areas in 1812 and 1887 are given in Table 5.1 as 3.19 *shih mou* and 2.70 *shih mou*, respectively. Assuming that the composite grain yield stopped increasing at the end of the eighteenth century (that is, using the 1952 unit yield) and that about 80 percent of farmland was devoted to grain production, we may obtain the following estimates of per capita output: for 1812, 3.19 × 0.8 × 238 = 607 catties; for 1882, 2.70 × 0.8 × 238 = 514 catties.

Or, taking the eleventh century level as 100, the indices of per capita grain output for the subsequent periods would be: eleventh century, 100%; 1812, 83%; 1882, 70%; 1949-52, 64%. The early Ming and the early Ch'ing were probably two short respites in the long trend of deteriorating conditions as the result of the temporary improvement in the man-land ratio.

The per capita grain output in 1949-52 was both the end result of the long worsening process and the very lowest point ever reached in Chinese agricultural history. The trend of deterioration after the Sung had the unfortunate and ironic effect that the Chinese populace suffered a reduced per capita output although they were working longer and harder. The population increase was so large that the combined effects of farmland expansion and the rising unit yields under intensified farming were not enough to offset the reduced returns to labor.

The foregoing situation may be viewed from another angle. Agricultural development in China after the Sung dynasty was characterized simultaneously by an increase in the marginal product of land and a decrease in the marginal product of labor. The latter change should be reflected in a secular trend of declining real wages, especially the wages of farm laborers. In a recent study, I have compiled historical data of wages for workers—most were figures of actual wage payments and some were wage rates stipulated or announced by the employers.[77] They are converted into monthly wages, if originally otherwise reported, and then converted into quantities of millet or rice—that is, in real terms,

217

TABLE 9.2
Real Wage Rates for Various Types of Work, 50 B.C.-A.D. 1818

Approximate date	Location	Type of worker	Monthly cash wage (*wen* or *chien*)	Grain equivalent (*sheng*)[a]
50 B.C.	Ho-hsi	farmer	424	131.9
50 B.C.	Ho-hsi	farmer	700	217.8
27 A.D.	Ho-hsi	farmer	—	120.0
150	unknown	servant	1,000	342.5
770	Ch'ang-an	farmer	—	160.0
1107	Szechwan	tea picker	1,800	165.0
1080	K'ai-feng	servant	3,000	400.0
1080	K'ai-feng	worker	3,000	400.0
1086	K'ai-feng	draft worker	6,000	800.0
1132	Hang-chou	factory worker	—	132.8
1132	Hang-chou	general service	—	112.8
1136	Fukien	tea picker	2,100	15.0
1180	unknown	servant	1,350	—
1180	Kiangsi	servant	900	—
1181	Hang-chou	winemaker	1,000	—
1580	Chekiang	farmer	183	16.6
1580	Chekiang	oil presser	2,400	201.0
1640	Su-chou	river cleaner	600	51.0
1640	Chekiang	farmer	250	22.7
1640	Nan-shun	silk reeler	1,200	109.0
1732	Shansi	farmer	333	32.8
1732	Shansi	farmer	1,200	117.0
1734	Shantung	farmer	2,280	220.0
1737	Kwangtung	cane cutter	450	27.0
1738	Su-chou	silk worker	—	30.0
1738	Su-chou	silk worker	—	51.7
1738	Su-chou	silk worker	—	31.1
1738	Su-chou	silk worker	—	41.4
1738	Su-chou	silk worker	—	30.0
1747	Nanking	silk worker	960	55.0
1747	Nanking	painter	500	28.6
1747	Nanking	silk worker	1,500	86.2
1747	Nanking	silk worker	608	34.9
1741	Shansi	farmer	300	18.0
1742	Shensi	farmer	400	24.3
1744	Anhwei	farmer	292	17.7
1744	Kiangsu	farmer	167	10.0
1749	Shensi	farmer	1,200	78.0
1752	Chekiang	farmer	683	51.2
1760	Chekiang	farmer	333	17.3
1761	Honan	farmer	1,200	45.0
1765	Hopei	farmer	1,428	73.5
1773	Honan	farmer	375	14.3
1773	Honan	farmer	275	10.5
1773	Kwangtung	farmer	300	11.5
1778	Kiangsu	farmer	600	21.0
1789	Kiangsu	farmer	300	11.5
1797	Kwangtung	farmer	667	22.3

Table 9.2—cont.

Approximate date	Location	Type of worker	Monthly cash wage (*wen* or *chien*)	Grain equivalent (*sheng*)[a]
1797	Kwangsi	farmer	600	20.7
1798	Hupei	farmer	600	20.7
1798	Kweichow	farmer	217	7.4
1798	Yunnan	farmer	300	10.4
1799	Kiangsu	farmer	500	17.1
1801	Szechwan	farmer	333	11.2
1801	Honan	farmer	275	9.5
1801	Shensi	farmer	417	14.3
1802	Kansu	farmer	250	8.7
1803	Anhwei	farmer	300	10.4
1804	Kiangsi	farmer	480	16.5
1805	Yunnan	farmer	108	3.7
1809	Fukien	farmer	1,000	34.5
1810	Szechwan	farmer	500	17.3
1818	Hopei	farmer	433	12.0

SOURCE: Chao and Chen 1984, table 6-1.

[a] 1 *sheng* equals 0.01 *shih*.

according to the grain prices in the same localities and same years from which the wage rates are taken. All data are presented in Table 9.2.

As expected, the real wage varied over a wide range in any period, reflecting differences in skills, regions, and so on. The ranges between the lowest real wage and the highest real wage shown in Table 9.1 are summarized as follows:

Period	Real wage (*sheng*)	Period	Real wage (*sheng*)
Han (206 B.C.-220 A.D.)	120-343	Ming (1369-1644)	17-201
T'ang (618-907)	160	Ch'ing, Yung-cheng reign (1723-1735)	33-220
Northern Sung (961-1127)	165-800	Ch'ing, Ch'ien lung reign (1736-1795)	10-86
Southern Sung (1128-1279)	15-133	Ch'ing, Chia-ch'ing reign (1796-1820)	4-35

Both the lowest and the highest wages showed more or less similar secular trends—a gradual rise between the Han and the Northern Sung and a decline thereafter, with a respite during the early Ch'ing.

The lower end of the wage scale is more meaningful than the upper end as a measure of the marginal product of labor in general and the prevailing standard of living. High wages were renumeration for highly skilled workers determined by the scarcity of that special category of labor, whereas low wages were payment to unskilled workers and farm laborers, hence indicative of the general state of labor supply in the time. Moreover, many of the lowest wages, such as those for the Han, T'ang and Ming, represent the original figures of wages in kind (certain quantities of grain) paid to farm laborers, which are completely free from any conversion errors.

It should be pointed out that it was an established custom in traditional China for employers to provide meals for their workers during the time period of employment. If 30 *sheng* (about 42 catties of grain) is allowed for as the subsistence cost for hiring farm laborers, the total cost at the low end of the wage scale in various historical periods may be estimated (in *sheng*) as:

Han	150	Ming	47
T'ang	190	Ch'ing (1723-1735)	63
Northern Sung	195	Ch'ing (1736-1795)	40
Southern Sung	45	Ch'ing (1796-1820)	34

The sharp drop in the agricultural wage rate occurred in the Southern Sung. By the mid-Ch'ing, landlords barely paid the subsistence cost to their hired hands, signifying an extremely low marginal productivity of labor at that time. As explained in Chapter 7, managerial landlords felt that hiring farm laborers was less profitable even at this low wage rate than leasing out their lands. Consequently they were inclined to give up self-operation and became tenurial landlords.

IO

Conclusions

FAILING TO SEE the close resemblance between Chinese and European economic history that is claimed by many historians, we must now take a new look at the development of China's economy. Instead of clear-cut stages characterized by distinct modes of production replacing each other in succession, we have seen strong indications that in the past two millennia or so China was very close to a market economy, with the same basic option space found in ordinary market economies. I have therefore made the following hypotheses: (1) The numerous participants in such an economy would make decisions independently to maximize their economic gains subject to existing constraints. (2) One important constraint faced by the premodern Chinese populace was probably the limited amount of farmland relative to population size. (3) Certain institutional and technological developments in traditional China may be interpreted as results of the populace's revised preferences in responding to this changing constraint.

In spite of the danger of overemphasizing a single factor in interpreting historical events, historical data appear to be consistent with these hypotheses. The impacts of population pressure on farm institutions and on the choice of farming technologies are obvious.

A careful examination of historical records of population and cultivated acreages indicates that these data, though poor in quality by modern statistical standards, do reveal meaningful trend lines. This is particularly true when our main concern is the man-land ratio, because the two sets of statistics were usually subject to the same types of biases, which tend to offset each other to a large extent when the two variables are put in the ratio form. After proper adjustments on the original data, the measured man-land ratio showed some slight improvement, or at least did not deteriorate, until the tenth century. Thereafter it began to fluctuate along a declining trend line, a decline that became more noticeable and more rapid after the seventeenth century.

Because of resilient economic institutions, overpopulation did not express itself in the form of open unemployment and high population pressure can be detected only indirectly. The twelfth century appears to be a crucial turning point, for by this time the average sown area per household had decreased from its previous maximum of 80 *shih mou* to less than 25 *shih mou*. This circumstance suggests a change in the use of labor. Put in a comparative perspective, at the same time that each serf in the English manorial system had a land allotment not substantially short of the 30 acres recorded by the Domesday Book of 1086, the average peasant household in China tilled less than 5 acres of land.[1]

The twelfth century also witnessed the beginning of a process in which farmland became fragmented and the beginning of a long declining trend in the proportion of urban population to total population. These effects I believe to be not sheer coincidence but a further manifestation of overpopulation.

The Chinese populace made economic choices according to comparative gains. As a result, parallel modes of production existed for more than two thousand years. In terms of ownership systems, the basic land institution was private ownership; in terms of operation systems, owner-cultivators, managerial landlords, and tenurial landlords; and in terms of labor sources, slaves, indentured workers, and tenants. Serfs, however, were never a part of the Chinese agrarian system, and the Chinese form of slavery differed in many significant respects from its European counterpart. All these alternative institutions were drawn on freely until a general equilibrium was reached.

The simultaneous existence of different modes of production in premodern China does not mean that no changes occurred in land institutions. The relative importance of various modes of production did change over time, and drastically. These alterations were responses to changed economic conditions and comparative gains.

No one denies that farmland as wealth was unequally distributed in traditional China. Yet no evidence survives that clearly demonstrates either that land distribution in traditional China was more unequal than in most other countries or that a situation of poor distribution had worsened over time. It is the increasing man-land ratio, not the poor distribution of farmland, that produced China's impoverishment.

The continued gains in population affected the distribution of private land ownership. When increasingly more people wished to buy land while increasingly fewer people were willing to alienate property, land owner-ship gradually became dispersed and the number of major landlords tended to decrease. The available quantitative data on land distribution since the Northern Sung seem to support this contention. By the early twentieth century, only a handful of large landlords had survived; roughly 70 percent of farmland in the country had devolved into the hands of small- and medium-sized owner-cultivators.

The dispersion of land ownership implies that fairly large numbers of participants were present on both sides in the factor markets. This pre-sumption is further supported by the circumstance that landlords often adopted different tenure systems simultaneously because they could not determine such matters purely on the basis of their own preferences.

Another interesting discovery is that the standard distribution shares under sharecropping tenancy were fixed at 50-50 in China for more than two thousand years. This finding helps resolve a dispute in land tenure theory. On the basis of the partial equilibrium theory of share tenancy, the portion of income owed to sharecroppers is equivalent to the price at which landlords hire them. It follows naturally that as the man-land ratio in the economy rises, so does the landlord's share, whereas the share-cropper's portion tends to decline, an effect analogous to price fluctuation in response to demand variation in ordinary markets. In contrast, the general equilibrium theory contends that landlord and sharecropper are partners who negotiate an equilibrium compromise. Such a compromise may be attained through negotiating distribution shares, or relative con-tributions of land and labor, or both. It is possible, therefore, for them to fix the distributive shares for the sake of simplicity and merely negotiate their relative contributions of resources. This finding conforms with gen-eral equilibrium theory, because such a remarkable stability of distri-bution shares over such a long time, in spite of the continuously rising man-land ratio, is utterly inconceivable on the basis of partial equili-brium analysis.

Chinese tenure systems and farming technology also changed in re-sponse to mounting population pressure. Beginning in the late Northern Sung, overpopulation resulted in the adoption of production organiza-tions that were more flexible in matching productive factors with some types of labor-intensive technology. This evolution assumed a cyclical pattern, as did population growth in China.

From that time onward, the proportion of owner-cultivators seems to

have risen, whereas managerial landlordism gradually gave way to tenurial landlordism. Surplus population, as defined by marginal theorists,
depended on their families for a living. Since more labor inputs were
used on tenant farms than on latifundia, the land productivity of the former was relatively high. This in turn led to the high rent income of tenurial landlords relative to the profits of managerial landlords, a situation
clearly illustrated by the cost comparison of the two types of farms presented in Shen's *Nun Shu*.

The tendency to make production units and family units coincident
after the twelfth century was not confined to agricultural production. To
a certain extent, nonagricultural production showed a similar gain in do-
mesticity. The institutional flexibility of premodern China permitted
such a shift as long as it was technically feasible. As explained in Chapter
1, a landless person had the option of either working in a handicraft factory as a full-time worker or engaging in nonagricultural subsidiary production on a part-time basis in his rural home. This dichotomy paralleled
the distinction between working as a hired farmhand and being a tenant.
After overpopulation reduced the marginal product of labor to below the
subsistence level, subsistence cost constituted a wage floor for both latifundia and handicraft factories. Just like tenant farming, rural subsidiary
production by household members had no such cost rigidity. Because
surplus labor had no opportunity cost, individual families could use such
labor until its marginal product approached zero. In other words, because the family was obliged to support its members regardless of their
respective contributions, encouraging an idle member to earn a penny
was superior to his earning nothing at all.

The other profound impact of overpopulation was on the technological preference of producers. Again, the twelfth century may serve as
the approximate line dividing two patterns of technological orientation
in the agricultural history of China. Up to that time there had been a
flow of inventions of new farm implements, including the improved
plow that required less draft power, the shareplow that could turn over
the sod to form a furrow, and the deep-tooth harrow. All of these devices
were labor saving by nature. This stream of inventions had run its course
by the end of the twelfth century. According to Dwight Perkins, 77 different kinds of farm implements, not including irrigation equipment,
were listed in Wang Chen's *Nung Shu* (Treatise on Agriculture), published in 1313; of these devices, all but one were also included in agricultural handbooks published several hundred years later. Perkins is

right in saying that to assume that Chinese peasants were either too conservative or too unimaginative to try new tools is inconsistent with the
fact that they were quite capable of developing such a range of new implements. As a matter of fact, the Chinese people not only did not invent
any new implements in the later period, they also rejected the mechanical
principles that were introduced to China by foreign missionaries during
the Ming-Ch'ing and that could be easily embodied in farm implements.
Obviously, this is not a sign of lack of inventiveness but rather of changed
technological preference.

The technological development of farm tools in China literally stopped.
Implements used in the thirteenth century were still in use in the early
twentieth century. The few new tools invented during this time interval
were the so-called hand tools (*shou-kung-chü*) that were employed to replace animal-drawn implements. Labor-intensive in nature, they represented a backward trend in technological preference.

The primary direction of Chinese agricultural development after the
twelfth century was towards intensified farming. Beginning approximately at this time, the populace made increasingly great efforts to reclaim lands previously deemed unsuitable for agricultural use. They developed hilly, sandy, marshy, and other low-lying lands. Terraced fields
on mountains and diked fields or polders along seacoasts or surrounding
large lakes became very common during the Southern Sung.

Another important factor in Chinese agricultural development after
the twelfth century was the transformation of cropping systems. The index of multiple cropping was still below unity during the early Northern
Sung. Fallowing and slash-and-burn methods every two or three years
were still practiced in many areas. I believe that the index quickly
reached unity and continued to ascend in the Southern Sung. Many
double-cropping systems were introduced, including rice-rice, wheat-
rice, and wheat-barley, depending on local conditions. In addition, rice
crops were gradually extended northward wherever the length of the
frostfree period and the water supply permitted. Rice, the most labor-
intensive crop, was able to supply more calories per unit of land than any
other crop. It should be noted that these changes in cropping systems not
only absorbed a great deal more labor per unit of land but also created
labor shortages during the juncture when farmers had to simultaneously
reap the first crop and prepare the land and sow or transplant the second
crop.

Because of resilient land institutions and their timely adjustment, overpopulation was never directly observable. Yet the fact that very few in the Chinese countryside were visibly idle has misled many scholars into harboring the belief that no surplus population existed at any time. This notion has been reinforced by the observation that more labor would be needed during peak seasons in double-cropping areas. What these scholars continue to overlook is that, given the Chinese family system, labor was a variable productive factor only before the point where the marginal product of labor was equal to subsistence cost, but became a fixed productive factor after that point. Thus, labor would be used up as a fixed factor. Instead of maximizing net income by equating the marginal product of labor to marginal cost, the family tended to maximize total output until the marginal product of labor became zero. Therefore, idle labor would not be observable even after that point, not until the marginal product actually reduced to zero.

After the production institutions had adjusted themselves and technological preference had reversed to the labor-intensive variety, more labor was absorbed into the Chinese system. Everyone was made to work, regardless of his contribution. Full employment was apparent. During peak seasons, all members of the family were mobilized. Even school children were sent home to work, for they were still "helpful." Under such conditions, the term "labor shortage" is to be construed in an altogether different way than its ordinary meaning.

Declines in per capita grain output and in real wages after the Sung dynasty are discernible from historical data. These declines may be either too gradual to capture the attention of historians or, while acknowledged, attributed to a deterioration of wealth distribution or a malfunctioning of the feudal system. This hidden surplus population constituted a burden to society in economic terms.

The foregoing observations and analyses offer some interesting hypotheses about Chinese economic history. It is generally believed among Western economists that the market system provides an efficient mechanism to allocate resources. We may thus reasonably assume that the more impressive economic performance of China up to the twelfth century as compared to that of feudal Europe was attributable mainly to the country's relatively efficient economic institutions. Conditions in China were also conducive to accumulation of engineering knowledge and advances in technology.

These institutions, however, were too flexible to serve in checking population expansion. In time they became more labor absorbing in the face of deteriorating economic conditions. Thus, the population continued to expand. Meanwhile, scientific and engineering knowledge accumulated over time, a development that was initially fast paced. In a sense, there was a race between population growth and technological advancement in this early part of Chinese history, but unfortunately, the latter lost the race and dropped out. This hypothesis may help explain the so-called "Needham paradox," namely: Why did an industrial revolution take place in eighteenth century England but not in Sung China? Why did Chinese till with iron plows when Europeans used wood, and why did they continue to use plows when Europeans used tractors? What caused China to stagnate technologically for more than eight centuries? To answer these questions, we may resort to supply-demand analysis as taught in elementary economics. The item to be analyzed is the availability of machines. The European Industrial Revolution was characterized by the use of machines that saved enormous amounts of labor and made mass production feasible. Furthermore, all subsequent economic progress in the West has been associated with the invention of better and more labor-saving machines.

Production of machines involves supply and demand. On the supply side the most crucial element is not iron or coal, but a threshold level of technology for inventing new machinery. This threshold depends on the accumulation of scientific knowledge and engineering acumen over a long period of time. According to Marco Polo—or more reliably, Joseph Needham—Sung China had already approached the threshold of technological invention and was far more advanced than Europe in craftsmanship and engineering skill. By this time, however, the Chinese population had grown to the point where there was no longer any need to save labor. There was no longer a demand for labor-saving devices because people were concerned with the problem of how to dispose of unused labor gainfully. Without requisite demand, no production or invention can take place, even if it was technologically feasible. England—or, for that matter, all of Europe—was more fortunate than China in the sense that even though its scientific development and engineering ability lagged behind China's, by the time sufficient knowledge was accumulated to the point of permitting the invention of machines, a strong need to save labor was still acutely felt. The presence of both supply and demand in the West at this critical point made production of machines viable.

China, meanwhile, had fallen into a trap of overpopulation, and institutional flexibility only worsened the situation. Overpopulation induced the populace to adopt more labor-intensive technology and labor-absorbing institutions, which in turn raised the limit of tolerance for overpopulation. The population would then expand still further, and the flexible institutions would adjust themselves still further. While capable of alleviating short-run human suffering, China's institutional resiliency prolonged its economic stagnation.

Appendixes

Appendix A
Selected Traditional Units of Measure

Dynasty	Period	Cm. per _ch'ih_	Meters per _li_	Sq. m. per _mou_	Liters per _shih_
Chou	1121-221 B.C.	22.50	405.0	182.25	19.3
Ch'in	220-206 B.C.	23.10	415.8	461.04	19.3
Western Han	205 B.C.-A.D. 8	23.10	415.8	461.04	34.2
Eastern Han	9-220	23.75	427.5	487.34	19.8
Wei	221-265	24.12	434.2	502.65	20.2
Western Chin	266-316	24.12	434.2	502.65	20.2
Eastern Chin	317-420	24.45	440.0	516.50	20.2
Southern and Northern Dynasties	421-580	29.51	531.2	752.40	39.6
Sui	581-618	29.60	532.8	757.00	59.4
T'ang	619-906	30.00	450.0	540.00	59.4
Five Dynasties	907-960	31.00	465.0	576.60	59.4
Sung	961-1279	31.00	465.0	576.60	66.4
Yuan	1280-1368	34.00	510.0	693.60	94.8
Ming	1369-1644	34.00	510.0	693.60	107.3
Ch'ing	1645-1911	34.00	510.0	693.60	103.5
Republic	1912-	33.33	500.0	666.53	100.0

Appendix B
Political Subdivisions in Traditional China

Dynasty	Highest level	Intermediate level	Lowest level
Western Han	*chou*	*chun* or *kuo*	*hsien*
Eastern Han	*chou*	*chun* or *kuo*	*hsien*
Wei	*chou*	*chun*	*hsien*
Western Chin	*chou*	*chun* or *kuo*	*hsien*
Eastern Chin	*chou*	*chun* or *kuo*	*hsien*
Southern and Northern Dynasties	—	—	—
Sui	—	—	—
T'ang	*tao*	*chou* or *chun*	*hsien*
Five Dynasties	—	—	—
Sung	*lu*	*chou, fu, chun,* or *chien*	*hsien*
Yuan	*sheng* (1)	*lu* (2), *fu* (3), *chou* (4)	*hsien* (5)
Ming	*sheng*	*fu*	*hsien*
Ch'ing	*sheng* (1)	*tao* (2), *fu* (3)	*hsien* (4)

NOTE: "—" means no standard subdivisions.

232

Appendix C
Unit Yields and Farm Sizes in the Ch'ing Period

With the selective publication of the K'ung Fu (Mansion of Confucius) archives, it is possible to calculate the changes in grain yield, as well as the average farm sizes of tenants who rented lands from K'ung Fu.[1] Although the K'ung Fu management maintained fairly complete records of farm operations and rent collection on its estates over a period of five or six hundred years, the published volume of archives includes only selected estates in a few benchmark years spanning approximately the years 1653-1940. These estates were located in Chü-fu, Ssu-sui, Tsou-hsien, and Wen-shang counties in the province of Shantung.

In terms of type of management, K'ung Fu's land fell into three categories—those under the estate's direct operation, those leased to tenants under sharecropping contracts, and those leased to tenants on a fixed-rent basis. The fact that all three types of management were found in the same localities and lands in each category were divided into various grades suggests that neither the location nor the quality of land was the criterion determining the form of management.

Judging from the records, the sharecropping contract stipulated a 50-50 division between the tenants and K'ung Fu for the crop to be grown. Lands under the fixed-rent arrangement, however, were classified into two types: two crops, wheat and beans, were grown annually in the so-called wheat land, but only one crop of millet, *kaoliang*, or some other coarse grain was planted annually in the so-called *ch'iu tien* (autumn land). Rental payments were predetermined for all crops to be produced, either in crops or in cash. In the case of wheat land requiring a rental payment in kind, the sum of wheat rent and bean rent represented the total annual rent.

K'ung Fu maintained its own measurement gauges, which differed considerably from the official measurement systems in use during the Ch'ing and the Republican periods. Under the K'ung Fu system, each *mou* consisted of 1,666 square meters, or 2.5 times the size of the Ch'ing *mou*. The size of K'ung Fu's *tou*, a volume measurement for grain, is not clear, however. One of the published archives states: "For measuring wheat, each *tou* contains 64 catties. For measuring beans, each *tou* contains 60 catties. For measuring millet, each *tou* contains 56 catties."[2] These numbers suggest that the K'ung Fu *tou* was substantially larger than the standard unit. On the other hand, the editors of the volume of selected archives use a conversion ratio that makes 2.5 *tou* of the K'ung Fu system equivalent to a standard *tou*.[3] As long as the K'ung Fu estate managers used their own measurement systems consistently throughout, we may unambiguously detect changes in yield and farm size.

Yields Under Fixed-Rent Contracts

In traditional China, the rent level of fixed-rent tenancy was generally set at 50 percent of the "normal" yield and was held constant regardless of variation in actual output. It was subject to adjustment, however, if the normal yield had changed. Thus, rent adjustments over a long period of time indicate yield changes. Because the rent data (*tou* per *mou*) in this study have been selected from different years, and because the classification of land was not uniform for different localities, we can tabulate the data only separately for each locality, as given in Table C.1.

Among the seven localities, the exceptional case is Hung-miao Chuang, where the rent levels for all four grades of land rose. In the other six localities, there are eleven cases of reduced rents, nine instances of unchanged rents, and only two cases of increased rents. The general trend of declining yield during the period is quite obvious. Or, to say the least, there is no sign suggesting a clear trend in the opposite direction. Among the eleven instances of rent reduction, the extent of reduction ranges from 20 percent to 43 percent; four of them were reduced by one-third. Though it is impossible to determine the exact time of rent adjustments on the basis of these data, the adjustments appear to have taken place before 1890.

Yields on Self-Operated Lands and Sharecropping Lands

Some of K'ung Fu's lands were directly operated by its estate managers with hired hands or leased out to tenants under the sharecropping arrangement. From the records of annual output and rent collection of those lands, I have obtained the actual yields for the years reported, which may or may not have been "normal" years. Unfortunately, this

TABLE C.I

*Rents Under Fixed-Rent Contracts for Selected Estates
in Shantung Province, 1653-1926*

(*tou* per *mou*)

Grade of land	Ch'un-ting Chuang			Nan-chi Chuang				
	1655	1891	1911	1653	1853	1889	1919	1930
Upper	5	6	6	6	4	4	4	4
Upper-medium	4	4	4	—	—	—	—	—
Medium	3.5	3.5	3.5	4	3	3	3	3
Lower-medium	3	2	2	—	—	—	—	—
Lower	1.5	1.5	1.5	2	2	2	2	2
Lower-lower	1	1	1	—	—	1	0.8	—

Grade of land	Ch'i-wang Chuang			Ta Chuang				
	1655	1885	1925	1653	1889	1925	1928	1939
Upper	6.5	4	4	4.5	3	3	3	3
Medium	4	2.8	2.8	3.5	2.5	2.5	2.5	2.5
Lower	2	2.4	2.4	2	2	2	2	2
Lower-lower	—	—	—	—	—	1	1	1

Grade of land	Chang-yang Chuang		Hung-miao Chuang		An-chi Chuang			
	1653	1856	1653	1925	1655	1798	1901	1926
Upper	7	4	3.5	4	4	4	4	4
Medium	4	2.5	2.5	3	3	2	2	2
Lower-medium	3	—	—	—	2	—	—	—
Lower	2	2	1.5	2	1	1	1	1
Lower-lower	—	1	0.8	1.5	0.5	0.5	0.5	0.5

NOTE: "—" means no data.

compilation of archives has included only a small quantity of such materials. This is particularly true for self-operated lands, for which data are only available for two years; it is unclear whether self-operation of farm production in the K'ung Fu estates was entirely discontinued thereafter.

The 1655 output for the locality of Ch'i-wang Chuang alone was:

Land	Acreage (*mou*)	Rent per *mou* (*tou*)	Yield per *mou* (*tou*)
Wheat land, self-operation	182.9		6.16
Wheat land, sharecropping	69.9	2.28	4.56
Bean land, self-operation	37		8.78
Bean land, sharecropping	39	4.49	8.98

Based on the same rules of computation used in the previous section, the annual yields (i.e., the sum of wheat and bean yields) in 1655 were 14.94

235

TABLE C.2
*Rents and Yields for One K'ung Fu Estate, Ch'i-wang Chuang,
Selected Years, 1788-1807*

Year	Type of crop	Highest rent per *mou*	Lowest rent per *mou*	Average rent per *mou*	Average yield per *mou*
1788	wheat	1.733	0.058	1.087	2.174
1803	beans	0.300	0.174	0.202	0.404
1803	buckwheat	—	—	0.305	0.610
1805	wheat	—	—	0.807	1.614
1805	*kaoliang*	—	—	1.224	2.448
1805	millet	—	—	1.554	3.108
1805	sorghum	—	—	1.003	2.006
1805	beans	—	—	0.203	0.406
1807	wheat	1.087	0.072	0.710	1.420

tou for lands under self-operation and 13.54 *tou* for sharecropping lands.
It may be recalled that normal yields in Ch'i-wang Chuang during the
period around 1655, as indicated by the amounts of fixed rents, were:
upper grade, 13 *tou*; medium grade, 8 *tou*; lower grade, 4 *tou*. A comparison of the two sets of yield data suggests that 1655 was a better than
normal year as far as the grain output in that region was concerned.

By 1788, the second year for which yield data of Ch'i-wang Chuang
have been selected for publication, the total acreage of wheat land had
been reduced from the original 252.8 *mou* to 246.5 *mou*. Moreover, self-
operation of farmland had been discontinued; the entire 246.5 *mou* were
leased to sharecroppers. The manager of the Ch'i-wang Chuang estate
made the following estimates for various grades of land shortly before
harvesting:

Land	Acreage (*mou*)	Estimated yield (*tou* per *mou*)	Expected rent (*tou* per *mou*)
Upper grade, wheat	29.3	5.0	2.5
Medium grade, wheat	105.9	2.4	1.2
Lower grade, wheat	108.5	2.0	1.0
Barley land	2.8	2.0	1.0

The weighted average of yields for the four grades of land is 2.52 *tou* per
mou, or an expected average rent of 1.26 *tou* per *mou*. After the harvest,
only the total amount of actual rent collection was recorded, without any
breakdown for different grades of land. This gave an average rent of
1.087 *tou* per *mou*, or an average yield of 2,174 *tou* per *mou*.

Yield data for the selected years after 1788 were recorded in such a
way that it is no longer possible to distinguish preharvest estimates from
actual yields measured after harvesting. In view of the closeness between

TABLE C.3
Yields for One K'ung Fu Estate, Wen-shang County, 1736-1775

Year	Wheat	Kaoliang	Brown and black beans	Miscellaneous grain
1736	5.27	3.28	3.37	6.32
1737	3.09	5.06	2.57	8.61
1738	4.39	6.52	2.27	6.98
1740	3.71	4.79	3.01	3.86
1742	2.17	4.88	1.08	4.21
1743	2.59	4.03	2.24	5.31
1744	3.19	5.33	3.39	4.90
1750	3.21	4.52	2.65	2.24
1751	2.15	0.94	0.28	0.83
1752	2.00	2.46	0.73	1.92
1754	2.17	3.00	0.37	2.86
1755	3.46	3.13	1.62	2.55
1756	2.61	2.82	0.47	1.56
1766	2.64	2.48	0.42	2.60
1767	1.98	3.13	1.13	2.64
1768	1.28	2.62	0.80	2.67
1770	1.82	3.72	2.44	3.11
1771	1.73	0.65	0.14	0.23
1772	3.14	5.05	1.96	2.03
1773	2.52	4.10	1.86	4.75
1775	2.11	4.02	0.66	3.41

the estimates and actual yields shown here, however, we have treated all such data as actual yields. They are listed in Table C.2. It is obvious from these data that grain yields in Ch'i-wang Chuang during 1788-1807 were lower than that in 1655 by a large margin, too large to be explained by cyclical fluctuations caused by variation in cropping and climatic conditions. Moreover, because the data for 1788-1807 are taken from four different years, the probability that all were below-normal years is extremely slight.

The best set of data is from Mei-hua Chuang in Wen-shang county, where K'ung Fu leased out about 900 *mou* of farmland to tenants, mostly under 50-50 sharecropping contracts.[4] Both rent payments and yields are known for 21 years between 1736 and 1775. As shown in Table C.3, the landlord's share of yield (*tou*) per *mou* clearly declined for all four types of crop during the period.

There are scattered data of the same type for K'ung Fu estates in other localities that, although they cannot be used to construct an intertemporal comparison of yields in the strict sense, are nevertheless indicative of the direction of change. Those data are presented in Table C.4. The general picture revealed by these yield data is almost identical with what

TABLE C.4
Rents and Yields for Assorted K'ung Fu Estates,
Various Locations, 1653-1788
(*tou*)

Crop	Highest rent per *mou*	Lowest rent per *mou*	Average rent per *mou*	Average yield per *mou*
Nan-chi Chuang, 1653:				
Self-operated, wheat, medium	—	—	—	8.917
Sharecropping, wheat, medium	—	—	2.679	5.357
Ma-p'o-ch'uan Chuang, 1653: Sharecropping, sorghum	—	—	3.520	7.040
Ta Chuang:				
1788, wheat	1.836	0.625	1.665	3.330
1803, beans	0.371	0.048	0.167	0.334
1803, buckwheat	1.133	0.092	0.872	1.744
1803, millet	2.350	1.000	1.643	3.286
1803, *kaoliang*	0.629	0.407	0.450	0.900
1806, wheat	1.359	0.884	1.187	2.374
Chang-yang Chuang:				
1788, wheat	2.286	0.643	1.324	2.648

we have seen in Ch'i-wang Chuang, suggesting that reduction in grain yields was probably a common phenomenon in this area during the eighteenth century.

Changes in Farm Size

No Ch'ing dynasty population data are available for the four counties in which the K'ung Fu estates were located, but there is little doubt that the population of this region must have grown substantially during the period. This should be fairly evident from the changes, given more or less constant total acreage, in size of tenant farms on the K'ung Fu estates. In calculating farm sizes, two adjustments have been made. First, out of the listed names of tenants, the K'ung Fu manager or family head designated several managing agents, known as *chia-shou*, each of whom was in charge of a number of regular tenants and had the responsibility of collecting rents from them. As a compensation for his managerial role, the estate allotted the managing agent a much larger portion of land for his own use. Whether the *chia-shou* had to pay rent at the regular rate, or whether he had to pay rent at all, is not clear from the archives. In my

TABLE C.5

Average Acreage per Tenant in Assorted K'ung Fu Estates, Three Counties, 1655-1947

Year	Location	Average acreage per tenant (mou)	Year	Location	Average acreage per tenant (mou)
1655	Chu-yeh Tun:		1878	Chu-yeh Tun:	
	first *chia*	44.98		third and sixth *chia*	3.31
	second and third *chia*	60.11		ninth *chia*	6.80
	fourth and fifth *chia*	42.49	1889	Ta Chuang	1.92
	sixth and seventh *chia*	64.50	1889	Nan-chi Chuang	1.24
	eighth and ninth *chia*	32.06	1901	An-chi Chuang	1.54
	tenth *chia*	13.02	1913	Chung-chia Chuang	6.12
1678	Er-ya Ch'ang	113.18	1921	Niu Ch'ang	2.02
1759	Yun-ch'eng Ch'ang	5.38	1922	Ch'i-wang Chuang	1.55
1788	Ta Chuang	5.76	1923	Chun-t'ing Chuang	1.49
1788	Chang-yang Chuang	3.16	1925	Wu-shi Chuang	1.87
1803	Ta Chuang	4.57	1925	Ch'i-wang Chuang	2.20
1806	Ta Chuang	6.14	1925	Hung-miao Chuang	1.52
1816	Ping-yang Tun	11.40	1930	Wu-shi Chuang	1.85
1823	Ch'uan-to Chuang	4.42	1933	Chang-yang Chuang	0.72
1853	Nan-chi Chuang	1.04	1940	Ch'i-wang-p'o Chuang	1.39
1855	Ch'i-wang Chuang	3.12	1943	Ch'i-wang-p'o Chuang	1.49
1856	Chang-yang Chuang	1.29	1947	Nan-chi Chuang	1.08
1867	Ping-yang Tun	10.02			

calculations I have excluded the *chia-shou* in order to obtain the average size of farmland that regular tenants could lease.

Second, plots were categorized in the archives according to grades of land, and the name of a tenant appeared several times on the roster if he rented several plots of different grades. For each case of this kind, I have computed the sum of acreages leased by the tenant. If the published rosters are incomplete, however, understatement has likely been embodied in the average farm size I have computed. Furthermore, there is no way to determine the degree of such distortions. The results are chronologically tabulated in Table C.5.

In spite of the variation among different localities and the possible underreporting just mentioned, the secular trend of decline in the size of tenant farms over the three centuries or so is beyond doubt. The most drastic drop seems to have taken place between 1655 and the mid-eighteenth century.

Conclusions

From the recently published K'ung Fu archives of land and rent records we have been able to glean the following information: First, between 1653 and sometime around 1940, the estate managers of K'ung Fu substantially lowered the rental rates in fixed-rent contracts. This trend I believe to reflect the declining productivity of those lands. The yield data from self-operated farms and from sharecropping lands covering the same time span demonstrate an equally noticeable declining trend. The combined rent and yield data leave little doubt that decrease in yield was a true and nearly universal phenomenon on the K'ung Fu estates. Third, over the same three centuries, the average size of tenant farms shrank at an astonishing rate because of rapid population growth in the area. The combined effect of these two forces was inevitably a severe reduction in grain output per tenant. The situation appears to be much worse than what we found for the Su-chou area, where the average yield of grain per unit of cultivated land was nevertheless improving, though not sufficiently to prevent per capita output from declining in the face of rapid population growth. The K'ung Fu data thus provide strong evidence for a worsened standard of living in rural China after the seventeenth century.

Reference Matter

Notes

Complete authors' names, titles, and publication data are given in References Cited, pp. 255-63.

Chapter 1

1. *Ta k'uang*, "Kuan tzu" section.   2. *Wen wu*, no. 5 (1978): 50.
3. *Four Books*, pp. 184-85.   4. Ssu-ma Ch'ien, p. 411.
5. Elvin, p. 313.   6. Boserup, *Agricultural Growth*.
7. Perkins, pp. 23, 51, 186.   8. Hsu 1980, ch. 5.
9. Boserup, p. 40.   10. See, for example, Mendels.

Chapter 2

1. The following are the studies most relevant to our discussion: Ta Chen, *Population in Modern China*; Ping-ti Ho, *Studies on the Population of China, 1368-1953*; John D. Durand, "The Population Statistics of China, A.D. 2-1953"; Dwight H. Perkins, *Agricultural Development in China 1368-1968*, appendix A; Y. C. Yu, "The Demographic Situation in China"; and Tsui-jung Liu, "The Demographic Dynamics of Some Clans in the Lower Yangtze Area, ca. 1400-1900."

2. United Nations, *Population of Asia*.   3. Tsui-jung Liu, p. 148.
4. Hollingsworth, pp. 103, 117.   5. Ibid., p. 163.
6. See, for example, Lee, pp. 537-39.   7. Silver, p. 315.
8. Durand, p. 218.   9. Ta Chen, p. 32.

10. Durand suspects that the population figure for A.D. 2 contains a serious understatement on the ground that the average number of persons per household was too small. Using six persons per household, he has raised all official Han enumerations by a large margin. But this adjustment seems unwarranted because other historical data also indicate a relatively small number of persons per household during the Han.

11. Chen I-p'ing, p. 31.

12. *Wen-hsien t'ung-k'ao*, vol. 11, Household Registration, sec. 2.

13. The three cases with the lowest ratios of persons per household in Table 2.1 are suspected to reflect this type of bias. The 1201 relief operation was to

make provision for refugees after a major fire broke out in Lin-an in which the houses of 1,321 families had been destroyed and 5,345 persons were left homeless; presumably many lives were lost as well. The resulting ratio for the refugee families is 4.05 persons per household. The 1208 and 1209 relief operations, which assisted refugees who had traveled a considerable distance from the Huai River areas to Lin-an, Chekiang, the capital of the Southern Sung, showed two ratios of person to household, respectively, 3.72 and 4.33. It is difficult, however, to substantiate the bias of exaggerating family size.

14. A census based on the yellow register system was supposedly taken every decade. The second census of this series was taken in 1391, but for unknown reasons two conflicting national totals were recorded for that year. The total accepted here is taken from Hou-hu Chih, the local gazetteer of the site Hou-hu, where yellow registers were deposited during the Ming times.

15. Perkins, p. 216.

16. Sun and Chang, "Ch'ing-tai."

17. Parker, "Statistics"; Rockhill, "Population of China."

18. Now held in the library of the Economics Institute, Chinese Academy of Social Sciences (CASS), Peking.

19. Kuo, p. 13.

20. Ibid., p. 58.

21. See the life tables in Coale and Demeny.

22. Buck, pp. 383, 387.

23. Coale and Demeny, p. 184.

24. Perkins, p. 197.

Chapter 3

1. Pounds, p. 7.

2. Nai-ruenn Chen, p. 7.

3. For a detailed discussion of the standard layout of ancient Chinese cities and the measurement of city size and urban population, see Chao and Chen 1985, ch. 6.

4. Clark, p. 339.

5. Each ward or block in Ch'ang-an during the Han measured 266 double steps on each side. In the T'ang, the *li* was changed to the *fang*; each side of a *fang* was approximately 300 double steps long. See Appendix A and the detailed discussions in Chao and Chen 1985, ch. 6.

6. *Pei-shih*, vol. 40, biography of Chou Shen.

7. Hino, pp. 1-34.   8. Chou Pao-chu, p. 51.

9. Hsu Chu-yun 1980a, p. 1055.   10. Kuan, pp. 64, 108; Ke, p. 150.

11. As cited in Chao and Chen 1985, ch. 6.

12. For a list of the 100 counties, see ibid.

13. This figure was given to the king of Chi by Su Ch'in. See *Chan-kuo t'se*, the "Ch'i t'se" section.

14. Fujimoto, p. 38.

15. Sung Min-chiu, *Ch'ang-an chih* (Gazetteer of Ch'ang-an), vol. 1, as cited in Chao and Chen 1985, p. 375.

16. See Hartwell; Shiba; Kracke, pp. 13-48, 49-78; Schneider, pp. 168-69; Hollingsworth, pp. 246-47; and most important, Kato, pp. 839-54.

17. By using a smaller average family size of five persons, Kracke (p. 65) arrives at a lower total population figure.

18. Here the city wall is assumed to be square in shape; Kracke (p. 66) derives a slightly larger area by assuming a circular shape.

19. The minimum density of the old inner city is estimated by Kracke (p. 66) as about 210 persons per hectare.

20. Chou Pao-chu, p. 51.

21. Hartwell, p. 392.

22. Kato, p. 852; Shiba, p. 22.

23. Shiba, p. 23.

24. Kato, p. 842; Schneider, p. 168.

25. Only a few taverns are said to have five stories (Meng, p. 73).

26. Schneider, p. 168.

27. Wu Chih-mu, p. 180; Nai Te-weng, p. 91.

28. *Nan-sung lin-an liang-chi*, p. 22.

29. Ibid.

30. Kato, p. 843.

31. Kato, p. 848.

32. Wu Chih-mu, p. 148.

33. Sudo 1965, pp. 843-47.

34. Chang Po-chuan, p. 71.

35. Kato, p. 265.

36. Shiba, pp. 21-22.

37. Liang Keng-yao 1981, pp. 17-18.

38. Chao and Chen 1985, pp. 387-88.

39. Rozman, p. 1.

40. Ibid.; Skinner, p. 287.

41. Nai-ruenn Chen, pp. 128-30.

42. Shiba, p. 19.

43. Ibid., p. 31.

44. K'ung, p. 213; Tsou I-jen, p. 90.

Chapter 4

1. Tseng, pp. 162-82.

2. *Hou-han shu*, vol. 1, sec. 2, biography of Emperor Kuang Wu.

3. *Sung-shih*, vol. 1, biography of Emperor T'ai Tsu.

4. *Yü-hai*, sec. 176.

5. A stone tablet surviving from the Southern Sung records all the names of persons who had donated lands to the public school system in Canton, states that a few landowners concealed some land in the *chen chi pu* registration, but their dishonesty was reported by other people; these concealed plots were consequently confiscated by the local government and then transferred to the public school system. See *Chin-shih hsü-pien*, vol. 19, Sung section 7, p. 7.

6. Another stone tablet recording the sources of lands of a public school sys-

tem in Shao-hsing during the Southern Sung mentions a case in which a person presented a fake deed and claimed the ownership of a portion of the school lands. The dispute was resolved by cross-checking against the original documents of the *chen chi pu* registration; the person who falsified the deed was then punished by the government. See *Liang-che chin-shih-chih*, 13: 3.

7. *Ming-hui-tien*, section on the twenty-fourth year of the Hung-wu reign.

8. For a detailed explanation of various technical points, see Chao 1980.

9. Ibid., p. 47. The original verbal description of the new measuring technique seems to mean that, regardless of the shape of the plot, a rectangle would have to be drawn to contain it in order to measure its area. An alternate measuring method was also used, however, as shown by a fish-scale register displayed in the Chinese History Museum in Peking. The survey map of the lot registered as number 1812 in the 6th *chia*, 3d *tu*, 13th *t'u*, owned by Chao Ming-li, is reproduced in the accompanying figure to show the alternative measuring technique actually used:

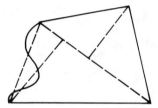

Solid lines represent the plot's boundary lines; broken lines are drawn to measure area. Specifically, a diametrical line is drawn between two opposing corners; then two lines are drawn from the other two corners perpendicular to the diametrical line; the areas of the two triangles divided by the diametrical line can now be determined.

10. Ibid., p. 48.

11. I am grateful to the Institute of Economic Research, the Academy of Social Sciences, and the History Department of Nanjing University for allowing me access to these archives.

12. Shimizu, pp. 477-592.

13. Ping-ti Ho, pp. 101-23.

14. Perkins, p. 232.

15. Ping-ti Ho, p. 114.

16. Fu Kwang-che, pp. 8235-51.

17. Chen Pao-chung, pp. 10037-42.

18. Sudo 1954, p. 479.

19. Shimizu, pp. 477-592.

20. Fujii, pp. 60-87.

21. For details of this derivation process, see Chao 1980, pp. 57-58.

22. Ibid., p. 56.

23. Buck, p. 164.

Chapter 5

1. *Chin-shu*, vol. 47, biography of Fu Hsüan.
2. *Wei-shu*, vol. 53, biography of Li Hsiao-po.
3. Wu Chang-ch'üan, p. 2.
4. Ibid., p. 10.
5. *Hsin t'ang-shu*, 120: 327.
6. *Tse-fu yüan-kuei*, vol. 495.
7. Liang 1978, p. 43.
8. Ibid.
9. Sudo 1954, p. 187.
10. Buck, pp. 181-5.
11. *Chiang-su chin-shih chih*, 13: 32.
12. Ibid., 15: 3.
13. Ibid.
14. *Liang-Che chin-shih chih*, 13: 3.
15. *Chiang-su chin-shih chih*, 17: 10.
16. *Chin-shih hsü-pien*, 13: 34.
17. Ibid., 13: 46.
18. Ibid., 19: 7.
19. *Chiang-su chin-shih chih*, 13: 32.
20. Ibid., 14: 4.
21. Ibid.
22. Ibid., 14: 19.
23. Ibid., 17: 19.
24. *Liang-Che chin-shih chih*, 15: 13.
25. Ibid., 14: 7.
26. *Chiang-su chin-shih chih*, 17: 19.
27. Ibid.

Chapter 6

1. Chiang, p. 167.
2. Ibid., pp. 181-2.
3. Myers 1972, pp. 173-92.
4. Elvin, ch. 5.
5. Ibid., p. 250.
6. This issue was carefully discussed by a seventeenth-century scholar, Chang Ying, in his *Heng-ch'an so-yen* (Remarks on real estate).

7. When commenting on my early draft, Thomas Rawski suggested that the reproduction rate of landless families was probably rather higher. A recent empirical study by Linda Gail Arrigo (unpublished) has found that the reproduction rate of landless families in China was indeed relatively low.

8. For a detailed discussion, see Chao and Chen 1982, pp. 335-38.

9. *Hsu-tzu-chih-t'ung-chien*, vol. 27, memorial of Chao P'u in the second year of the Yung-hsi reign.

10. Ibid., vol. 219, on the events in January of the 4th year of the Hsi-ning reign.

11. The new data consist of 57 volumes of local government land and household registers, mostly in the form of fish-scale registers; 84 volumes of land purchase records from private households; 175 volumes of rent collection records from landlord families; and numerous land transaction deeds. Except for three fish-scale registers in the library of Wuhan University, the materials are held in the Economic Research Institute, Peking and Nanking University. The original sites of three fish-scale registers cannot be identified; the rest come from Huei-chou prefecture in Anhwei; Ch'u-chou, Yen-chou, and Hang-chou prefectures

in Chekiang; and Kuang-hsin prefecture in Kiangsi. These districts were adjacent, though they were under the jurisdiction of three different provinces. The materials were first collected by a used book dealer in T'un-hsi, Anhwei and were then sold to Nanking University and the Economic Research Institute in the 1950's.

12. The Ch'ang-chou data were taken from a fish-scale register held in the Japanese Diet Library.

13. Muramatsu, p. 701.

14. Ching and Lo, pp. 50-51, 69, 76, 82.

15. Li Wen chih 1957, 1: 177-91.   16. Muramatsu, p. 550.

17. Land Commission, table 23.   18. Buck, p. 196.

19. Myers 1970, pp. 220-22.   20. Land Commission, p. 36.

21. Rural Reconstruction Commission, Rural Survey of Kiangsu Province, pp. 51-2.

22. Hinton, p. 209.   23. Perkins, p. 93.

24. Ibid.   25. Beattie, p. 14.

26. Hwang and Wang, pp. 4-5. There is also a monetary theory that attempts to explain the fluctuations of grain prices and land prices in Ming-Ch'ing times. According to this theory, falling prices in the second half of the 17th century were caused by the curtailed influx of silver from abroad, the result of the ban on foreign trade by the Manchu government because of the campaigns against resistance in Taiwan. See Peng, p. 560.

27. Yeh Meng-chu, vol. 1, section on Landed Property.

Chapter 7

1. *Han-shu*, 24: 100.

2. Ho Ching-ku, pp. 47-51.

3. *Kuan-tzu*, "Ch'ing-chung chia-pien."

4. *Han-fei-tzu*, "Wai-chu-pien."

5. *Chan-kuo-t'se*, "Ch'i t'se."

6. *Shih-chi*, vol. 48, biography of Chen She.

7. Chao and Chen 1985, p. 79.

8. Ibid.

9. Ho Chang-chün, p. 147.

10. *Chin-shu*, vol. 93, biography of Wang Shun.

11. *Nan-ch'i-shu*, vol. 27, biography of Li An-min.

12. *Nan shih*, vol. 70, biography of Kuo Tsu-shen.

13. See the mandate issued by Emperor Wu of the Northern Chou in the eleventh month of 575. *Chou-shu*, 6: 11.

14. For a detailed discussion of *chuang yüan* and the related literature, see Chao and Chen 1982, ch. 6.

15. Ching and Lo, pp. 64, 68, 80.
16. Chao and Chen 1982, p. 282.
17. *T'ai-p'ing Kuang chi*, vol. 37, "Yang-p'ing tse-hsien."
18. *Huang Pu-chih*, vol. 5.
19. Chao and Chen 1982, p. 287.
20. Ibid., p. 282.
21. *Ta-ming-lü*, vol. 4, section on Household.
22. Fu I-ling 1961, p. 63.
23. Feng, vol. 28.
24. Chao and Chen 1982, p. 293.
25. Li Wen-chih 1981, p. 9.
26. Ibid., p. 150.
27. Chen Heng-li, p. 76.
28. Ibid.
29. Tao Shu, pp. 17-19.
30. Ching and Lo, *Ch'ing-tai Shan-tung*.
31. All the cases are taken from ibid., appendix table 2.
32. Ibid., pp. 57, 140.
33. Ibid., p. 89.
34. Li Wen-chih 1957, 1: 682.
35. Liu Yung-ch'eng 1982, p. 65.
36. *Ch'ing-shih-kao* (Draft History of the Ch'ing), Chung-hua ed., 15: 4207.
37. Liu Tzu-yang et al., p. 98.
38. Liu Yung-ch'eng 1962, p. 120.
39. See the standard interpretation of the 1588 law during the Ming time as cited in Chu Shih, p. 241.
40. Wei Chin-yü, p. 128.
41. Liu Yung-ch'eng 1962, p. 120.
42. Ibid., p. 121.
43. Li Wen-chih 1957, 2: 811-39.
44. *Han-shu*, 1: 8.
45. Wei et al., "Ch'ing-tai nu-pei chih-tu."
46. Wang Pao, *T'ung-yueh*, as cited in *Tai-ping yü-lan*, vol. 598.
47. *Chou-shu*, 6: 11.
48. Chao and Chen 1982, p. 318.
49. *Wen-hsien t'ung-kao*, vol. 11, section on Household Registration.
50. *Chu wen-kung wen-chi*, vol. 14, as cited in Chao and Chen 1982, p. 393.
51. Fu I-ling 1980, p. 3.
52. Ku, vol. 13, section on Slaves and Servants.
53. Wang Shih-hsing, vol. 3, section on Kuang-shan.
54. Ray Huang, ch. 3.
55. Niida, pp. 657-64.

Chapter 8

1. *Han-shu*, vol. 24.
2. Wang Mang's statement, however, has been variously interpreted. See Chao and Chen 1982, pp. 326-28.
3. *Hou-han-shu*, vol. 65, biography of Cheng Hsuan, and vol. 84, biography of Yang Chen.

4. *Chin-shu*, vol. 26, Food and Money.

5. *T'ung-tien*, vol. 35, section on Office Land.

6. Sudo 1965, ch. 1.

7. *Sung-hui-yao*, vol. 66, Food and Money.

8. These terms have varying interpretations. For a detailed discussion, see Chao and Chen 1982, p. 338.

9. *Hsu-tzu-chih-t'ung-chien*, vol. 397, section on the second year of the Yuan-yu reign.

10. Hsueh, vol. 17.

11. Buck, statistical volume, tables for various provinces.

12. Land Commission, p. 37. 13. Chao and Chen 1982, p. 335.

14. *San-kuo-chih, Wei shu*, 16: 53. 15. Chao and Chen 1982, ch. 7.

16. *Chin-shu*, K'ai-ming ed., 109: 292.

17. Sudo 1965, p. 73; Sun Ta-jen, "Tui t'ang chih wu tai . . . fen-hsi."

18. Chao and Chen 1982, p. 360. 19. Ibid.

20. *Sung-hui-yao*. 21. Sudo 1954, pp. 133-37, 140.

22. Sudo 1965, p. 309. 23. Ibid.

24. Niida, 3: 781, 809. 25. Fu I-ling 1961, p. 30.

26. Muramatsu, p. 165.

27. See, for instance, *Hsien-hsien-chi*, compiled in the Ch'ien-lung reign, vol. 3.

28. Niida, 3: 768.

29. Ting, p. 11.

30. Liu Yung-ch'eng 1979, p. 43.

31. For details, see Chao and Chen 1982, pp. 370-71.

32. For details, see ibid., p. 380.

33. For details, see ibid., p. 381.

34. South Manchuria Railway, *Kida si noson gaikyo chosa*, 1940, 2: 105, cited in Chao and Chen 1982, p. 382.

35. Li Wen-chih 1957, 1: 260. 36. Buck, pp. 198, 216.

37. *Han-shu*, 29: 143. 38. *Chin-shu*, 47: 136.

39. Hu Hung, *Wu-feng-chi*, vol. 2, cited in Chao and Chen 1982, p. 392.

40. *Sung-shih*, 201: 502.

41. *Sung-hui-yao*, vol. 66, section on the fifth year of the reign of Tien-sheng.

42. Ibid., section on the eleventh year of the reign of Tsun-hsi.

43. Ibid.

44. *Sung-shih*, 173: 423.

45. As cited in Elvin, p. 72.

46. *Wen-hsien t'ung-k'ao*, vol. 167, sec. 6.

47. As cited in Chao and Chen 1982, p. 392.

48. As cited in Elvin, p. 242.

49. As cited in Chao and Chen, 1982, p. 395.
50. McDermott, pp. 675-701.
51. Fu I-ling, 1961, p. 3.
52. *Chiang-su chin-shih chih*, vol. 17, p. 19.
53. Hu Hung, vol. 2, letter to Liu Hsin-shu.
54. As cited in Chao and Chen 1982, p. 400.
55. Fu I-ling 1961, p. 34.   56. Sudo 1954, pp. 215-32.
57. Ibid., p. 198.   58. Ibid., p. 193.
59. *Ch'ung-ming-hsien chih*, vol. 4, section on land systems.
60. Li Wen-chih 1957, 1: 251.

61. According to a recent study of the Wu Ch'i-hsien family, the tenants were actually all tenant-servants. It is indeed surprising that people of a status inferior to free tenants could successfully resist rent payments. See Yeh Hsien-en, p. 191.

Chapter 9

1. Tang, p. 198.   2. Elvin, p. 113.
3. Hsu 1980b, chap. 5.   4. Boserup, p. 33.
5. Shen and Chao, p. 9.   6. Huan K'uan, sec. 1.
7. Yang K'uan, p. 94.
8. Chang Tse-hsien and Kuo Sung-i, p. 154.
9. Perkins, p. 56.
10. Li Po, pp. 126, 128.
11. Ibid., p. 69.
12. Pan Hung-sheng, "Chieh-fang-ch'ien . . . nung-chü."
13. Li Po, p. 79.
14. For a detailed discussion, see Chao and Chen 1982, pp. 1-18.
15. *Hsin t'ang-shu*, vol. 53, sec. 3.   16. See Chapter 6.
17. Amano, p. 229.   18. Hsu 1980b, p. 111.
19. Honda, p. 49.   20. Ibid.
21. Chang Tse-hsien and Kuo Sung-i, p. 160.
22. The index was 1.30 in 1952. See State Statistical Bureau, p. 128.

23. A different explanation was offered in the *Ch'i-min-yao-shu*, an agricultural handbook published in the sixth century. See Hsu, 1980, p. 83, and *Nung-shih yen-chiu chi-kan*, p. 94. Hsu contends that because the lightweight grain of millet would easily shatter from the spikelet and thus grow by itself the following year, to plant millet on the same piece of land for two consecutive years would entail additional work in ground dressing and weeding during the second year. In traditional China this problem was resolved by the fallowing system, under which the self-regenerated millet would be burned along with other grass. I think that the above statement is not a convincing reason for planting

wheat the second year, because the extra work of ground dressing and weeding would still be necessary even if millet were replaced by wheat, or for that matter any other crop, during the second year.

24. Shen Tsung-han and Chao Ya-shu, p. 50.

25. Ibid., p. 23.

26. Ibid., p. 28.

27. See, for example, Amano, pp. 211-56, and Ho, pp. 169-79.

28. The 1952 distribution figure is based on detailed agricultural statistics supplied by the Chinese government in 1981.

29. See, for example, Shih et al. 1981, 1982; Shih 1963, 1981; Huang Sheng-Chang, 1982; Chu K'o-chen, 1972.

30. Shih 1981, 2: 232-313.

31. Ibid., p. 305.

32. Hou pp. 110-21.

33. Ibid., p. 110.

34. Chu K'o-chen 1972.

35. Tan, p. 20.

36. Tsou I-lin, p. 77.

37. *Huang-ho shui-li-shih shu-yao*, p. 27.

38. Yüan Chieh, vol. 7, "Wen-chin-shih-pien."

39. Li Chien-nung, pp. 19-27.

40. Lin, p. 75.

41. Li Chien-nung, pp. 12-19.

42. Perkins, app. H.

43. Lin, p. 75.

44. Ibid., p. 76.

45. Ibid., p. 75.

46. Ibid., p. 76; *Jen-min jih-pao* (People's Daily), Sept. 3, 1981.

47. *Jen-min jih-pao*, ibid.

48. Perdue, "Official Goals."

49. Lin, p. 77.

50. Hsu Ch'in-chih, p. 185.

51. Perkins, pp. 13-29 and app. G.

52. Boserup, p. 41.

53. The conversion rates are taken from Chao and Chen 1982, p. 67, and Wu Ch'eng-lo, p. 70.

54. The ratios are taken from Chang Tse-hsien and Kuo Sung-i, 160, and Chen Heng-li, p. 13.

55. Chang Tse-hsien and Kuo Sung-i, p. 160.

56. Ibid.

57. See Chapter 7.

58. See Chang Tse-hsien and Kuo Sung-i, p. 160. The use of Chou gauges is also supported by other relevant data. If the new Han *mou* is used for conversion, 100 *mou* would be equal to 69 *shih mou*, which is considerably higher than both the average farming ability of a husband and wife and the average size of a piece of property during the West Han.

59. Ibid.

60. Hu Chi, pp. 74-75.

61. Chang Tse-hsien and Kuo Sung-i, p. 161.

62. Ibid.

63. *Ssu-ming shu-chih*, vol. 4, section on Kuang-hui Yuan.
64. Li Wen-chih 1957, 1: 619-21.   65. Buck, p. 225.
66. Chao 1970, pp. 217-18.   67. Ibid.
68. Li Wen-chih 1957, 1: 755-60.
69. Chang Tse-hsien and Kuo Sung-i, p. 161.
70. The average rice yields are taken from Perkins, p. 21, and the cultivated acreages from ibid., p. 229, table B.8. For the Sung dynasty, acreages of Kiangsu and Anhwei are combined. We use 69 percent as the proportion for Kiangsu, a figure shown by the Ming statistics in the same table.
71. Muramatsu, pp. 19-20.
72. Chen Heng-li, pp. 13-19.
73. The multiple-cropping index for all crops was 130.9 in 1952, but no such index is given for grain crops. See State Statistical Bureau, p. 128.
74. Perkins, p. 27.
75. Ibid.
76. State Statistical Bureau, p. 119, and Nai-ruenn Chen, p. 124.
77. Chao and Chen 1985, ch. 6.

Chapter 10

1. Dillard, p. 51. The average allotment was about the same in France, but somewhat smaller in Germany (25 acres), during the same period of time. See *Cambridge Economic History of Europe*, 1: 301, 303.

Appendix C

1. The data used in this study are taken from *K'ung-fu tang-an shüan-chi*, pp. 251-447.
2. Ibid., p. 353.
3. Ibid., pp. 260-63.
4. Ho Hsiu-ling et al., pp. 228-29.

References Cited

Amano Motonosuke. *Chūgoku nogyoshi kenkyū* (A study of Chinese agricultural history). Tokyo, 1962.

Beattie, Hilary J. *Land and Lineage in China*. Cambridge, 1979.

Boserup, Ester. *The Conditions of Agricultural Growth: The Economics of Agrarian Change Under Population Pressure*. Chicago, 1965.

Buck, John L. *Land Utilization in China*. Nanking, 1937.

Bureau of Meteorology, *Chung-kuo chin-wu-pai-nien han-lao fen-pu-t'u chih* (Yearly charts of dryness and wetness in China for the last 500 years). Peking, 1981.

Cambridge Economic History of Europe. Cambridge, 1966.

Chan-kuo-t'se (Strategies of the Warring States).

Chang lu-hsiang. *Pu nung-shu* (Supplement to the Treatise on Agriculture).

Chang Po-chuan. *Chin-tai ching-chi shih-lueh* (A brief economic history of the Chin Dynasty). Shenyang, 1981.

Chang Tse-hsien and Kuo Sung-i. "Lueh-lun wo-kuo feng-chien-shih-tai ti liang-shih sheng-ch'an" (A brief essay on food production in the feudal period of our country), *Chung-kuo-shih yen-chiu*, no. 3 (1980): 144-65.

Chang Ying. *Heng-ch'an so-yen* (Remarks on real estate).

Chao, Kang. *Agricultural Production in Communist China, 1949-1965*. Madison, Wisc., 1970.

——. "Ming-ch'ing ti-chi yen-shiu" (A study of Ming and Ch'ing land registers), *Journal of the Modern History Institute, Academia Sinica*, no. 19 (1980): 37-59.

Chao Kang and Chen Chung-i. *Chung-kuo t'u-ti chih-tu shih* (Land institutions in Chinese history). Taipei, 1982.

——. *Chung-kuo ching-chi chih-tu shih* (A history of Chinese economic institutions). Taipei, 1985.

Chen Fu. *Nung shu* (Treatise on agriculture).

Chen Heng-li. *Pu-nung-shu yen-chiu* (A study of Pu-nung-shu). Peking, 1958.

Chen I-p'ing. "Pei-sung ti hu-k'ou" (The population and household returns of the Northern Sung), *Shih Huo Monthly*, 6, no. 7 (1977): 28-34.

Chen, Nai-ruenn. *Chinese Economic Statistics: A Handbook for Mainland China*. Chicago, 1967.

255

Chen Pao-chung. *An-hui t'ien-fu mu-fa yen-chiu* (A study of the land tax law of Anhwei Province). Taipei, 1977.

Chen, Ta. *Population in Modern China*. Chicago, 1937.

Chi-min yao-shu (Important techniques for the common people).

Chiang-su chin-shih chih (Artifacts in Kiangsu).

Chiang Tai-hsin. "Ch'ing-ch'u k'en-huang cheng-t'se chi ti-chuan fen-p'ei ch'ing-k'uang ti k'ao-tsa"(A survey of early Ch'ing reclamation policy and land distribution), *Li-shih yen-chiu*, no. 5 (1982): 160-72.

Chin-shih hsü-pien (A new list of artifacts).

Chin-shu (History of the Chin).

Ching Su and Lo Lun. *Ch'ing-tai Shan-tung ching-ying ti-tsu ti she-hui hsing-chih* (The social nature of managerial landlords in Shantung during the Ch'ing dynasty). Tsinan, 1959.

Chiu-chang suan-shu (Nine chapters of arithmetic).

Chou Pao-chu. "Sung-tai tung-ching ch'eng-shih ching-chi ti fa-chan chi ch'i tsai chung-wai ching-chi wen-hua chiao-liu chung ti ti-wei" (The position of the Sung capital in urban economic development and international economic and cultural relations), *Chung-kuo-shih yen-chiu*, no. 2 (1981): 49-55.

Chou-shu (History of the Chou). K'ai-ming ed.

Chu Hsi. *Chu-wen-kung wen-chi* (Collected writings of Chu Hsi).

Chu K'o-chen. "Chung-kuo chin-wu-ch'ien-nien-lai ch'i-hou pien-ch'ien ti ch'u-pu yen-chiu" (A preliminary study of the climatic changes in China in the past 5,000 years), *K'ao-ku hsueh-pao*, no. 1 (1972).

Chu Shih. "Kuan-yü chung-jih-hsueh-che tui ming-ch'ing liang-tai ku-kung-jen shen-fen ti-wei wen-ti yen-chiu ti ping-chieh" (An evaluation of the studies of Chinese and Japanese scholars of the problem of the status of hired hands during the Ming and Ch'ing dynasties), *Ching-chi yen-chiu-so chi-kan*, no. 3, pp. 240-50.

Ch'ung-ming-hsien chih (Gazetteer of Chung-ming county).

Clark, Colin. *Population Growth and Land Use*. London, 1967.

Coale, Ansley J., and Demeny, Paul. *Regional Model Life Tables and Stable Populations*. Princeton, N.J., 1966.

Dillard, D. *Economic Development of the North Atlantic Community*. Englewood Cliffs, N.J., 1967.

Directorate of Statistics. *An Analysis of the Tenancy System in China*. Nanking, 1946.

Durand, John D. "The Population Statistics of China, A.D. 2-1953," *Population Studies*, 13 (Mar. 1960): 209-57.

Elvin, Mark. *The Pattern of the Chinese Past*. Stanford, Calif., 1973.

Feng Meng-lung. *Hsing-shih heng-yen* (World-waking stories).

Four Books (English translation of *Shih Shu*). Taipei, 1979.

Fu I-ling. *Ming-ch'ing nung-tsun she-hui ching-chi* (Rural society and economy in Ming and Ch'ing times). Peking, 1961.

————. Ming-tai chiang-nan shih-min ching-chi shih-t'an (An inquiry into the economics of the urban population in Kiangnan during the Ming dynasty). Shanghai, 1963.

————. "The Chinese Feudal Society Included Remnants of Village System and Slave System," Universitatis Amoiensis ACTA, *Scientiarum Socialium*, no. 3 (1980).

Fu Kwang-che. *An-hui-sheng t'ien-fu yen-chiu* (A study of land revenue in Anhwei Province). Taipei, 1977.

Fujii Hiroshi. "Mintai dendo tokei ni kan suru ichi kosatsu" (A critical examination of cultivated acreage statistics in the Ming dynasty), *Toyo-gakuho*, 30, no. 3 (Aug. 1943): 60-87.

Fujimoto Eijirō. *Chūgoku keizaishi* (Chinese economic history). Kyoto, 1967.

Han-fei-tzu (Works of Han-fei-tzu).

Han-shu (The history of the Han). K'ai-ming ed.

Hartwell, Robert. "The Demographic, Political, and Social Transformation of China, 750-1550," *Harvard Journal of Asiatic Studies*, 42, no. 2, (Dec. 1982): 365-442.

Hino Kaisaburo. "Todai zioyu no bosi no kado sumi ni tsuide" (Fang, Shih, Chiao, and Yu in the cities of the T'ang period), *Toyo-gakuho*, 47, no. 7 (Dec. 1964): 1-34.

Hinton, William. *Fanshen, A Documentary of Revolution in a Chinese Village.* New York, 1967.

Ho Chang-chün. *Han-T'ang chien feng-chien t'u-ti-so-you-chih hsing-shih yen-chiu* (A study of the forms of the system of feudal land ownership from the Han to the T'ang). Shanghai, 1964.

Ho Ching-ku. "Lueh-lun chan-kuo shih-ch'i ti ku-yung lao-tung" (A brief study of hired workers during the Warring States period), *Shansi shih-ta hsueh-pao*, no. 4 (1981): 47-51.

Ho Hsiu-ling et al. *Feng-chien kuei-tsu ta-ti-chu ti tien-hsing* (A typology of feudal aristocratic landlords). Peking, 1981.

Ho, Ping-ti. *Studies on the Population of China, 1368-1953.* Cambridge, Mass., 1959.

Hollingsworth, T. H. *Historical Demography.* Ithaca, N.Y., 1969.

Honda Osamu. "So-gen zidai no hinkaida kaihatsu ni tsuide" (The development of coastal land during the Sung and Yuan periods), *Toyoshi Kenkyu*, 40, no. 4, p. 49.

Hou Jen-chih. "Wo-kuo si-pei feng-sha-ch'ü ti li-shih ti-li kuan-k'uei" (A study of the historical geography of the windy and sandy areas in the northwestern region of our country), in Shih Nien-hai et al., 2: 110-21.

Hou-hu chih (Gazetteer of Hou-hu county).

Hou-han shu (History of the later Han).

Hsien-hsien chih (Gazetteer of Hsien county).

Hsin t'ang-shu (New history of the T'ang). K'ai-ming ed.

Hsu Cho-yun. "Chou-tai tu-shih ti fa-chan yu shang-yeh ti fa-ta" (Development of cities and commerce in the Chou dynasty), in Yu Chung-hsien, ed., *Chung-kuo ching-chi fa-chan-shih lun-wen hsüan-chi* (A collection of essays on the history of Chinese economic development), pp. 1053-80. Taipei, 1980a.

———. *Han Agriculture*. Seattle, Wash., 1980b.

Hsu-tzu-chih-t'ung-chien (History as a mirror for rulers).

Hsueh Chi-hsuan. *Lang-yu chi* (Collected writings of Hsueh Chi-hsuan).

Hu Chi. "T'ang-tai liang-shih mu-ch'an-liang" (Unit yields of grain in the T'ang dynasty), *Hsi-pei ta-hsueh hsueh-pao*, no. 3 (1980): 74-5.

Huan K'uan. *Yen-t'ieh-lun* (On the monopoly of salt and iron).

Huang Pu-chih. *Chi-lei chi* (Chicken ribs).

Huang, Ray. *Taxation and Government Finance in Sixteenth-Century Ming China*. Cambridge, 1974.

Huang Sheng-chang. *Li-shih ti-li lun-chi* (Essays on historical geography). Peking, 1982.

Huang-ho shui-Li-shih shu-yao (A brief history of water conservancy in the Yellow River basin).

Huang Pu-chi. Peking, 1982.

Hwang, Kuo-shu, and Wang, Yeh-chien. "The Secular Movement of Grain Prices in China, 1763-1910," *Academia Economic Papers*, 9, no. 1.

Kato Shigeru. *Shina keisaishi kōsho* (Studies in Chinese economic history), translated into Chinese (Chung-guo ching-chishih k'ao-cheng). Taipei, 1976.

Ke Chien-hsiung. "Hsi-han jen-k'ou-k'ao" (A study of the population of China during the Western Han), *Chung-kuo-shih yen-shiu*, no. 4 (1981): 148-512.

Kiang-su Chin-shih chih (Artifacts of Kiangsu).

Kracke, E. A., Jr., "Sung K'ai-feng: Pragmatic Metropolis and Formalistic Capital," in John W. Haeger, ed., *Crisis and Prosperity in Sung China*. Tuscon, Ariz., 1975. pp. 49-78.

Ku Yen-wu. *Jih-chih lu* (Daily notes on learning).

Kuan Chung. *Kuan-tzu* (Works of Kuan Chung).

Kuan Tung-kuei. "Demographic Changes Between the Warring States Period and the Early Han," *Bulletin of the Institute of History and Philology*, no. 54, part 4, pp. 64-108.

Kuan-tze (Works of Kuan-tze).

K'ung Hsi-an. "Chung-kuo liu-ta-shih ti jen-k'ou chi ch'i tseng chien" (Population changes in the six large cities in China), in *Chung-kuo li-tai jen-k'ou wen-t'i lun-chi* (Essays on the population problems of past dynasties), pp. 209-17. Hong Kong, 1965.

K'ung-fu tang-an shüan-chi (Selected archives of K'ung-fu). Peking, 1982.

Kuo Sung-i. "Lun t'an-ting ju-ti" (On the policy of merging of the land tax and labor service), *Ch'ing-shih lun-tsung*, no. 3 (1982): 1-62.

Land Commission. *Ch'üan-kuo t'u-ti tiao-ch'a pao-kao kang-yao* (Summary report of the national land survey). Nanking, 1937.

Lee, Ronald D. "A Historical Perspective on Economic Aspects of the Population Explosion: The Case of Preindustrial England," in Richard A. Easterlin, ed., *Population and Economic Change in Developing Countries*, pp. 517-66. Chicago, 1980.

Li Chien-nung. *Sung-yuan-ming ching-chi-shih-kao* (A draft history of the Chinese economy in the Sung, Yuan, and Ming dynasties). Peking, 1957.

Li Po. *Chung-kuo ku-nung-chü fa-chan-shih chien-pien* (A brief history of the development of traditional farm implements in China). Peking, 1981.

Li Wen-chih. *Chung-kuo chin-tai nung-yeh-shih tzu-liao* (Historical materials on agriculture in modern China). Peking, 1957.

———. "Lun Chung-kuo ti-chu-ching-chi-chih yü nung-yeh tzu-pen-chu-i meng-ya" (Landlordism and the embryo of agricultural capitalism in China), *Chung-kuo she-hui ko-hsueh*, no. 1 (1981): 143-60.

Li Wen Chih et al. *Ming-ch'ing shih-tai ti nung-yeh tzu-pen-chu-i meng-ya wen-t'i* (Problems of embryonic agricultural capitalism in Ming and Ch'ing times). Peking, 1983.

Liang-che chin-shih-chih (Artifacts in Kiangsu and Chekiang).

Liang Keng-yao. "Nan-sung nung-tsun ti t'u-ti fen-p'ei yü tsu-tien chih-tu" (Rural land distribution and tenancy in the Southern Sung), *Shih Huo Monthly*, 8, no. 1 (1978): 40-45.

———. "Nan-sung ch'eng-shih ti fa-chan" (Urban development in the Southern Sung), *Shih Huo Monthly*, 10, no. 10 (1981): 4-27.

Lin Ching-ch'ien. "Wei-hu-tsao-tien ti li-shih chiao-hsün" (Historical lessons of enclosing lakes and creating polders), *Ching-chi yen-chiu*, no. 2 (1981): 73-76.

Liu, Tsui-jung. "The Demographic Dynamics of Some Clans in the Lower Yangtze Area, ca. 1400-1900," *Academia Economic Papers*, 9, no. 1 (Mar. 1981): 115-60.

Liu Tzu-yang et al. "Ku-kung ming-ch'ing tang-an kai-lun" (A brief study of the Ming and Ch'ing archives in the Imperial Palace), *Ch'ing-shih lun-tsung*, no. 1 (1980): 79-98.

Liu Yung-ch'eng. "Lun ch'ing-tai ku-yung lao-tung" (On labor employment in the Ch'ing dynasty), *Li-shih yen-shiu*, no. 4 (1962): 110-20.

———. "Lun Chung-kuo tzu-pen-chu-i meng-ya ti li-shih ch'ien-t'i" (The historical prerequisites for embryonic capitalism in China), *Chung-kuo-shih yen-chiu*, no. 2 (1979): 33-45.

————. *Ch'ing-tai ch'ien-chi nung-yeh tzu-pen-chu-i meng-ya ch'u-t'an* (A preliminary inquiry into the embryonic agricultural capitalism during the early Ch'ing). Foochow, 1982.

McDermott, Joseph P. "Bondservants in the Tai-hu Basin During the Late Ming: A Case of Mistaken Identities," *Journal of Asian Studies*, 40, no. 4 (Aug. 1981): 675-701.

Mendels, Franklin F. "Proto-Industrialization: The First Phase of the Industrialization Process," *Journal of Economic History*, 32, no. 1 (Mar. 1972): 241-61.

Meng Yuna-lao. *Tung-ching meng-hua-lu* (The prosperity of Tung-ching). Peking, 1961. Reprint ed.

Ming shih-lu (Verifiable records of the Ming).

Ming Wan-li hui-tien (Government documents of the Ming Wan-li reign).

Ming-hui-tien (Documents of the Ming).

Mu Chao-ching. "Liang-sung hu-chi chih-tu wen-t'i," in *Lishi Yanjui*, 1 (1982): 157.

Muramatsu, Yuji. *Kindai konan no sosen* (Bursaries in the Kiangnan area in recent history). Tokyo, 1970.

Myers, Ramon H. *The Chinese Peasant Economy*. Cambridge, Mass., 1970.

————. "The Commercialization of Agriculture in Modern China," in W. E. Willmott, *Economic Organization in Chinese Society*, pp. 173-92. Stanford, Calif., 1972.

Nai Te-weng. *Tu-ch'eng chi-sheng* (The prosperous capital). Hangchow, 1980. Reprint ed.

Nan-shih (History of the southern dynasties).

Nan-sung lin-an liang-chi (Two gazetteers of Lin-an published in the Southern Sung). Hangchow, 1983. Reprint ed.

National Agricultural Research Bureau, *Crop Reports*, 5, no. 12 (Dec. 1937).

Niida Noboru. *Chūgoku hōseishi kenkyū* (A study of the legal system in Chinese history). Tokyo, 1960.

Nung-shih yen-chiu chi-kan, no. 2 (1960).

Pan Hung-sheng. "Chieh-fang-ch'ien ch'ang-chiang huang-ho liang-liu yü shih-er-sheng-ch'ü shih-yung ti nung-chu" (Farm implements used in the twelve provinces in the Yangtze and Yellow river regions before Liberation), *Nung-shih yen-chiu chi-kan*, no. 2 (1956): 186-206.

Parker, E. H. "Notes on Some Statistics Regarding China," *Journal of the Royal Statistical Society*, 1899.

Pei-shih (History of the Northern Dynasties).

Peng Hsin-wei. *Chung-kuo huo-pi-shih* (A history of money in China).

Perdue, Peter D. "Official Goals and Local Interests: Water Control in the Dong-
ting Lake Region During the Ming and Qing Periods," *The Journal of Asian
Studies*, 41, no. 4, (1982): 747-66.

Perkins, Dwight H. *Agricultural Development in China, 1368-1968*. Chicago,
1969.

Pounds, N. J. G. *An Economic History of Medieval Europe*. New York, 1974.

Pu Nung-shu chiao-shih.

Rockhill, W. W. "An Inquiry into the Population of China," *Annual Report of the
Smithsonian Institution*, 47, no. 2, part 3 (1905).

Rozman, Gilbert. *Urban Networks in Ch'ing China and Tokugawa Japan*. Princeton, N.J., 1973.

Rural Reconstruction Commission. *Chiang-su-sheng nung-ts'un tiao-ch'a* (Rural
survey of Kiangsu Province). Nanking, 1934.

San-kuo-chih (History of the Three Kingdoms). K'ai-ming ed.

Schneider, W. "Babylon Is Everywhere," in his *The City as Man's Fate* (trans. I.
Sammet and J. Oldenburg), pp. 168-69. London, 1963.

Shen. *Nung-shu* (The Agricultural Treatise). Peking, 1983. Reprint ed.

Shen Tsung-han and Chao Ya-shu. *Chung-hua nung-yeh-shih lun-chi* (Agricultural development in China, the past and the present). Taipei, 1979.

Shiba, Yoshinobu. "Urbanization and the Development of Markets in the Lower
Yangtse Valley," in John W. Haeger, ed., *Crisis and Prosperity in Sung China*,
pp. 13-48. Tucson, Ariz., 1975.

Shih Nien-hai. *Ho-shan chi* (Writings about rivers and mountains). Peking, 1963
(vol. 1), 1981 (vol. 2).

Shih Nien-hai et al. *Chung-kuo li-shih ti-li lun-tsung* (Essays on the historical
geography of China). Sian, 1981 (vol. 1), 1982 (vol. 2).

Shih-chi (Records of the historian).

Shimizu Taiji. *Mindai tochi seido shi kenkyū* (Studies of land institutions in the
Ming dynasty). Tokyo, 1968.

Silver, Morris. "Births, Marriages, and Income Fluctuations in the United Kingdom and Japan," *Economic Development and Cultural Change*, 14, no. 3 (Apr.
1966): 305-20.

Skinner, G. William, ed. *The City in Late Imperial China*. Stanford, Calif., 1977.

South Manchuria Railway. *Mantetsu chosa geppo* (Monthly survey reports), 18, 1
(1938).

———. *Kida si noson gaikyo chosa* (Report of the survey on general conditions
in the rural areas in north China). 1940.

Ssu-ma Ch'ien. *Records of the Historian* (Trans. Yang Hsien-yi and Gladys Yang).
Hong Kong, 1974.

Ssu-ming shu-chih (New gazetteer of Ssu-ming county). 1259.

State Statistical Bureau. *Ten Great Years*. Peking, 1960.

261

Sudo Yoshiyuki. *Chūgoku tochi seido shi kenkyū* (Studies of Chinese land institutions). Tokyo, 1954.

―――. *Toso shakai kezai shi kenkyū* (Studies in socioeconomic history in the Sui and T'ang dynasties). Tokyo, 1965.

Sun Ta-jen. "Tui t'ang chih wu-tai tsu-tien-ch'i-yueh ching-chi nei-yung ti fen-hsi" (An analysis of the economic nature of land leases from the T'ang to the Five Dynasties), *Li-shih yen-chiu*, no. 6 (1964): 97-107.

Sun Yü-tang and Chang Chi-chien. "Ch'ing-tai ti ken-t'ien yü ting-k'ou ti chi-lu" (Farmland and population records of the Ch'ing dynasty), *Ch'ing-shih lun-tsung*, no. 1 (1980): 110-20.

Sung-hui-yao (Documents of the Sung).

Sung-shih (History of the Sung).

T'ai-p'ing kuang-chi (Stories of peaceful days).

Ta-ming lu (Legal codes of the Ming).

Tan Chi-hsiang. "Ho i huang-ho tsai tung-han i-hou ch'u-hsien i-ke ch'ang-ch'i an-liu ti chü-mien (Reasons for the occurrence of a long period of stability for the Yellow River after the Eastern Han), *Hsueh-shu yueh-kan*, no. 2 (1962): 1-13.

Tang, Anthony M. "The Agricultural Legacy," in C. M. Hou and T. S. Yu, *Modern Chinese Economic History*, pp. 231-50. Taipei, 1979.

Tao Shu. *Chu-he* (On rent). 1927.

Ting I-tseng. *Nung-p'u pien-lan* (Guide to farming and gardening).

Ts'e-fu yuan-kuei (Collection of government documents).

Tseng Wu-hsiu. "Chung-kuo li-tai ch'ih-tu kai-shu" (A study of measuring rods in Chinese history), *Li-shih yen-chiu*, no. 3 (1964): 162-82.

Tsou I-jen. *Chiu-shang-hai jen-k'ou pien-hua chih yen-chiu* (A study of population changes in old Shanghai). Shanghai, 1980.

Tsou I-lin. "Ts'ung ti-li huan-ching chiao-tu k'ao-ch'a wo-kuo yun-ho ti li-shih cho-yung" (An examination of the historical function of canals in China from the viewpoint of the geographical environment), *Chung-kuo-shih yen-chiu*, no. 3 (1982): 70-80.

T'ung-tien (Collected statutes).

United Nations, Department of Economic and Social Affairs. *The Population of Asia and the Far East*. New York, 1959.

Wang Chen. *Nung shu* (Treatise on agriculture).

Wang Pao. *T'ung-yüeh* (Slave contracts), reprinted in *Tai-ping yü-lan* (Collection of ancient publications).

Wang Shih-hsing. *Kuang-chih-i* (Collected writings of Wang Shih-hsing).

Wei Chin-yü. "Ming-ch'ing shih-tai tien-nung ti nung-nu ti-wei" (The serf status of tenants during Ming and Ch'ing times), *Li-shih yen-chiu*, no. 5 (1963): 120-40.

Wei Ch'ing-yüan et al. "Ch'ing-tai nu-pei chih-tu" (The bond-service system of the Ch'ing dynasty), *Ch'ing-shih lun-tsung*, 2 (1981): 1-55.

Wei-shu (History of the Wei).

Wen-hsien t'ung-k'ao (Collected records).

Wu Chang-ch'üan. *T'ang-tai nung-min wen-t'i yen-chiu* (A study of agrarian problems in the T'ang dynasty). Taipei, 1963.

Wu Ch'eng-lo. *Chung-kuo tu-liang-heng shih* (A history of Chinese weights and measures). Shanghai, 1957.

Wu-chiang-hsien chih (Gazetteer of Wu-chiang county).

Wu Chih-mu. *Meng-liang-lu* (Recollections of Lin-an). Hangchow, 1980. Reprint ed.

Yang K'uan. "Wo-kuo li-shih-shang t'ieh-nung-chü ti kai-ke chi ch'i tso-yung" (The functions of and improvements in iron farm implements in Chinese history), *Li-shih yen-chiu*, no. 5 (1980): 90-98.

Yeh Hsien-en. "Kuan-yü hui-chou ti tien-p'u chih" (On the tien-p'u system in Hui-chou), *Chung-kuo she-hui ko-hsueh*, no. 1 (1981): 180-95.

Yeh Ming-chu. *Yueh-shih-pien* (Collected writings of Yeh Meng-chu).

Yu, Y. C. "The Demographic Situation in China," *Population Studies*, 32, no. 3 (1978): 427-47.

Yüan Chieh. *Tsu-shan wen-chi* (Collected writings of Yüan Chieh).

Yuan-feng chiu-yü chih (Histories of nine regions).

Yü-hai (A dictionary of literary terms).

Index

Library of Congress Cataloging in Publication Data

Chao, Kang, 1929–
  Man and land in Chinese history.

  Bibliography: p.
  Includes index.
    1. China—Population density—History.   2. Land
use—China—History.   I. Title.
HB2114.A3C45   1986   304.6'1   84-51715
ISBN 0-8047-1271-9 (alk. paper)